Event Planning and Management

CIPR

Event Planning and Management

A practical handbook for PR and events professionals

KoganPage

PR in Practice

Ruth Dowson & David Bassett

Publisher's note

Every possible effort has been made to ensure that the information contained in this book is accurate at the time of going to press, and the publishers and authors cannot accept responsibility for any errors or omissions, however caused. No responsibility for loss or damage occasioned to any person acting, or refraining from action, as a result of the material in this publication can be accepted by the editor, the publisher or either of the authors.

First published in Great Britain and the United States in 2015 by Kogan Page Limited
Reprinted 2015

2nd Floor, 45 Gee Street
London
EC1V 3RS
United Kingdom

1518 Walnut Street, Suite 1100
Philadelphia PA 19102
USA

4737/23 Ansari Road
Daryaganj
New Delhi 110002
India

© Ruth Dowson and David Bassett, 2015

The right of Ruth Dowson and David Bassett to be identified as the authors of this work have been asserted by them in accordance with the Copyright, Designs and Patents Act 1988.

ISBN   978 0 7494 7139 2
E-ISBN   978 0 7494 7140 8

British Library Cataloguing-in-Publication Data

A CIP record for this book is available from the British Library.

Library of Congress Cataloging-in-Publication Data

Dowson, Ruth.
   Event planning and management : a practical handbook for PR and events professionals/
Ruth Dowson, David Bassett.
      pages cm
   ISBN 978-0-7494-7139-2 (paperback) – ISBN 978-0-7494-7140-8 (ebook)   1. Special events–
Planning.   2. Special events–Management.   I. Bassett, David, 1975-   II. Title.
   GT3405.D69 2015
   394.2–dc23
                                                                    2015021103

Typeset by Graphicraft Limited, Hong Kong
Print production managed by Jellyfish
Printed and bound by CPI Group (UK) Ltd, Croydon CR0 4YY

To Matt with gratitude and love;
thanks for the endless cups of tea and patience.
To 'my boys', Luke and Asher; and to Karoline 'my girl'.
To Poppa Glyn (the original event manager in my life)
and in loving memory of Jacqui, Stuart and Mariette.

RUTH

Mum – this is dedicated to you;
I really couldn't have done it without you.
I love you.

Dad – thanks for all the memories of
fun family gatherings, birthday parties
and school discos that made me want to
organize events just like yours.

DAVID

CONTENTS

LIST OF FIGURES

LIST OF TABLES

LIST OF IMAGES

FOREWORD

The facts speak for themselves. The UK business events sector is worth £39 billion to the UK economy and the 25,000 businesses involved employ more than half a million people. In Australia business events attract 900,000 international delegates a year and they spend A$2.7 billion, or 21 per cent of all international visitor spend per year. In the USA the meetings industry contributed $115 billion to the economy and provided 1.8 million jobs. Make no mistake: the events industry is a very serious business and it is growing.

With these sorts of numbers and levels of income it is very timely that *Event Planning and Management* should join the very successful CIPR/Kogan Page series *PR in Practice*. Events are a mainstay of public relations and they are at the same time thoroughly enjoyable and an immense challenge.

So what exactly is an event? According to the authors of this book, Ruth Dowson and David Bassett an event has three key elements: it is a planned gathering with purpose, it is memorable or special, and it is temporary. Behind that simple description lies a complex question: how do you make an event a success? The purpose of this book is to provide a step-by-step guide to doing just that, irrespective of the size of the event or where it is held.

Dowson and Basset's systematic approach starts off by defining an event and then takes the reader through a useful overview of the kinds of events that fall in to different categories, from music festivals to set-piece sporting events. Peppering the early chapters with case studies and examples, the authors then move on to the basics of event planning, choosing locations, developing the content, through to site planning and logistics.

The middle chapters of the book cover those vital elements of building event teams, collaboration and working with partners, with the key requisite – building effective relationships – featuring large. Again, numerous case studies illustrate the main points. There is a good solid chapter on promotion and publicity including how essential it is to use social media to get the word out and add interactivity before the event actually takes place. Getting the finances and procurement of an event right is absolutely critical. Besides offering good practical templates to help with such things as organizing budgets, expenditure and service level agreements, the authors do not shy away from tackling some of the tougher issues such as what to do when sponsors withdraw.

In the last two chapters Dowson and Bassett look at evaluating events, both online and in more traditionsl ways. Again, by using examples like the longer-term economic impact of the Beijing Olympics and advice on how to develop a sustainability monitoring and evaluation plan, the book brings a wealth of knowledge and practical assistance to anyone wanting to create an event.

It's a very readable book. It is full of examples, advice, practical suggestions and tips. It is grounded in a deep understanding of the industry and many years' experience. It's a must-have for any serious event planner and for the absolute beginner.

Anne Gregory, Series Editor
Professor of Corporate Communication
University of Huddersfield

PREFACE

We were delighted, but not entirely surprised, when we heard the CIPD wanted to add to their *PR in Practice* series with a book on event planning and management. Having both been involved in the events industry for most our working lives, we have witnessed the rapid growth of the industry as well as the numbers of individuals and organizations working in the industry. Indeed, there are now many individuals and organizations that would not consider themselves events professionals but who do in fact play an essential role in the industry, such as PR, marketing and creative design specialists.

With almost 50 years' combined experience in events, we have found that writing this book has given us a chance to share our practical advice, best practice, top tips, checklists and templates to help others plan and manage their events. We want our readers to be able to use the book as a 'how to' guide, to make things easier for them whatever their ability or experience, helping them to gain confidence.

The book can be read either from cover to cover or by starting with a particular chapter for advice on a specific aspect of the events planning process. The structured approach we recommend is not written in stone, but we recognize that in this industry it is easy to forget something very simple that can adversely affect the outcome of your event.

We hope that you enjoy reading our book and that your events will benefit from reading our stories and experiences.

ACKNOWLEDGEMENTS

Thank you to the following individuals without whose contributions and support this book would not have been written.

To Anne Gregory for inviting us to write this book and the team at Kogan Page for their efforts in publishing it.

To our wonderful colleagues and fantastic students (past and present) at the UK Centre for Events Management for inspiring us. We've learned so much from you over the years, we thought we would return the favour. A special mention to our 'Brontë Family', Dan, Bernie, Michelle, John, Richard and Anna for always being there (with cake!).

To Jakki for helping to plug the gap in our knowledge of social media.

To Eliza and Ivan for giving up your time to feedback on the drafts.

To Jeanette and Julie for allowing us to use their images to create the mood board.

To the Team Tennis Schools Team for giving us permission to include their tournament poster.

To each other for the laughter therapy which helped us to persevere!

And finally to our amazing case study authors, thank you, Imran Ali, Rhiannon Bates, James Boardman, Faye Briggs, Linda Broughton, Ken Brown, Sophie Bunker, Julia Calver, Alex Clarke, Jonny Clegg, Ivan K Cohen, Charlotte Exley, Rosie Ford, Holly Glover, Phil Hadridge, Philippa Hallam, Emma Heslington, Emma Heslington, Eliza Hixson, Kevin Holdridge, Becky Hughes, Charlotte Jarman, Karen Livingstone, Zoe Pickburn, Olivia Pole-Evans, Tony Rogers, Ben Southall, Ben Southall, Phoebe Southall, Antje Strietholt, Bernadette Theodore-Saltibus, Dominique Wallace, Libby Willetts, Yanning Li, Emma Wood, Richard Wright and Xi Wang.

Introduction to events

It is often said that there's never a dull day working in events. While this statement might not be entirely accurate, it's certainly true that a career in the events industry offers variety, continually throws up new challenges, is fast-paced, often sociable, and may even offer a touch of glamour. But what exactly does a career in events planning entail? Some people are surprised to discover that there's more to it than simply organizing parties and weddings. While party and wedding planning make up a significant part of the industry – each year weddings are worth around £10 billion in the UK (Hitched W.I.F.E, nd) and a staggering $54 billion in the USA (The Wedding Report, 2013) – events also include business meetings and conferences, music concerts and festivals, food and drink festivals, religious celebrations, art and cultural exhibitions and sporting competitions.

As an events planner, you are likely to find yourself organizing a number of different events at any one given time. A typical working week (if there is such a thing in the events industry) might involve travelling to a number of different locations, visiting a variety of possible event sites (both indoor and outdoor) as well as meeting several clients, suppliers and customers. If you're someone who adheres to the motto 'variety is the spice of life' then a career in events planning might well tempt you.

In this opening chapter, we will begin by:

- defining an event;
- examining classifications and categories of events;
- assessing the size and structure of the events industry;
- considering the relationships between events and other industry sectors.

Defining an event

When events professionals talk about an event, they are not talking about natural phenomena, such as earthquakes and freak storms, but about planned gatherings of people. Some gatherings might involve family and friends, work colleagues or work contacts from other businesses. Other gatherings might include a room full of strangers – as is often the case when attending live events such as concerts or sporting competitions. The purpose of the gathering will inevitably vary. Sometimes people gather simply to be entertained while at other times people gather to be educated. But the important point here is that the gathering is planned and there is a purpose to it. The first part of our definition is:

'An event is a planned gathering with a purpose'

Stop for a moment and think about a recent event that you attended. Which event did you immediately think of? A special occasion such as a birthday or wedding perhaps, or a sporting competition or a music concert? Maybe you thought of it as a particularly enjoyable experience? You may have been fortunate enough to have shared the company of close family and friends. Maybe the event took place somewhere exotic or on a glorious sunny day. Whatever the event, it was obviously something memorable. This brings us to the second part of our definition:

'An event is memorable or special'

One of the most recent and memorable events that we attended was an open-air concert performance. The concert took place in beautiful leafy surroundings, in an outside venue with attendees gazing up at the stars while enjoying a picnic with family and friends. It was a truly wonderful evening in a magnificent setting. But, as they say, all good things come to an end. The concert performance, like all events, lasted only for a fixed length of time. Some events last only a matter of hours – a concert performance or a football match. Other events may last a few days – an outdoor festival or industry trade show. Some events might last a few weeks such as an art exhibition or festive Christmas market. Whatever the length of time, all events have a predetermined life cycle with a planned start and end date. This brings us to the third part of our definition:

'An event is temporary'

FIGURE 1.1   Defining an event

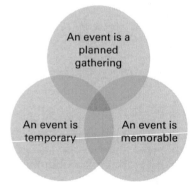

The box below shows some further definitions and descriptions of an event given by some of the leading events management authors:

'An occurrence at a given place and time; a special set of circumstances; a noteworthy occurrence.'
Getz (2007)

'Those non routine occasions set apart from the normal activity of daily life of a group of people.'
(Shone & Parry, 2013)

'An occasion, a gathering of people at a certain place at a certain time for a specific reason.'
(Kilkenny, 2011)

'A gathering of human beings, generally lasting from a few hours to a few days, designed to celebrate, honour, discuss, sell, teach about, encourage, observe, or influence human endeavours.'
(Matthews, 2008)

'Every event experience is unique arising from interactions of setting, programme and people.'
(Getz, 2007)

Classifications and categories of events

One of the most enjoyable aspects of a career in the events industry is the opportunity to work on a variety of different events. Below we consider some of the main ways of grouping or categorizing events.

Categorization by type

Events are most often categorized according to their type. So, for example, although a family birthday and wedding might be very different, they can both be grouped as private events. Similarly, a business meeting or trade show can be grouped under the category of business events.

Getz' Typology of Events is the most commonly used method of categorizing events by type. Table 1.1 shows the eight different types of events as categorized by Getz (2007) and includes examples of each.

TABLE 1.1   Getz typology of events

Cultural celebrations	Business and trade	Arts and entertainment	Educational and scientific
Festivals	Meetings	Concerts	Conferences
Carnivals	Product launches	Performances	Seminars
Religious events	Trade shows	Awards ceremonies	Training
Political & state	**Private events**	**Recreational**	**Sport competition**
Political summits	Parties	Games	Individual/Team
Royal occasions	Weddings	Outdoor activities	Amateur/Professional
State visits	Family occasions	Adventure activities	Local/International

Top Tip

If you are thinking about a career in the events industry then it's a good idea to gain experience of different types of events. This could be through volunteering to help at different events, putting on your own events in the local community or even simply attending several kinds of events. By getting involved in a variety of types of events you will learn new things, try out different types of work (you may even discover a hidden talent) and, most importantly, make new contacts. We've all heard that it's often 'not what you know but who you know', and that couldn't be more true than when it comes to forging a career in the events industry.

Categorization by size and impact

Events vary in their size and impact, with terms such as 'community event' or 'mega event' used to describe and categorize them. A local event might include a village fete or networking lunch aimed at businesses in the local community. These events are unlikely to draw in a huge attendance or generate a great deal of media interest outside the locality. The amount of time and resources needed to plan an event of this type should also be reasonably limited. A mega event, such as the Olympic Games or the FIFA World Cup, will attract viewing figures of billions from all around the globe. The organizing committee work for several years to ensure the success of an event of this magnitude.

Bowdin *et al* (2012) identify four categories of events – 'local', 'major', 'hallmark' and 'mega'.

Local events

As mentioned above, a good example of a local event is a village fete bringing members of the local community together. Indeed, members of the local community as well as local businesses would be likely to be involved in planning and running an event of this type. The main purpose here is to engage members of the local community.

Major events

Unlike a local event, major events are likely to attract visitors from outside the local region and often in large numbers. Examples of major events for a region include an art and cultural festival or an international business convention. The main purpose of hosting such events is to generate increased visitor spend in local shops, restaurants, cafes, hotels and other local businesses. Major events are also likely to attract interest from the media, which in turn will attract more visitors to the region.

Hallmark events

Hallmark events as those events that become so identified with a particular town, city or region that they become synonymous with the name of the place. An excellent example of a hallmark event is the Wimbledon Tennis Championships. If you were to tell a friend that you were going to Wimbledon they'd probably assume you had tickets to watch the tennis tournament, rather than think you'd be travelling to south-west London. The Glastonbury Festival is another excellent example of a hallmark event although, as case study 1.1 shows, the festival is in fact held in a village called Pilton rather than Glastonbury itself.

Mega events

As the name suggests, mega events are the largest in terms of their size and impact. Perhaps the best example of a mega event is the Olympic Games which every four years attracts participants and spectators from all over the world to the host city as well as commanding TV audiences of billions. For the host city the Games has the potential to generate substantial economic gains but the high costs of hosting the Games can mean huge debts if not managed carefully by the organizing committee.

CASE STUDY 1.1   Glastonbury Festival: A hallmark event

Alex Clarke, Event Production Freelancer, UK Centre for Events Management Graduate, 2013

Glastonbury is a market/pilgrimage town situated in the heart of Somerset, in the south-west of England, with a population of almost 10,000. It is often described as a 'new age' town with many people visiting for its spiritual connections, myths and legends. However, the main attraction to the area is undoubtedly the Glastonbury Festival.

In 1970, Michael Eavis, a farmer, inspired by a local blues festival, put on an event on his own farm in Pilton – then called the Pilton Festival. Tickets were only £1 and all milk from the farm was free to the 1,500 attendees. Over 40 years later the Glastonbury Festival is one of the largest, most renowned festivals in the world with bands scrambling for a slot on the line-up. Attendance at the Festival has slowly increased from 1,500 to nearly 200,000 in 2014.

While Glastonbury Festival has made the town of Glastonbury famous, it is worth pointing out that Worthy Farm (where the Festival is held) is actually in Pilton village, and is closer to the town of Shepton Mallet (3.3 miles), than to Glastonbury itself (6.7 miles). This is worth noting for two reasons. The first being that although the hallmark Festival is synonymous with the town of Glastonbury, its physical connections are tentative. Secondly, because although the people of the town of Glastonbury are affected by the Festival, it affects those in the two closer towns to a much greater extent. The impact on local residents around the Festival can be astronomical: traffic, people and bad behaviour all play a part, with many local residents finding it impossible to get to work, or to function in their normal day-to-day lives.

John Clarke, the Site Manager of Glastonbury Festival, explains: 'The impact of traffic congestion on the local communities of Shepton Mallet and Glastonbury is probably the biggest impact they feel from the Festival. Although our set up/break down can take up to three months, it is from the Monday before the Festival that the major disruption starts. We call this "Manic Monday" as this is when traders are allowed onto site and staff/crew numbers increase dramatically.'

However, the local economy does benefit from spending in surrounding towns. Shepton Mallet is home to a large superstore and local shops, which are often the last port of call before the Festival for drinks, food and other forgotten items. Funding is put back into the surrounding communities by the Festival organizers, and every year a 'thank you' concert is held for local residents only, at the end of the summer season. The Festival also tries to help local residents carry on with life by encouraging Festival attendees to use trains and shuttle buses and also providing local residents with transport passes that entitle them access to certain areas surrounding the Festival, in theory making their journeys more manageable.

The local population are given a break from the Festival usually about every five years. These are known as the 'fallow' years (a farming term) when the farmland, the villagers and the organizers are all given a year off to recover.

Read more:

Glastonbury Festival (2014) **History 1970**, [Online] Glastonbury Festivals Ltd available from **www.glastonburyfestivals.co.uk/history/history-1970/** [Accessed: 18 July 2014]

Hatherley, O (2014) Glastonbury: the pop-up city that plays home to 200,000 for the weekend, **The Guardian** [Online] 23 June, available from **www.theguardian.com/ cities/2014/jun/23/glastonbury-city-pop-up-weekend-festival** [Accessed: 18 July 2014]

Other ways of categorizing events

Frequency

Christmas and New Year celebrations are obvious examples of events that occur annually. Business events such as half-yearly sales meetings, monthly staff awards and prize-givings as well as daily team meetings are also events that can be categorized by their frequency.

Geography

Sporting competitions are a good example of events that can easily be categorized by geography. In the sport of athletics there are World and European Championships, with each event occurring every two years. Many countries around the world also host both regional and national athletic championships each year.

Sector

When asked 'what do you do?' an events professional might explain that they manage events in a particular sector, such as the corporate, public or charitable sector. In addition, somebody specializing in a particular sector might tell you that they specialize in a specific sub-sector. For example, an events planner specializing in corporate events might work predominantly with clients in sub-sectors such as the banking, legal or medical industries.

Internal or external

Examples of internal events include staff team-building events and staff meetings. These events are usually only attended by employees working within a particular organization and are often referred to as 'in-house' events. External events, on the other hand, are used by an organization to engage with people from outside the company. These include events such as product launches and media events.

Size and structure of the industry

Size

With events taking place each and every day all around the world, providing any accurate data about the size of the industry is extremely difficult. Table 1.2 shows the host cities and countries for the world's biggest sporting spectacle (the Summer Olympics) and one of the most global political events (the G20 Summit), which demonstrates that events are truly global.

Furthermore, the events industry is fragmented, with many small companies (often employing only one or two people) operating in the sector. Consequently, it is challenging to calculate the number of companies that exist, or even the number of people employed in the industry. To further complicate matters, there is significant overlap between events organizations and those in other closely related sectors (eg tourism, hospitality and sport), which means that categorizing or grouping businesses neatly into a specific sector is almost impossible.

Despite the difficulties in obtaining accurate data about the size of the events industry, nearly everyone agrees that the sector is growing quickly and that it is an exciting time to be a part of it. However, a number of global studies and research reports do attempt to provide us with an indication of the size, scale and growth of the industry. Below are some key facts and figures regarding the economic value of the events industry.

TABLE 1.2 Host cities and countries for the Summer Olympics and G20 Summit

Summer Olympics	G20 Summit
2000 Sydney, Australia	2011 Cannes, France
2004 Athens, Greece	2012 Los Cabos, Mexico
2008 Beijing, China	2013 St Petersburg, Russia
2012 London, England	2014 Brisbane, Australia
2016 Rio de Janeiro, Brazil	2015 Antalya, Turkey

Facts and figures

The British Visits and Events Partnership (BVEP) provide key facts and figures about the value of business events and conferences to the British economy:

- UK business events sector is worth £39.1bn to the UK visitor economy.

- Around 80 million people attend 1.5 million conferences and meetings annually.

- The sector's 25,000 businesses employ 530,000 people.

UK Music have undertaken a study on the economic benefits festivals and concerts bring to the UK music industry:

- The major music festivals and concerts in the UK attract 7.7 million music tourists a year.

- Music tourists at festivals and concerts spend £1.6 billion in total during their trips.

- This boosts the UK economy to the tune of at least £864 million a year, providing 19,700 full-time jobs.

The Association of Australian Convention Bureaux (AACB) provide statistics to show the importance of international business events to the Australian tourism market:

- Business events held in Australia attract 900,000 international delegates a year.

- International business event delegates spend $2.7bn in GDP in total (21 per cent of all international visitor spend).

- 30 per cent of international business event delegates are from Asia where growth prospects are greater than any other market.

- The business events sector creates 22,500 jobs.

Research commissioned by the Convention Industry Council (CIC) identified positive growth in the US meetings industry between 2009 and 2012:

- 1.83 million meetings and events were attended by 225 million participants (an increase of 10 per cent).

- The meetings industry contributed more than $115 billion to the economy (an increase of 9.6 per cent) surpassing that of the air transportation, motion picture, sound recording, performing arts and spectator sport industries.

The meetings industry provides jobs for nearly 1.8 million people in the United States (an 8.3 per cent increase).

Top Tip

It is important for an event professional to keep up to date with current research that indicates the growth of the events industry – whether this is the growth of a particular sector or a specific country or region of the world. Economic growth means that there will be a greater demand for events, which in turn will create new opportunities for work. Likewise, it's important to identify any patterns of decline in the industry. In this case, it may be necessary for a professional to diversify their offer (ie have the ability to work with a wide range of clients on different types of events.

Structure

We have seen that the very nature of an event brings people together (attendees), but an event also brings together a range of individuals and organizations whose involvement and interaction is necessary to ensure the smooth running of an event.

It is possible to group these into three categories:

1 Event clients
2 Event organisers
3 Event suppliers

Event clients

Events clients are the 'buyers' of events, who hire or employ event organizers to plan, organize and run the events on their behalf. Typically, it is corporate companies who have a budget to hire professional event organizers, although private individuals hosting elaborate parties and weddings may also require the expertise of a professional event organizer.

Event organizers

Event organizers are professional individuals and groups who plan, organize and run an event on behalf of their clients. An event organizer acts as liaison between their client and suppliers and is ultimately responsible for the smooth running of the event. An event organizer can be tasked with running an event on behalf of their own organization as well as being hired by an external client. For example, in larger companies, events such as Annual General Meetings (AGMs) and annual conferences are often run by an 'in-house' event organizer.

Event suppliers

Event suppliers constitute a wide range of specialist organizations providing elements of the goods and services needed by the professional event organizer to ensure the success of an event. The larger the event, the greater the need for goods and services, and the more complex the event, the greater the need for increased technical and specialist support, eg sound and lighting engineers or pyrotechnics operators.

FIGURE 1.2   Key players in the events industry

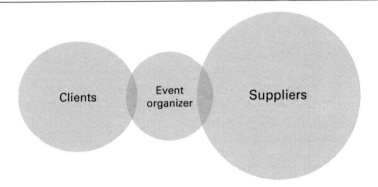

Figure 1.2 (although not to scale) represents the relative position and size of the event organizers, suppliers and clients in the industry. At the heart of any event, you will find an event organizer tasked with managing the event on behalf of their client and liaising with various suppliers to ensure the smooth running of the event. In essence their role is to work as an intermediary between their client (or buyer) and the suppliers.

You will notice that each of the circles in Figure 1.2 is a different size with the smallest circle representing the event organizer who, as already

mentioned, is often only one or two people. The event organizer is likely to be setting up a number of events at any one time and dealing with multiple clients, and so the circle representing the event's clients is larger. The last circle, the biggest of all, represents the event' suppliers who for any given event (particularly larger and more complex ones) will include a plethora of organizations providing the goods and services needed to make the event happen.

This case study looks at the key players contributing to the success of the Great North Run – 'The World's Greatest Half Marathon' – taking place annually in the north-east of England and the first run in the world to reach the milestone of its one-millionth finisher.

CASE STUDY 1.2　Great North Run

Jonny Clegg, UK Centre for Events Management Graduate, 2015. Placement Student at The Children's Foundation, 2012–2013

The iconic Great North Run is currently the second-largest half marathon in the world (after the Gothenburg half marathon), attracting over 57,000 runners; in September 2014 it was the first International Association of Athletics Federations (IAAF) event in the world to reach its one-millionth finisher. The Great North Run is held in the north-east of England, stretching across Newcastle, Gateshead and South Shields, and has achieved IAAF Gold Label Road Race status, signifying it as one of the leading road races in the world. In 2014 the race attracted people from over 40 different countries, establishing the event as 'The World's Greatest Half Marathon'. The race sees world-class athletes competing, including Mo Farah, Haile Gebrselassie and Paula Radcliffe.

The Great North Run brings together a multitude of sponsors, partners and organizers who all contribute to its success, including three local authorities. Bupa has been the title partner for the last 22 years, making it one of the longest sports sponsorships agreements ever. Bupa is also the title partner for the Great Run series, which is part of Nova International sporting group, which specializes in the development, design, organization and rights management of mass participation and televised sporting events. Joe Milner from Nova explains: 'Here at Nova we aim to create events which engage the local community and year-on-year there are tens of thousands of supporters lining the route cheering on participants and showing their support.'

In 2009, Powerade became the category sponsor for the Great Run and Great Swim series in an aim to become more popular within the running community. Over the five years they have been sponsors, Powerade have been able to reach 1 million runners, 2.2 million spectators, and 50 million TV viewers, while 2 million bottles of Powerade have been sampled. Sponsors such as Powerade and Bupa are also present at associated events such as the Pasta Party, which is held the night before the run. As well as sponsors benefiting from the event, the Great North Run has an economic impact of £38 million on the region.

Many participants take part to raise money for charity and on average £28 million is raised each year. There are 298 official charities from across the country working all year round recruiting runners, advising on training, and waiting to meet and greet runners in the Charity Village at the end of the Run.

Libby Nolan, Fundraising Manager for The Children's Foundation explains: 'In the months leading up to the Great North Run we help to prepare the runners with advice on training and are on hand for any questions they may have.'

The Great North Run is an event that takes months of planning but leaves behind a legacy that lasts a lifetime. From the hundreds of bus drivers who transport the runners' baggage to the finish line, to the thousands of workers who hand out water, direct runners and ensure the safety of participants, there is an extensive range of organizations associated with this event, and without them the Great North Run would not be such a success.

Read more: **www.greatrun.org/events/Information.aspx?ctid=317&id=1**

Having the necessary equipment, facilities and infrastructure at your event is an essential part of the planning process (more about this in Chapter 5). The following checklist contains a list of event suppliers and support services that may be needed to make your event a success. This list will need to be amended as the equipment, facilities and services required will vary according to the type of event and the activities you have taking place.

CHECKLIST: Event suppliers and support services

ORGANIZERS

☐ Professional event organizers
☐ Event management companies
☐ Event production companies
☐ Party and event planners

VENUE

☐ Venue hire
☐ Room hire
☐ Equipment hire
☐ Outside catering
☐ Toilets and public facilities
☐ Car parking
☐ Security

TEMPORARY STRUCTURES/SITE

☐ Staging company
☐ Portable accommodation supplier
☐ Roadway/walkway supplier
☐ Fencing/barrier supplier
☐ Site vehicle supplier
☐ Toilets and public facilities
☐ Waste management
☐ Traffic management
☐ Crowd management
☐ Health and Safety
☐ CCTV
☐ Telecomms
☐ Wifi

TRAVEL & ACCOMMODATION

☐ Travel agencies
☐ Transport companies
☐ Hotel booking agencies
☐ Destination marketing organizations (DMOs)
☐ Local tourism bodies

CONTENT

☐ Theming companies
☐ Guest speakers
☐ Workshop facilitators
☐ Artists and performers

STAFF

☐ Security
☐ Stewards
☐ Volunteers
☐ Agency staff
☐ Bar staff
☐ Uniform providers

FOOD & BEVERAGE

☐ Bars
☐ Food concessions
☐ Specialist hospitality
☐ Mobile catering

ENTERTAINMENT

☐ Local attractions
☐ Tour guides
☐ Ticketing agencies
☐ Photographers and video makers
☐ Music and entertainment
☐ Costume hire services
☐ Florists

AUDIO VISUAL

☐ Lighting companies
☐ Sound companies
☐ Multimedia companies
☐ Live streaming companies
☐ Pyrotechnics operators

Relationships with other industry sectors

There are many individuals and organizations that would not consider themselves to be part of the events industry but who do in fact spend a significant amount of time planning, organizing, hosting and running events (you may be one of them!). This is because there is significant overlap between the events industry and other closely related sectors such as the tourism, hospitality and sport industries.

Tourism

Earlier we explained how large events can attract visitors (eg spectators, participants, suppliers and media) from outside a region. Getz (2007) refers to this as the 'drawing power' of events to destinations, which can be measured by how many visitors come to a region to attend an event, as well as how much money they spend, for example, on accommodation, travel, eating, drinking and entertainment.

In recognition of the 'drawing power' of events, more and more tourism organizations (both local and national) are developing a destination-based event tourism strategy to increase the economic benefits of events. The City of Edinburgh promotes itself as the world's leading festival city with 12 major annual festivals taking place all year round. Festivals such as the Edinburgh International Festival, the Edinburgh Fringe, the Edinburgh International Film Festival and the Edinburgh Military Tattoo have become a permanent part of the city's identity and help to attract 4.2 million attendees from 70 countries (Edinburgh Festival City Official Website, nd).

Hosting an event also plays an important role in enhancing the image of a particular destination, which in turn will help to attract visitors to the region even after the event has finished. The following case study explains how the world's biggest annual sporting event – The Tour de France – has helped to put Yorkshire on the tourist map.

CASE STUDY 1.4   Yorkshire *Grand Départ* of the Tour de France 2014

Julia Calver, Senior Lecturer – UK Centre for Events Management

The Tour de France is the biggest annual sporting event in the world. Organized by the Amaury Sport Organisation (ASO) it attracts a global television audience of 3 billion and a roadside audience of 12 million. It offers incredible profile for participants, funders and sponsors over the 21 stages of the race. The first two stages in particular, known as the *Grand Départ*, offer increased attention by being the start of the event and are regularly located in countries other than France.

It was because of this that Gary Verity, Chief Executive of tourism agency Welcome to Yorkshire, saw the opportunity to put the county in the global spotlight by bidding for the right to host the *Grand Départ* of the Tour de France 2014.

The bid was developed during the latter half of 2011 and submitted to ASO in mid-2012. The bid required the development of partnerships and networks between Welcome to Yorkshire, the local authorities within the region, the tourism sector, the wider business community and high-profile individuals. This was in order to demonstrate the enthusiasm and willingness not only of Welcome to Yorkshire but of all the participating agencies. Wider value beyond the basic hosting was recognized during this process, for example in the plans to hold a county-wide arts festival and to set up a Legacy Board to harness the benefits post-event. Much emphasis was put on public engagement with the collection of over 130,000 pledges of support through the consumer-facing Back le Bid campaign.

This proactive approach paid dividends when it was announced in December 2012 that Yorkshire would host the *Grand Départ* in 2014 with 6,000 attending the January 2013 public launch in Leeds City Centre.

The period between the announcement of winning the bid and the event was characterized by partner organizations capitalizing on opportunities open to them. This ranged from using the event to maximize bookings for hotels, to value-added visits to local attractions. Farmers created pop-up camp sites and brewers brewed commemorative ales. Welcome to Yorkshire worked with the Arts Council, local authorities and the private sector sponsor, Yorkshire Water, to present the Yorkshire Festival 2014, a celebration of arts in Yorkshire, in the 100-day lead-up to the *Grand Départ*. It also worked with local authorities and British Cycling to leave a cycling legacy known as Cycle Yorkshire, a 10-year programme to build participation in cycling.

The event weekend began on 3 July with the presentation of the teams at Leeds Arena. Watched by a live audience of 11,000, a British TV audience of over a million and a worldwide TV audience of 3.5 billion, the event heralded a spectacular spectator turnout for the race days. Over the two days, more than 4 million people turned out to cheer, as the race unfolded over beautiful countryside in gorgeous summer weather, fulfilling the dream of putting Yorkshire on the global destination and sporting map.

Read more: **www.letour.yorkshire.com, www.yorkshirefestival.co.uk,**
www.cycle.yorkshire.com

Hospitality

Hospitality is often described as the business of making people feel welcome and relaxed and helping them to enjoy themselves. A great event organizer understands the importance of being hospitable to those attending the event (eg providing a warm and friendly welcome on arrival, or a meal or drink in a pleasant environment), and takes pride in the delivery of excellent hospitality. While the concept of hospitality may appear simple, it isn't easy to get right. A survey of 300 UK conference organizers found that the most frequent cause for complaint from delegates was related to the food and beverage, which demonstrates that great hospitality can set your event apart from other events (UK Conference Market Survey, 2006).

The hospitality sector includes all businesses that provide food, beverages and/or accommodation services. The sector includes restaurants and hotels which often provide the space event organizers need to put on an event. Many private events, such as birthday parties, are held in restaurants and business conferences often take place in hotels. Hotels also provide accommodation for conference delegates staying overnight.

VIP hospitality is a feature at many large spectator events (in particular sporting events) and is extremely attractive to corporate clients looking to entertain their clients or potential prospects. At larger events you will find a wide range of hospitality packages to suit a range of budgets and preferences. Increasingly, there has been a 'democratization' of corporate hospitality, with companies such as Vodafone introducing VIP event packages for all its customers in 2010. Typically the 'VIP treatment' at an event involves good quality food and drink, some of the best seats in the house, as well as being entertained.

Sport

Sport by its very nature involves competitions and events to determine the winners. The very biggest sporting spectacles usually attract spectators and television audiences from around the world but, interestingly, the world's largest annual participation sports event is the Gothia Cup – The World Youth Cup. This is a week-long youth football tournament held annually in Gothenburg for both boys and girls, with 1,600 teams, from 80 nations participating in 4,500 matches on 110 pitches. While the Gothia Cup may not attract the same level of attention as other sporting spectacles, it undoubtedly requires careful planning, organizing and running for an event of this size and scale (Gothia Cup Official Website, nd).

Sporting stadiums are among the largest venues in the world – the largest sporting venue in the world, the Indianapolis Motor Speedway, has a permanent seating capacity for more than 257,000 (World Stadium's Official Website, nd) – and as such, host some of the world's largest events. Wembley Stadium, the 'home of football' and the second largest football stadium in Europe, each year hosts major events such as the finals of the football

FA Cup and League Cup, as well as international fixtures for the England team, and in 2011 and 2013 hosted the UEFA Champions League Final. The stadium also hosts major events for sports other than football including the Rugby League Challenge Cup Final and American football NFL International Series matches. However, there are even more events hosted at the stadium each year that are not related to sport, from major concerts to private events such as weddings and conferences. Indeed, it is an economic necessity for the modern sporting stadiums to host non-sporting events given the costs of building and maintaining the stadium.

Chapter summary

- An event is a planned gathering of a temporary nature, which is often a memorable or special occasion for the attendees.
- Many different types of event are hosted and these can be grouped (or categorized) according to their type, size and impact, frequency, geography or sector.
- With planned events taking place each and every day all around the world, the events industry is a truly global industry which continues to grow quickly.
- The structure of the events industry is complex with a plethora of organizations and individuals providing the goods and services needed to make an event happen.
- There is significant overlap between the events industry and other closely related industry sectors such as tourism, hospitality and sport.

Reference list

Association of Australian Convention Bureaux (2014) *Business Events: Delivering Economic Prosperity for Australia*, [online] available from: http://aacb.org.au/exfiles/Delivering%20Economic%20Prosperity%20-for%20Australia.pdf [Accessed: 30 December 2014]

Bowdin, G, Allen, J, Harris, R, McDonnell, I and O'Toole, W (2012) *Events Management*, 3rd edn, Elsevier Butterworth Heinemann, Oxford

British Visits and Event Partnership (2014) *EVENTS ARE GREAT BRITAIN: A report on the size and value of Britain's events industry, its characteristics, trends, opportunities and key issues – Executive Summary (published in March 2014)* [online] available from www.businessvisitsandeventspartnership.com/research-and-publications/research/category/4-bvep-research [Accessed: 5 November 2014]

Convention Industry Council (2014) *FACT SHEET 2014: The Economic Significance of Meetings to the US Economy* [online] available from: www.conventionindustry.org/Files/2012%20ESS/140210%20Fact%20Sheet%20FINAL.pdf [Accessed: 30 December 2014]

Edinburgh Festival City Official Website (nd) [online] available from: www.edinburghfestivalcity.com/the-city [Accessed: 31 December 2014]

Gothia Cup Official Website (nd) *Tournament Brochure for 2015*, [online] available from: www.gothiacup.se/trycksaker/2015/pageflip_eng/ [Accessed: 5 November 2014]

Getz, D (2007) *Event Studies: Theory, Research and Policy for Planned Events (Events Management)*, Elsevier Butterworth Heinemann, Oxford

Hitched W.I.F.E Wedding Industry Facts and Economics (nd) *Each year UK weddings are worth £10 billion*, [online] available from: www.theweddingreport.com/wmdb/index.cfm?action=db. viewdetail&t=s&lc=00&setloc=y [Accessed: 5 November 2014]

Kilkenny, S (2011) *The Complete Guide to Successful Event Planning*, 2nd edn, Atlantic Publishing, Florida

Matthews, D (2008) *Special Event Production: The Process*, Butterworth Heinemann, Oxford

Shone, A and Parry, B (2013) *Successful Event Management: A Practical Handbook*, 4th edn, Cengage Learning EMEA, Andover

The Wedding Report (2013) *2013 Wedding Statistics Summary for United States* The Wedding Report [online] available from: www.theweddingreport.com/wmdb/index.cfm?action=db.viewdetail&t=s&lc=00&setloc=y [Accessed: 5 November 2014]

UK Conference Market Survey (2006) in Rogers T (2008) *Conferences and Conventions: A Global Industry*, 2nd edn, Elsevier Butterworth-Heinemann, Oxford

UK Music (2011) *Destination Music – The Contribution of Music Festivals and Major Concerts to Tourism in the UK*, UK Music [online] available from: www.ukmusic.org/assets/media/UK%20Music%20-Music%20Tourism.pdf [Accessed: 5 November 2014]

World Stadiums Official Website (nd) [online] available from: www.worldstadiums.com/stadium_menu/stadium_list/100000.shtml [Accessed: 1 January 2015]

Event planning

Planning an event can be great fun – it unleashes the creative side in us (even those of us who don't consider ourselves to be particularly creative). It gives us the opportunity to dream up unique and unusual venues to host an event, to conjure up new and exciting activities for the event attendees to enjoy, and to create weird and wonderful menus for the guests to sample. And this part can be a lot of fun. But planning an event is no easy task and, with much to do, it can prove quite stressful. As an event organizer, you are only too aware that much of the success of the event will be down to how well you plan it and so it's not uncommon to find yourself worrying about things you might have forgotten or overlooked. Indeed, it is often said that what makes the difference between a good event organizer and a great event organizer is an exceptional 'eye for detail'.

Fortunately the process of planning an event becomes a little easier with experience. This is because planning any event involves a certain amount of repetition because there are specific key tasks that you will carry out for most events. We call these the 'essential' planning tasks. For example, no matter whether an event planner is tasked with organizing a local village fete or a national sports tournament, many of the 'essential' tasks, such as drawing up a detailed site map, creating a schedule for the event, or promoting the event to the target audience, will include the same processes.

For larger, more complex and more elaborate events, however, relying on experience alone is unwise, and it is sensible for even the most experienced of event organizers to adopt a more systematic process for planning and organizing the event. Following an event-planning process will help to guide an event organizer through the different stages of planning an event and make sure that they don't overlook anything important.

In this chapter we will explain:

- The importance of adopting a systematic approach to event planning
- The distinct phases of the event-planning process
- The essential planning tasks and activities to be carried out at each distinct phase.

Event planning

The success of any event is largely a result of what happens long before the day of the event: that is, how well-planned and organized it is in the build-up to the event. An event organizer knows that, if they spend the right amount of time and effort on the various planning activities and tasks, then the chances of developing and delivering a successful event are increased. This, however, is not without its challenges, with the task of an event organizer having been likened to that of: 'a ring master, a juggler, a magician...' (O'Toole and Mikolaitas, 2002).

While the unique nature of an event means that no two events are the same, this means that the process of planning an event is never quite the same, but we have already identified that there are certain essential tasks the event organizer will be required to carry out for any event. These essential tasks include:

- Developing the concept
- Determining the budget
- Establishing the objectives
- Prioritizing (mapping) the stakeholders
- Preparing a proposal
- Carrying out a feasibility study
- Selecting the location and venue
- Planning the programme and content
- Planning the site layout
- Logistics planning
- Recruiting the event team
- Sourcing suppliers and contractors
- Promotion and publicity
- Financial and procurement planning
- Event debrief and evaluation

Event-planning process

Depending on the size, type and format of an event, an event organizer will prioritize different planning tasks and allocate different amounts of time to these tasks. But the tasks will be carried out in a similar sequence because, for example, it is very difficult to choose a suitable venue or choose a menu until you have a clear idea of what the budget will allow.

Many authors have attempted to outline the specific steps or stages in the event-planning process and we are no different. The Dowson and Bassett (2015) Event-Planning Model includes all of the tasks we consider to be

FIGURE 2.1   The Dowson and Bassett (2015) Event Planning Model

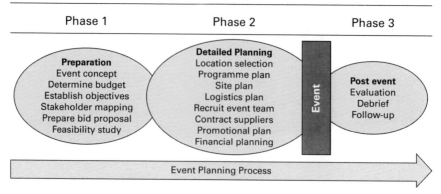

'essential' when planning an event and these are grouped into three distinct phases. Figure 2.1 includes all that we consider to be the 'essential' planning tasks carried out by an event organizer when putting on an event.

Dowson and Bassett Planning Model

Here we briefly describe each of the three phases of the Dowson and Bassett (2015) model.

Phase 1: preparation

The preparation phase is about the event organizer getting themselves properly prepared. There is always the temptation to rush this stage but you do so at your peril! Once the detailed planning is under way, an event organizer rarely gets the opportunity to pause, reflect and re-evaluate. An experienced event organizer will tell you how important it is, for example, to take the time to work closely with a client to develop the event concept and reach an agreement around the primary objectives for the event (as we will discuss shortly, not all objectives will be given the same level of priority by your client).

Phase 2: detailed planning

The detailed planning phase can feel like a whirlwind of activity for an event organizer as they race against the clock to be ready for the big day. This can include travelling to a shortlist of venues, meeting and booking guest speakers, entertainers and performers, tasting menus and sampling drinks (as we said planning events can be great fun!). With lots to do at this stage (and sometimes not a lot of time to do it) the likelihood is that, certainly for larger events, you will carry out some tasks yourself, while others will be shared within the team, and some tasks may require the help of a specialist. Typically the larger and more elaborate an event, then the greater the need for specialist suppliers and support services (it may be helpful to refer back to the Chapter 1 Checklist).

Phase 3: post-event

It may seem a little strange to talk about planning activities occurring after the event has finished. There are, however, some extremely important actions to be undertaken post event, and none more so than completing a thorough event evaluation. Indeed we dedicate an entire chapter to event evaluation later in the book (Chapter 9). Carrying out a thorough event evaluation enables an organizer to assess what worked well and what didn't work well, providing them with useful lessons for planning future events. Evaluation can also be a useful way of showing others (eg clients, sponsors and partners) that the event was a success, which can ultimately help to justify future events.

The value of this model is in its simplicity. There are, however, some important caveats:

- The diagram should only be used as a guide. The key tasks are not necessarily sequential and the order will depend upon the type of event as well as how an event organizer prefers to work.

- There is likely to be overlap between the different phases of the planning life cycle with tasks underway simultaneously.

- The amount of time spent on each task will vary depending upon the type, size and nature of the event.

This simple model is unlikely to be detailed enough for larger, more elaborate and more complex events. In this case, a more detailed model could be used.

Phase 1: preparation

The preparation phase is where the event organizer makes sure that they are ready for what lies ahead. Once the detailed planning phase begins, there is no turning back, and it is vitally important to spend enough time for the event organizer to be fully prepared for what lies ahead.

FIGURE 2.2   Phase One: Preparation

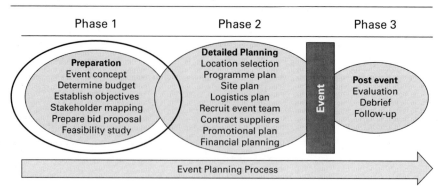

The 'essential' tasks at the pre-planning phase are listed below and subsequently explained in more detail:

- developing the concept
- determining the budget
- establishing the objectives
- prioritizing (mapping) the stakeholders
- preparing a proposal
- carrying out a feasibility study

Developing the concept

The initial idea for an event will usually come from the client, and can sometimes be a little vague or ambiguous. For example, a client may approach an event organizer to 'put on a huge event' which is held 'somewhere amazing' with 'lots of fun activities' taking place during the event. While this sounds like a great client to work for (already thinking of big and bold ideas for their event), as an event professional it is important to work with the client to develop a clearer concept of the event from the outset. The clearer the initial concept of the event, then the less likely the event organizer will spend time, effort and resources (including money) focusing on the wrong things. It is equally important that the client has both a clear and realistic idea of the event so that they are not ultimately disappointed that the event did not meet their initial ideas or expectations.

A simple but effective way of conceptualising an event is to use the 5Ws:

- **WHY** are you putting on the event?
- **WHO** is coming to the event?
- **WHAT** is happening at the event?
- **WHEN** is the event taking place?
- **WHERE** is the event taking place?

FIGURE 2.3   Developing the event concept using the Five Ws

WHY
Purpose
Motives
Objectives

WHERE
Location
Venue
Surroundings

**The
5 Ws**

WHO
Target audience
Customer profile
Attendee numbers

WHEN
Date & time
Season
Occasion

WHAT
Activities
Programme
Format

Top Tip

Having worked with your client to develop a clearer idea of the event concept (the who, what, where, when and why of your event) it is a good idea to condense this into a one-page event brief. This one-page brief, containing all of the important information, can easily be shared with members of your event organizing team as well as any external suppliers and contractors to help give them a clearer 'picture' of the event that your client has in their mind.

Developing the event concept is often an enjoyable part of the planning process, with the opportunity for the event organizer (as well as the client) to 'open up their minds to various possibilities and to try something different' (Powell, 2013). Even those of us who might not consider ourselves to be a creative person can still enjoy the process of generating new ideas. Creating a concept or 'mood' board for your event is also a lot of fun. Mood boards are collages of items such as photographs, clippings, drawings and fabrics which are created to capture or convey the concept of the event. The client can view the mood board and decide whether or not they like the main ideas the board represents. Figure 2.4 shows an example of a mood board capturing a wedding planner's ideas for using black and white polka dots for a wedding theme.

FIGURE 2.4   Mood board capturing a wedding planner's ideas

Photographs courtesy of:
Jeanette Sunderland (Netty's Cakes http://www.nettyscakes.co.uk/)
Julie Armitage (Picture Perfect http://www.pictureperfectphotographyuk.co.uk/)

Determining the budget

Even the most creative and resourceful event organizer is going to incur costs putting on an event. There are examples of events, most notably, charitable fundraisers, where financial goodwill and donations from charitable supporters mean that no financial commitment is needed to deliver the event. But it generally costs money to hire venues, book rooms, feed guests and entertain people at an event.

It is important for an event organizer to know how much money the client is prepared to spend. We agree with Judy Allen (2009), who goes as far as to suggest that, *'The first thing you need to do is to establish how much money you can set aside for the event.'* This is understandable, because if you don't achieve this, you are likely to find yourself spending time, effort and resources planning and organizing what is not realistic within the given budget. For example, there is no point visiting possible locations and venues only to discover that these would swallow up the entire client budget. Both the event organizer and the client are likely to end up feeling frustrated.

It is vital for an event organizer to discuss and agree with their client exactly what is, and is not, included in the budget. For instance, is the budget expected to cover transport and accommodation for guests? Is it expected to cover the cost of an open bar in the evening, or to cover the cost of attendees bringing their partners or spouses to the event?

Top Tip

Discussing the subject of money with your client can feel a little awkward, so it's better to get this difficult conversation out of the way right at the start of the planning process. Don't hesitate or feel nervous when you ask them. If you're nervous, then the client will be nervous too. Simply ask, 'What is your budget for this event?' And if a client isn't prepared to tell you about their budget then chances are that they are wasting your time.

Some costs may immediately spring to mind when planning an event, such as the cost of hiring a venue, but there are also likely to be 'hidden' costs as well. The following checklist shows a list of some of the top items that you might not consider when thinking about the event budget.

CHECKLIST: hidden costs of the event budget

☐ Stationery (eg menu cards)
☐ Printing (eg invitations)
☐ Postage
☐ Promotional materials
☐ Welcome gifts
☐ Prizes
☐ Travel expenses
☐ Overnight accommodation
☐ Tips and gratuities
☐ Photography and videography

Establishing the objectives

Working with the client to clarify the event concept certainly helps to steer an event organizer in the right direction but it is equally important (if not more so) to work with the client to establish the primary event objectives. These will subsequently help to guide the event organizer throughout the process of planning and organizing the event. It is a good idea involving not only the client but other key individuals when establishing the event objectives. Any good wedding planner, for example, will tell you how important it is to make sure the mother of the bride is on side with the plans for the big day (as well as the bride and groom of course).

FIGURE 2.5   Establishing the event objectives using the Five Es

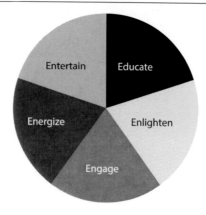

There are different ways of thinking about the objectives for an event and while there is no magic formula, here are some suggestions that will help:

Five Es

The Five Es is a simple approach to understanding more easily the emotions that event attendees will experience which in turn will help the event organizer to establish appropriate and relevant event objectives.

- Educate – training workshops are elements of an event programme that are primarily intended to educate attendees.
- Enlighten – a guest speaker could be invited to speak to event attendees, enlightening them about future issues and trends.
- Engage – motivational speakers can be used to engage attendees.
- Energize – icebreaker activities can be used to energize attendees.
- Entertain – don't forget to include time for social activities in the event programme for attendees to unwind and to enjoy themselves.

Hierarchy of objectives

A hierarchy means that different elements are organized in order of importance (in this case the objectives). As an event organizer, you must understand the most important objectives for the client for an event. It is important to prioritize the objectives for an event because there is rarely the luxury of infinite resources (namely time and money) to put on an event and so the event organizer must understand where to focus their time and effort.

Figure 2.6 should help you to determine which objectives should be considered as high priority (therefore requiring a great deal of time and effort) and those objectives which are of lower priority.

SMART objectives

It is important to ensure that your event objectives are SMART, an acronym for Specific, Measurable, Agreed, Realistic and Time-bound objectives. SMART

FIGURE 2.6 Hierarchy of event objectives

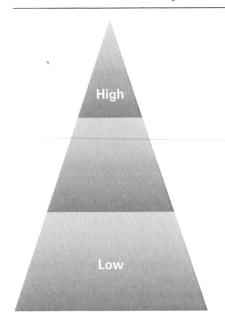

Failure to meet this objective means you are unlikely to be asked to organize another event for this particular client and they might even refuse to pay for the organizing of this event.

This objective may be seen as a 'nice to have' by the client or the client may even be unaware or not care if this particular objective is met.

is one of the most commonly used methods for developing well-written objectives but, at least in our own experience of working with event clients and event organizers, it is not always used correctly.

SPECIFIC – Objectives should clearly state what you are expected to achieve, using action verbs to describe what has to be done.

MEASURABLE – Objectives should each include a target or milestone so that you can measure whether or not you have achieved them.

AGREED – Objectives provide a definition of success and it is therefore important that the intended outcomes should be agreed upon with the client.

REALISTIC – Objectives should be challenging but not unrealistic. Objectives should take account of the skills, knowledge and resources of the event team.

TIME-BOUND – Objectives just don't seem to get done if there's no time frame tied to the objective-setting process.

Legacy objectives

Finally, when thinking about the event objectives it is easy to focus on the immediate (short-term) outcomes for an event. Take the Five Es for example (educate, enlighten, engage, energize, entertain) where the focus is on the feelings and emotions that event attendees will experience during or immediately after the event. But the outcomes can also be much longer term as well. A phrase that is often associated with larger events is the event 'legacy', which means the lasting benefits/outcomes as a result of hosting the event. For example, the legacy objectives associated with hosting a major sporting tournament – such as the Stag World Veteran Table Tennis Championship (see Case study 2.1) – typically include increasing participation in sport as well as promoting the social and health benefits of playing sport regularly. Indeed, promoting the legacy objectives for a major sporting event has become an important factor in the decision to award a particular event to a host city or nation and is a critical part of the bidding process (more about the bid process shortly).

CASE STUDY 2.1   Leveraging of legacy: Stag World Veteran Table Tennis Championships 2014

Richard Wright, Lecturer in Sports Event Management, Auckland University of Technology, New Zealand

The inaugural World Veteran Table Tennis Championships (WVC) took place in Gothenburg in 1982, attracting 450 players from 21 countries. Thirty years later, the 16th WVC returned to Sweden, having travelled the world and grown significantly in size and status. In May 2011, the hosting rights for the 17th WVC were awarded to Auckland, ahead of rival bids from Las Vegas (USA), the Gold Coast (Australia), Piran (Croatia), Ljubljana (Slovenia) and Alicante (Spain).

New Zealand's winning bid came at their third attempt and was jointly delivered by the Auckland Tourism, Events and Economic Development (ATEED) and Table Tennis New Zealand (TTNZ). It was won on a promise to 'change the face' of the WVC and showcase table tennis as a 'sport for life', accessible to players of all ages, genders, nationalities, ethnicities, social backgrounds and abilities.

Over the past two decades, the terms 'legacy' and 'leveraging' have emerged as arguably the two most powerful weapons in an event manager's arsenal. The concept of 'legacy' featured heavily from the outset of the ATEED-TTNZ bid, and a committee of 10 was subsequently tasked with the challenge of delivering these pre-event promises to an Antipodean audience where Rugby rules and other sports know their place. The Leveraging of Legacy (LoL) Committee was set up in August 2013 and their Strategic Plan 2014–2020 was launched in March 2014. The use of the LoL acronym was chosen to highlight the laughable attempts made by other major event organizers when it came to generating meaningful 'lasting' legacies. In sum, the LoL plan demonstrated this group's desire and determination to place legacy at the heart of the planning process and improve the local organizer's odds of offering a noteworthy long-term return on investment (ROI) by

TABLE 2.1   World Veteran Table Tennis Championships

Year	Country	City	Players	Nations
1982	Sweden	Gothenburg	450	21
1984	Finland	Helsinki	650	36
1986	Italy	Rimini	1100	38
1988	Croatia	Zagreb.	1650	45
1990	USA	Baltimore	1100	46
1992	Ireland	Dublin	1300	48
1994	Australia	Melbourne	1800	49
1996	Norway	Lillehammer	1950	49
1993	England	Manchester	1400	53
2000	Canada	Vancouver	1850	57
2002	Switzerland	Lucerne	2750	63
2004	Japan	Yokohama	2384	47
2006	Germany	Bremen	3650	59
2008	Brazil	Rio de Janeiro	1378	52
2010	China	Hohhot	2065	51
2012	Sweden	Stockholm	3263	61
2014	New Zealand	Auckland	1640	58

increasing the size and significance of a second-tier participant sports event that risked being overlooked by many living within the local community. The goal was to offer an unforgettable attendee experience that would enable the hosts (TTNZ) to establish a professional platform for six-years-worth of additional profile-raising leveraging opportunities.

Legacy-linked table tennis activities were delivered over a six-month period, which encompassed the six-day WVC. They were designed to turn existing awareness into attraction, attraction into attachment and attachment into affiliation. The expansion of an existing schools-based programme (Project Ping Pong) was identified as a viable tennis way of illustrating the social and health benefits associated with playing table tennis. Another notable WVC 2014 LoL action was the engagement of two Auckland tertiary education institutions: AUT University and Unitec Institute of Technology. The LoL events were initiated or inspired by students completing event-related degree courses, allowing the under-resourced, budget-restricted, operational team the chance to package and promote a series of value-adding leveraging activities to all attendees. In sum, the creation and consumption of a long-term plan provides the guardians of table tennis with a tangible legacy for the foreseeable future (ie something that should form the backbone of their sport's new strategic plan). Unlike a host of pre-event 'legacy' promises attached to other major events, the knowledge and experience offered by the LoL Committee, plus the lessons learned by the table tennis community, should ensure that WVC LoL opportunities continue to appear for future generations attracted to a true 'sport for life.'

Read more: **www.wvc2014.com/**

Prioritizing (mapping) the stakeholders

Perhaps with the exception of a birthday party, there is usually more than one person to consider when it comes to putting on an event. For most events there are a number of parties interested in the outcome of the event (the stakeholders). As the event organizer, it is important to consider what each stakeholder expects you to accomplish. The key stakeholders will also have a major influence on the outcome of the event (ie making it a success or making sure it's unsuccessful). With this in mind, it is essential to manage stakeholder relationships carefully to make sure that all of the important stakeholders are willing to work towards making the event a success.

For example, a large event such as a music festival will have a long list of stakeholders with both an interest in what is happening, and an influence on making the festival a success. As can be seen from the diagram in Figure 2.7 below, we have grouped the different stakeholders as either internal or external – that is whether they are from inside the client's organization (internal) or from outside the client's organization (external).

FIGURE 2.7   Internal and external stakeholders for a music festival

Internal Stakeholders
Festival Director
Event Manager
Employees
Volunteers

Event

External Stakeholders
Event attendees
Local community
Local authorities
Local businesses
Artists and performers
Media suppliers/traders
Emergency services

Different stakeholders will have different priorities for the same event, and it is not unusual for the interests of stakeholders to conflict with each other. A good question to ask is: How would each of the stakeholders like to see the largest portion of the budget spent? For the stakeholders for a music festival, the attendees will be delighted if the organizers 'blow' the biggest part of the budget by booking headline artists and performers, or upgrading camping, car parking or the food and drink area. The artists and performers would like to see the largest part of the budget spent on booking fees, with decent dressing rooms and other backstage facilities. The local community might want to see a portion of the budget allocated to upgrading facilities and amenities in the local area. But all too often, considerations of paying suppliers (such as sound engineers, with their equipment) are jeopardized by the desire to bring in a headline band (who won't be heard without sound equipment or technical support).

For an event organizer, keeping all of the various internal and external stakeholders satisfied is not always easy. In fact, it isn't always possible. As an event organizer, the key to putting on a successful event is being able to prioritize stakeholders (who are the most important) and to make sure that nobody significant gets upset or overlooked.

A helpful model for prioritizing (mapping) stakeholders is the Power and Interest Matrix shown in Figure 2.8.

This power and interest matrix model groups each of the stakeholders based on their power and interest in the event. It allocates the stakeholders to one of four quadrants/categories:

- Promoters (high power/high interest)
- Latents (high power/low interest)
- Defenders (low power/high interest)
- Apathetics (low power/low interest)

FIGURE 2.8   Mendelow's Stakeholder Power and Interest Matrix

Stakeholder power/interest matrix

High	Keep satisfied	Manage closely
Power	Monitor	Keep informed
Low	**Interest**	**High**

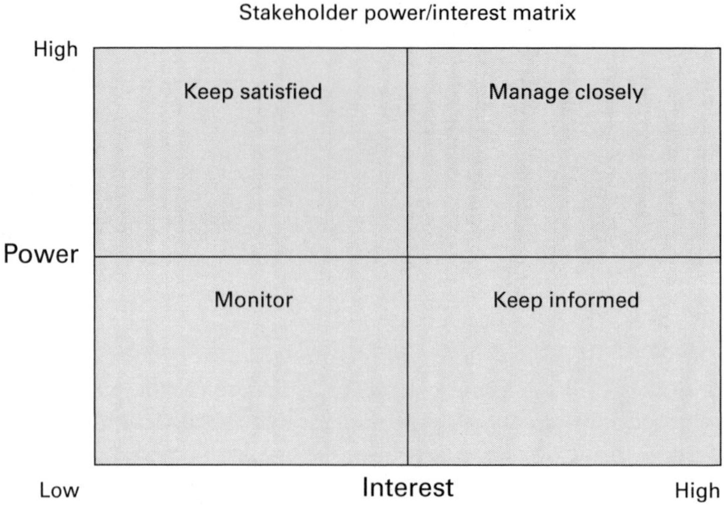

Adapted from Johnson, G, Scholes, K and Whittington, R (2010)

Depending on the category, the model suggests different strategies for the proper communication approach to each category of stakeholders. Stakeholders with high power and low interest need to be kept satisfied. Those with low interest and low power should be only monitored with minimum effort. A stakeholder with low power and high interest in the event should be kept informed and finally the high power, high interest stakeholders should be closely monitored and informed.

Once the various stakeholders have been mapped (prioritized) using the Power and Interest Matrix then a plan can be devised for a proper communications strategy for each stakeholder, eg manage closely, keep informed. Going back once again to the example of a music festival, if the festival organizers do not properly communicate and collaborate with the local community (including the local authority) then they are likely to find that, once detailed planning is under way, the objections to hosting the event begin and, in the worst case scenario, may mean they are not granted a licence or the permission needed to put on the festival.

The following case study expands on the relationship between an event agency and a key supplier – but it should be noted that at any one time, working on multiple events will involve managing multiple stakeholders, often with competing demands and with different priorities, demonstrating the complexity of the task.

CASE STUDY 2.2   Bracken Presentations: maintaining
relationships with stakeholders

Zoe Pickburn, Events Administrator at Bracken Presentations. UK Centre for
Events Management Graduate, 2014

Bracken Presentations is a small events company, based in Nottingham, which
was established by Managing Director, Jenny Gillmore, in 1997. Bracken largely
produces public sector events such as meetings, conferences and roadshows, as
well as offering support services for a variety of programmes. The importance of
establishing and maintaining relationships with all stakeholders of an event is
paramount for all events organizations: the event's ultimate success (or failure) is
dependent on the way that key stakeholders, such as the client and delegates,
feel towards the event (and, by extension, the organizers). These relationships are
also essential in the long term. The success of any business, and especially of a
smaller company like Bracken, relies on these relationships.

*The importance of relationships with all stakeholders cannot be stressed
enough. This is the aspect that I am most proud of at Bracken, and is
absolutely key to ongoing business.*

Jenny Gillmore (Managing Director)

An example can be seen in the strong relationship that Bracken have with KLN,
who are their preferred AV provider. Over the years Jenny has developed a close
relationship with Lee Malin, the owner. Both parties benefit from a high level of
trust. Bracken can trust KLN to produce high-quality recordings, removing risk
from the event, and in return KLN has a high level of autonomy. The relationship
also ensures that time isn't wasted searching for suppliers, and that Bracken are
quoted and charged a fair price for the service, creating cost-savings which can
be passed on to clients, adding value from their perspective, and ultimately
contributing towards return business.

Within any event, maintenance of relationships with key stakeholders is of
great importance. For Bracken, these stakeholders include venues and caterers
and, of course, the client, as well as delegates. All of these relationships remain
particularly challenging to maintain when dealing with public sector clients or any
large organization. Movement between departments can be frequent and sudden,
meaning that, although the client remains as a body (eg a government department),
the individual with whom you have built up a relationship and a rapport is liable to
change. This challenging aspect of working with public sector clients is resolved

at Bracken by having a clear chain of communication, as well as regular briefings, with both staff and clients, to ensure that everyone involved is kept 'up to date' with progress and that, should the contact change, there are always concise, up-to-date briefing and progress documents that can be consulted.

At a recent reception, which was a celebration of innovation-driven entrepreneurship for around 200 participants, the client was evidently a key stakeholder. Communication with the client included regular email contact, as well as routine reports and conference calls, beginning at fortnightly intervals and building up to weekly, and then daily during the final run-up to the event. Bracken also met the client at the venue in order to conduct a site inspection together and share ideas on the physical layout of the event, as well as the structure and content. The venue was another key stakeholder. As a prestigious government building was used, Bracken had to consider the high level of security in place, which made clear liaison essential. As well as meeting the client, they used the site inspection to confirm logistical elements of the layout and flow. Prior to the event they provided details of all attendees, including staff, crew and exhibitors, as well as delegates. As delegates are usually key stakeholders at events, strong communication with them is always essential; however, the high level of security at this reception meant that it required robust two-way communication channels, as Bracken had to collect a high level of information from all attendees in order to satisfy the requirements of the venue.

Read more: **www.brackenevents.co.uk**

Preparing the proposal

It is often the case that a potential client will 'shop around' to find the best event organizer to run their event. In this instance, a proposal is commonly prepared by an event organizer in order to persuade the client to hire them. The likelihood is that the client will have invited proposals from several professional event organizers and will ultimately choose which one to hire based on their assessment of the proposal. Therefore the 'art' of proposal writing is extremely important for a professional event organizer as this can often be how they secure most of their paid work. It is crucial that whoever assesses the proposal bids firmly believes that you are capable of putting on a great show!

Top Tip

You should do everything possible to improve the quality of your proposal writing. The cheapest way to do this is simply to make time to review it. It sounds obvious but ask yourself – how often do you review an important written document a matter of hours before the deadline? There are some excellent proposal and bid-writing courses and workshops that you can attend. These vary from short online instructional courses to more comprehensive training programmes delivered by professional bid-writers. You should also always ask the recipients for feedback on your proposals (especially for proposals which are unsuccessful). Sending a polite email that says, 'May I ask why my proposal was rejected?' might just help you to go on to win the next bid proposal.

The proposal itself could be anything from a simple one-pager, a detailed report or even a verbal presentation (more commonly referred to as a pitch). Whatever the form of the proposal, the purpose is the same: to sell your event concept (why, where, when, what and who) to a potential client and to sell yourself as a professional event organizer with the right skills and experience to stage the event. A simple template of what should be included in a proposal for a potential client is outlined in the following checklist.

CHECKLIST: event proposal template

Event details

☐ Event title

☐ Reasons for the event

☐ Objectives of the event

☐ Brief description of the event

☐ Event organizer details (including awards and accolades)

☐ Key members of the organizing team (including skills and experience)

Event concept

Why is the event happening?

- purpose
- goals and objectives
- key messages

Who is the event for?

- target audience

- profile (eg demographics)

- estimate of numbers

What will happen at the event?

- main activities

- event programme

- event format (eg reception, dinner, concert, lecture)

When and **Where** is the event taking place?

- date and time

- preferred location, surroundings

Event implementation (making it happen)

☐ Physical resource (venue, equipment, technology)

☐ Financial resource (budget, cash flow, ROI)

☐ Human resource (staff, volunteers, suppliers, contractors)

Other considerations

☐ Promotion and publicity

☐ Sponsorship

☐ Security

☐ Contingency plan

Perhaps the best-known examples of a competitive bidding process to put on an event is in the world of mega sporting events and competitions. Host cities and host nations compete against each other for the right to put on events such as the summer and winter Olympic Games and the FIFA World Cup. The bid procedure involves candidate cities or nations preparing a bid which demonstrates that there is political support and backing from the host region, that the necessary facilities and infrastructure to stage an international event will be in place and, of course, the ability of the host nation to organize the event. While not on the same scale as the competitive bidding process for a mega sporting competition, the Eventice competition is another excellent example of event organizers being asked to 'sell themselves' through a competitive bidding process. The Eventice is an Apprentice-style competition that allows final year Event Management students to compete to win their first job in the industry (read more about the Eventice competition in Case study 2.3).

But an event organizer does not have to create a proposal only when requested. O'Toole and Mikolaitas (2002) refer to the 'self generated proposal' where the idea for an event comes from the event organizer themselves. This is often the case in larger companies who host numerous 'in-house' events and ideas for new functions may well come from their in-house event team (eg where they have identified a gap in the current pro-gramme of events). Here the event organizer will pull together a convincing proposal to gain the support and financial resources needed to put on the event. It is imperative that the in-house event organizer is able to demonstrate the return on investment for their company. While they may not be competing with other event organizers to put on the function, they are competing with other internal departments and projects to secure funding. The return on investments might not be only financial but it could also be how the event will contribute to the company's mission statement, vision and values.

CASE STUDY 2.3   The Eventice competition

James Boardman: Project Manager at Blitz Communications Ltd. UK Centre for Events Management Graduate, 2013. Winner of The Eventice Competition, 2013

With the ever-growing popularity of the Event Management degree, with a UCAS course search revealing that over 60 institutions have a range of courses in event management, graduates are finding increasing competition and greater scrutiny when applying for their first role in the events industry.

> *Within such a highly competitive jobs market, it is essential that graduates show their passion for the industry and sell themselves and skills gained during any work experience, as well as highlighting the knowledge gained at University.*

(Liz Sinclair, ESP Recruitment)

Employers are expecting higher levels of competency, experience and skills and one of the many critical skills is bidding and pitching. ESP Recruitment, a company specializing in the event industry, launched, in 2011, The Eventice, an Apprentice-style competition that we run in association with *Event Magazine* and Bluehat Group, that allows final year Event Management students to compete to win two jobs in the industry. The competition, which is applied for by around 60 students annually from over 10 universities in the UK, sees 15 finalists go head-to-head to compete for the available job roles.

Graduates are required to take part in a number of activities and tasks to demonstrate their abilities to the judges who are industry professionals and potential employers. Munir Samji, CEO of Blitz Communications was responsible for judging candidates and stated, 'The competition was an excellent way for graduates to demonstrate their skills and previous experience to us. We were looking for graduates with the ability to sell themselves and their ideas, to persuade us that our clients would want them on their events. Above all, we were looking for positive attitude and affable personality.'

As the competition moves forward over three days, participants take part in a series of tasks to test their abilities. One of the critical tasks for judges to identify their new potential employee is the pitching and bidding task, where students go out into an exhibition hall of incentive travel stands, find an event venue, have two hours to develop an event concept, and then pitch the event back to the judges' panel in front of the opposition. Based on this task, judges make the decision which participants they would like to take through to the final.

The final aspect of the competition is based around presentation skills where finalists give two presentations to a theatre of industry professionals on topics such as upcoming event technology. Mike Hughes, winner of the Eventice in 2013, commented that 'the competition has given me a realistic perspective on the importance of bidding and pitching within the events industry; they are essential both within the recruitment process and as a key business skill'. This process demonstrates the importance of bidding and pitching skills to employers as it is often essential for job roles within the events industry.

Read more:

Walters, P (2009) Events management. *The Independent* [Online]
    www.independent.co.uk/student/career-planning/az-careers/
    events-management-1545878.html

Carry out a feasibility study

A formal feasibility study is usually carried out for larger, more complex, more elaborate events, which in turn usually means that the hosting of the event is more costly. With a greater financial investment needed as well as more time and effort to organize the event, the feasibility study focuses on helping to decide whether to proceed with the proposed event.

In determining the feasibility of an event there are two essential questions:

Is the proposed event the best solution?

Putting on an event is likely to be one way of achieving the desired objectives but it isn't necessarily the only solution (or even the best). An important part of the feasibility study is to consider alternative options and solutions for the proposed event. So, for example, if the purpose of a company hosting a staff party is to boost morale – why not just give everybody the day off or better still use the event budget to pay a bonus to staff? Similarly, if the objective of the event is to raise awareness of new products and services – why not spend the budget on increased advertising and new promotional literature?

Is the proposed event likely to succeed?

Some events planners will tell their client that 'anything is possible' when discussing their initial concept for an event. While we admire their optimism, the reality is that there are a number of crucial factors that will determine whether the event is likely to succeed. For instance, an event organizer will need to consider whether there is sufficient time, finance and support to put on the event, as well as ascertaining whether there is sufficient demand for an event from the intended target audience.

The following list includes the important questions to consider when determining if the proposed event is likely to succeed. Not all of these questions will be relevant to every event (as we've already said, no two events are ever the same) and you must choose the ones that are most appropriate given the circumstances.

Important questions to determine the feasibility of an event

- Is there enough time to organize the event?

- Is there enough time to secure a suitable location/venue?

- Is there enough time to promote the event to the target audience?

- Does the target audience have sufficient time to make arrangements to attend (eg book travel and accommodation)?

- Is there enough time to book guest speakers, artists, performers, entertainers and so on?

- Is the budget sufficient to put on the event?

- What is the likelihood of a favourable financial outcome (eg profit, break even)?

- What if the event is delayed, postponed or cancelled?

- Are there enough people willing to help organize the event?

- Is it likely there will be enough people to assist on the day of the event?

- Is support from participants, officials, media and other interested parties forthcoming?

- Is there enough support and interest from the target audience?

- Do we require specialist expertise and support to put on the event?

- Are the experts available/affordable?

Phase 2: Detailed planning

FIGURE 2.9   Phase Two: Detailed planning model

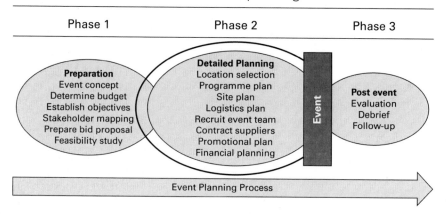

The detailed planning phase involves a whole host of different planning activities and tasks. Some of the tasks will be completed by the event organizer, others might be delegated to a team member while some tasks may require specialist expertise and support from outside the team.

Below we list the essential tasks during phase 2 – the detailed planning phase:

- Selecting the location and venue
- Planning the programme
- Planning the site layout
- Logistics planning

- Recruiting the event team
- Sourcing suppliers and contractors
- Promotion and publicity
- Financial and procurement planning

Each of the above tasks is only looked at briefly in this chapter but is discussed in more detail in subsequent chapters. It is, once again, also worth pointing out that these tasks are not necessarily carried out sequentially, with event organizers all working in their own way, and the various tasks will require different amounts of time and effort, depending on the nature of the event.

Selecting the location/venue

When choosing the event location (whether it be country, city or town), one of the most important factors is to consider the target audience. An event organizer needs to be confident that enough people will want to attend the event and so this involves thinking about how far people are willing to travel and also how accessible the location is by car or public transport as well as the cost of travel to and from the event. For example, an invitation to an event in an exotic location is likely to generate a lot of interest from the target audience but only if the time and cost of travel is affordable and available. You need to be confident that enough people will travel to attend the event.

Once the location has been decided upon, there may be a vast selection of venues to choose from (particularly in larger towns and cities) including purpose-built convention centres, hotels, sports stadiums, churches, museums, concert halls, universities, theatres, casinos, to name but a few. Outside the busier towns and cities your choice of venue may be more limited although with a little imagination even an empty field can be transformed into a glamorous event venue using temporary structures, marquees, tents and staging.

When choosing a venue there are obvious factors to consider like the availability of the venue, and the price and capacity of the venue. Depending upon the type of event, there will be other factors to consider which could include proximity to accommodation, availability of car parking at the venue or availability of free internet and so on. The image of a venue is another important factor to consider and whether this fits with the style of a particular event or the expectations of the event attendees. Closely linked to this is considering the reputation of a venue, but perhaps more important is the reputation of the venue staff – their capabilities and experience as well as their willingness to go the extra mile (customer service) with 62 per cent of event organizers/venue bookers saying that staff 'going the extra mile' was most important to their delegates (satisfaction) (Warwick Conferences, 2013).

When asked to research a city or region that you are unfamiliar with and therefore unlikely to know about the image or reputation of a location/

venue then a very good starting point is to contact the local Destination Marketing Organization (DMO), also sometimes referred to as a Convention and Visitor Bureau (CVB). DMOs can liaise with venues, secure permits, organize site visits and even help source local suppliers – and all free of charge. Destination Management Companies (DMCs) as well as Venue Finding Agencies (see our Case Study about Pineapple Events in Chapter 3) are also well known for their expertise in helping event organizers to put on an event in a city or region they are unfamiliar with – although in both cases this will be in return for a fee or commission.

Planning the programme

Having already developed a clear idea of 'who' will be attending the event (during the preparation phase), the next step is to create a programme of activities to meet the tastes of the target audience. For example, a music festival organizer will book headline acts that meet the musical tastes of festival goers, or a charitable fundraiser arranging a black tie dinner will select a menu which satisfies the culinary tastes of the guests.

The type of event and its main purpose will also influence the nature of the programme or schedule. A team-building event, for instance, will probably include activities such as raft-building and orienteering, whereas a staff Christmas party is more likely to include a line-up of singers, dancers and performers. The chosen location will often influence the programme of activities. For example, if a location is famous for a scenic view, a place of interest or even a popular night spot, it is likely that this will be incorporated into the event programme as part of the social activities.

The event programme is likely to include a combination of both 'formal' and 'informal' activities. A wedding service, the cutting of the ribbon at a shop launch, an opening address from a company owner are all likely to be considered as formal proceedings in an event programme whereas the 'informal' event will include social activities such as day trips and visits, music and entertainment, dinner, drinks and dancing. The event organizer needs to pull all of the various activities together into an event programme (or schedule) which clearly shows when everything is taking place. There is always the temptation to cram in lots of activities but be sure to give attendees the time to relax too, particularly if the event is being held over a number of days.

Planning the site layout

The event site may be indoors or outdoors but, wherever the event is taking place, a proper plan of the layout of the event site needs to be prepared. When designing a site plan, one of the first considerations is creating the right environment for the attendees. The 'right' environment will depend upon the type of event. Take, for example, attendees at a classical music concert who will want to have a good view of the orchestra playing as well as plenty of leg room to sit comfortably. Attendees at a rock concert, on the other hand, may well expect the hustle and bustle of a busy crowd to add to the atmosphere and their enjoyment of the concert. While a little hustle and bustle amongst the concert audience is acceptable, it is imperative to ensure the safety of the audience and this is another crucial consideration when planning the layout of the site. A well-planned site will mean the risk of crowd congestion and crowd crush is reduced.

The layout of an event will depend upon the size and scale of it, as well as the format and nature of activities taking place. When drawing up a site plan, there are certain fundamentals that apply to almost any event, such as: ensure that attendees can easily enter and exit the site, provide attendees with a central point (perhaps a helpdesk, registration desk) that can easily be found and ensure that facilities, such as toilets and cloakroom, are also obvious and not too far to walk to.

The event site plan is used by different people for different purposes. The organizing team will use the site map to get everybody set up and in the right place, the suppliers and contractors will refer to their site map to locate power supply and water and the attendees will refer to their copy of the site plan to find their way to the toilets or the nearest bar.

Logistics planning

Logistics planning at an event is primarily about ensuring the smooth flow and movement of people on to an event site, around the site and finally off it. It sounds simple but it is in fact one of the biggest challenges faced by an event organizer. Indeed the biggest logistical challenge is sometimes before the event is even under way. Take, for example, a conference organizer attempting to get hundreds of conference delegates from around the world to their event, which is likely to involve making hundreds of bookings for transport and accommodation as well as making arrangements for hotel check-ins and conference registration.

Event logistics planning is not only concerned with the flow and movement of the event attendees but also ensuring that suppliers, contractors and support services are all in the right place ahead of the event. For example, a festival organizer is likely to have a mammoth task on their hands getting all the suppliers and contractors on-site before the event begins and that's even before considering the challenges of getting an entire cast of artists and performers, celebrities, VIPs and media on and off the site during the festival.

A good logistics plan should also clearly set out the communication protocol for staff and key personnel. Using the example of a music festival once more, the plan should include contact details for stage managers, artist liaisons as well as for the artists and performers who are involved in the event in case there is a delay or change of plan.

Recruiting the event team

It may be that an event organizing team is already in place. This is often the case with larger, more complex events where the volume of the workload requires a team effort. For a private party the event organizing team might be made up of family, friends and neighbours whereas for a business event the organizing team might be made up of work colleagues, colleagues working in other departments as well as people from partner organizations outside the company. Whoever forms the organizing team, it is important to make sure that all agree upon their roles and responsibilities early on as, ultimately, the effectiveness of the organizing team can have a significant bearing on the success of the event. The key is to ensure that each member of the team has the role to which they are best suited. Profiling and diagnostic tools, such as Belbin's team roles or Myers Briggs personality types (see Case Study 6.2) can be used with teams to determine the most suitable roles and responsibilities.

As the event date draws closer, it is likely that additional team members will be recruited to help with arrangements. A music festival organizer, for example, will be looking for new recruits to assist with ticketing, wrist band exchange, stewarding and security roles. The number of staff needed will depend on the number of event attendees who are expected. The complexity of the event will also influence the number of staff required. For example, an international conference with several high-profile guest speakers, each giving presentations simultaneously in different rooms, will typically require a member of staff to be in place in each of the presentation rooms.

It is strongly recommended, for larger events such as the examples of a music festival or international conference, that one person in the organizing team is given overall responsibility for recruiting the event team. Getting the right event team in place will take a significant amount of time and effort. And, of course, it isn't only recruiting sufficient numbers of staff but training new team members, organizing shift patterns, dealing with payroll, organizing staff uniforms and many other essential tasks. There is certainly more than enough to keep one dedicated person busy.

Sourcing suppliers and contractors

The larger the event, the more likely it is that an event organizer will need to source external suppliers and contractors. The more complex or more elaborate an event, the greater will be the need for specialist goods and services (eg increased technical support). There are quite literally thousands of specialist suppliers who can provide elements of the goods and services needed by an event organizer, ranging from providing additional staff, to marquee tents and furniture, to flowers and gifts. Indeed, there is a supplier for just about any item or service you could possible imagine.

For the event organizer, the challenge is in selecting the right suppliers who will provide excellent service and support. While there is clearly much to consider when selecting suppliers, there are two simple factors which should always be a high priority. Firstly, it is important to know the past experience of a potential supplier. Have they done this type of work before? Do they have a proven track record? In some cases, it might be beneficial to select a new fledgling company, as the supplier will be keen and eager to impress (and more often than not cheaper too). Secondly, it is important to look into the reputation of a potential supplier. In most cases suppliers who have a good reputation in the industry do so because they are well-established and have been in the business for a long time. Where possible, event organizers should stick with suppliers with a proven track record (prior experience) and who come highly recommended.

Promotion and publicity

The methods used to promote an event will depend primarily on the target audience and the best ways to reach that audience within the allocated promotional budget. By now, the event organizer should already have a clear idea of the profile of the target customer. The next step in developing an effective promotional plan is to determine the best way to communicate information about the event to the target audience. The event organizer has a variety of promotional tools at their disposal including sending personal invitations, putting up posters and leaflets about the event or placing an advert in a newspaper or magazine. Generally speaking the most effective promotional methods are those that communicate directly with the target audience, eg a personal letter of invitation to the event or a telephone call to recommend that people 'hold the date'.

Creating promotional tools can be very costly and, if not chosen wisely, can take up a large portion of the event budget. In particular, advertising space in a glossy magazine or national newspaper is likely to be very expensive. With this in mind, it is essential to ensure that the quality of advertising material is up to standard. Be sure to allocate sufficient time for promotional matter to be designed and produced ahead of the event. There is such a thing as free publicity when it comes to promoting an occasion, with newspapers, magazines, radio and television stations all regularly featuring content related to upcoming events. That is, of course, assuming there is a newsworthy story related to the event for the media to run. It might be, for example, that the event coincides with another high-profile happening or that there will be VIPs attending.

Financial and procurement planning

As any business owner will tell you, cash is king. Cash flow is the life supply of any organization with more businesses going under because of cash flow problems than because of anything else. If an event organizer doesn't have the money to, for instance, pay the staff wages then things are likely to go rapidly downhill. The basic principle of good cash flow management is to make sure that there is more money coming in to the business than going out of it. But good cash flow management is also about making sure that the money comes in on time and this is where it can become problematic for some events. Take, for example, a 'pay at the door' ticketed concert. The majority of incoming money will only do so through ticket sales on the day of the event. If the event organizer has to pay out lots of money beforehand (eg booking artists, advertising the concert, etc) then that could be a large chunk of money going out before any money comes in from ticket sales. Good financial planning involves anticipating any shortfalls in money which allows the event organizer to make contingency plans for cash flow (eg extending credit and payment terms).

While it would obviously be good for an event organizer to have all the money they need to put on the event, they may need to raise additional funds. Traditionally, events have been quite successful at attracting sponsors. Contra deals are also commonplace in the events industry where, unlike a sponsorship deal, no money exchanges hands; instead there is a trade of mutually beneficial goods or services. So, for example, an event organizer might borrow some lighting and sound equipment for their event and in exchange will give the supplier on-site promotional and branding opportunities.

Sound financial planning also involves contingency planning (the 'what if' scenario). For example, what if the event is cancelled, abandoned or postponed? How will this impact on finances? Does the organizer have appropriate insurance to cover actual event costs?

Phase 3: Post-event

FIGURE 2.10   Phase Three: Post-event

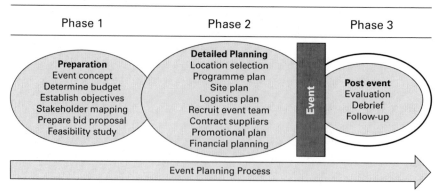

In order to make your event as successful as possible, it is important that certain key tasks are carried out after the event. Although each of these activities will be carried out post event, it is sensible to begin planning them in advance. For example, it is widely agreed that conducting a proper event evaluation is extremely important (indeed we have dedicated an entire chapter to event evaluation) and helps to make planning future events much easier. Post-event evaluation can be extremely complex but can also be fairly simple, eg planning a post-event debrief with key members of the event organizing team and distributing a simple survey to find out the event attendees' opinions. Furthermore, it is important to plan carefully any follow-up activities that need to be completed post event, eg sending a personal communication to thank guests for attending the event.

Evaluation

An evaluation after the event allows the event organizer to find out if they achieved their intended aims and objectives. A proper event evaluation will also help the organizer to assess what worked well and what didn't work well, providing them with useful lessons for planning future events. Evaluation can also be a good way of showing others (eg clients, sponsors and partners) that the event was a success, which can ultimately help to justify future events.

An important part of the evaluation will involve finding out the event attendees' opinions. One of the myths about evaluation is that it is extremely complicated and time-consuming but it doesn't have to be. For example, creating an evaluation survey is an easy way to gather valuable feedback from attendees (eg What did they most enjoy? What did they least enjoy?). The types of questions used in the survey are important and these should be linked to the intended aims and objectives. For an event such as a conference or seminar, where there is an educational purpose, it will be important to ascertain not just what attendees most enjoyed but also what the attendees have learned and how they will change what they do as a result of this learning. In this instance, it can be more beneficial to give attendees a survey some time after the conference or seminar (ie after they have been able to put some of their learning into practice) to find out their opinion.

As well as finding out the opinions of the event attendees, a proper event evaluation will take into account the opinions of the event participants (eg performers, artists, speakers) and also the event organizing team, as well as the thoughts of key suppliers, contractors and partner organizations. This leads us on to the importance of planning a proper event debrief.

Debrief

An important part of the post-event evaluation is a debrief meeting with key individuals from the event organizing team as well as key suppliers and partner organizations. The debrief meeting is an important part of the overall event evaluation as it looks at the event from the perspective of those 'experts' involved in putting it on. The very nature of the events industry means that immediately after an event the majority of the event organizing team as well as the wider team (suppliers, contractors and so on) will head off in separate directions, most likely en route to their next event. With this in mind, it is a good idea to carry out some sort of a debrief immediately at the end of the event while everyone is still on-site – this is often referred to as a 'hot debrief'.

In addition, scheduling a debrief meeting not too long after the event is also important. A 'cold debrief' gives everybody time for reflection and allows enough time for the evaluation data gathered from the attendees to be processed. While scheduling a 'cold debrief' with busy events professionals after the event has finished can prove extremely problematic, don't underestimate the importance of gaining valuable feedback from the 'experts'. The reality is that not everything will have gone to plan. There will be things that worked well but there will also be things that could have gone better. It is important to learn lessons from the 'experts' to improve the event for next time.

Follow-up

Event follow-up often involves sending out a personal communication to event participants (eg a thank you for their involvement). It can also involve sending out promotional materials that you did not give out at the event (eg sending a heavy brochure to an interested client) as well as distributing invites and information about upcoming events. It is easy to bombard people with mail-outs and emails so be sure to plan your follow-up campaign carefully to avoid this.

A final word on the event-planning process...

There is no 'one right way' when it comes to the step-by-step process for planning and organizing an event. That is to say – it's unlikely an event organizer will carry out the essential tasks in the same sequence that we've presented them. Indeed, nor is it likely that two event organizers will carry out the essential tasks in exactly the same sequence or dedicate the same amount of time to each task. This is perfectly acceptable because, like we said at the beginning of the chapter, the unique nature of an event means that no two events are the same, which in turn means the process of planning an event is never quite the same. However, for larger, more complex events it is essential that an event organizer adopts a more systematic approach to planning and organizing the event. Imagine, for a moment, trying to plan a week-long international trade show with more than 5,000 delegates attending from all around the world, using only the simple three-phase model we presented at the beginning of the chapter (refer to Figure 2.4). No matter how experienced and talented an organizer you might be, the reality is that relying on such a basic model means that you're bound to forget or overlook something important. In this situation, even the most experienced event organizer will adopt a more systematic approach to planning the event.

Top Tip

Developing your own 'bespoke' event-planning model is an excellent way of ensuring a consistent approach to organizing events. Using a standardized and consistent approach to plan each event will help to create a more cost effective, efficient way of organizing events. Furthermore, developing your own model means that you are continually able to test it out and implement changes to make your approach better and better (ie increasingly effective and efficient).

Case study 2.4 gives the story behind a team of event organizers working for the National Health Service who developed their own 'bespoke' event-planning model.

CASE STUDY 2.4 Developing an event planning model

Ken Brown, Centre Administrator at Kip McGrath, Former Lecturer at UK Centre for Events Management and **Ruth Dowson**, Senior Lecturer, UK Centre for Events Management, Former Head of Events at NHS Connecting for Health

From 2002 to 2007, we worked together as part of two in-house teams delivering events for two national programmes within the National Health Service (NHS). The first team had previously been made up of individuals tasked with delivering events but the problem was that each person had other responsibilities, and so they had each developed their own ways of working. None would have described themselves as an 'events professional' at the time. One of our first events was taken over at short notice, due to the original lead person being taken ill – as a result, no one really knew what was going on, and we ended up staffing an event for much larger numbers than actually attended. We then realized that we needed

FIGURE 2.11 Dowson & Brown event planning model –

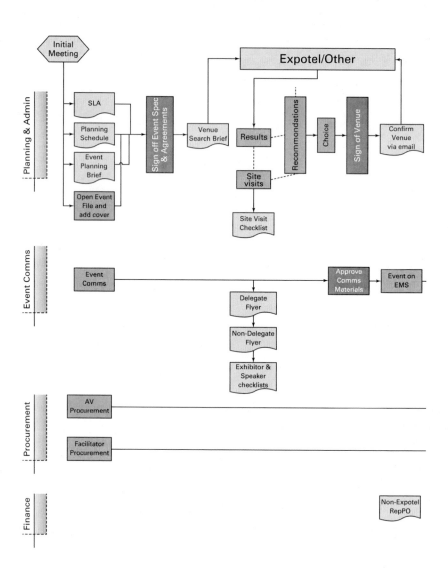

process map

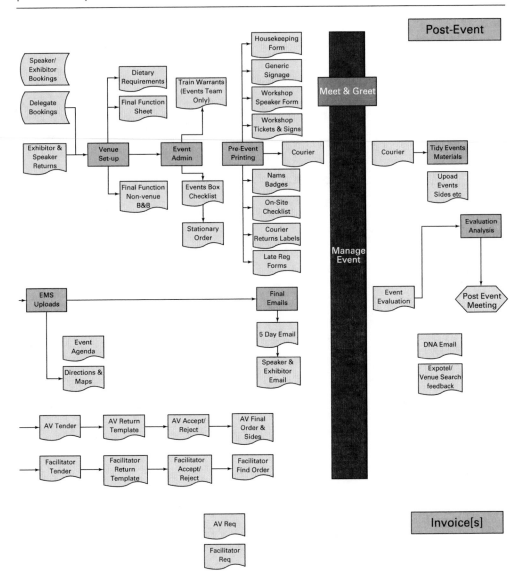

to develop more effective and efficient ways of working, so we gathered everyone in the core team together, along with a number of people who worked in the regions, to develop a shared process that would enable us to present a consistent experience to our event attendees and build in improvements into the process systems and content of the events we would run in the future. Our intention was to reduce the time involved in event planning, and to provide our event attendees with a professional experience that supported them in their roles in the NHS.

We asked everyone to bring with them copies of all the documentation they used, including emails, spreadsheets and handouts. We grouped these together into each step in the planning and communication processes, and stuck them all on the wall. Together, working in pairs, we went round every activity, adding our comments and thoughts. We then began to map out our delivery and communication processes, agreeing each step, to introduce a consistent approach, so that anyone coming to one of our organization's events would become familiar over time with the way we did things. Then we moved on to considering the content of the documentation, bringing together the 'best' of everyone's work and ending up with a series of templates that would be used by everyone delivering events in our organization. The process map, which is shown in Figure 2.11, became the way we delivered event planning, and we shared this with as many people who would listen. We set up an online shared drive (which would have been so much easier with Google Docs!) with a common file structure for events, populated with the templates that we had agreed, and branded for our organization. So every time we had a new event, we just copied and pasted the template file structure and renamed it for our new event.

Our mantra became 'why reinvent the wheel?'. We developed a 'buddy' system so no event was ever run by just one person; there was always a 'lead event manager' and a buddy, who knew what progress was being made. We also worked with our online partner to develop an online event management and booking system, that automated a lot of our administration and communications. Our office walls held poster-sized copies of our event-planning processes, (the process map is shown in Figure 2.11, the 'Dowson & Brown Model'), and we encouraged each other to consider improvements on an ad hoc basis, as well as having regular quarterly team meetings to review our processes and systems. As a result, the team was able to develop consistent high quality and improve our work, delivering hundreds of events around the country each year, attended by some 30,000 NHS employees.

Chapter summary

- The success (or failure) of any event is largely down to what happens long before the day of the event, in other words, how well it is planned.
- Planning any event involves a certain amount of repetition because there are various key activities and tasks that are carried out for most events.
- Prior to the commencement of detailed event planning it is essential to clarify the event concept, objectives (including stakeholder objectives) and budget as well as considering the feasibility of the event.
- Creating a convincing proposal document is essential to gain support for an event – whether this be from an external or internal client.
- The detailed planning of an event involves a whole host of different activities and for larger events it is likely an event organizer will need to delegate certain tasks.
- Post-event activities such as the event evaluation need to be planned well in advance in order to provide useful lessons for future events.
- Developing your own 'bespoke' event-planning model can help ensure a standardized, more consistent approach to planning events and will make sure that you don't overlook anything important.

Reference list

Allen, J (2009) *Event Planning: The ultimate guide to successful meetings, corporate events, fundraising galas, conferences and conventions, incentives and other special events*, John Wiley & Sons, Ontario, Canada

O'Toole, W and Mikolaitis, P (2002) *Corporate Event Project Management*, John Wiley & Sons Inc, New York

Powell, C (2013) *How to Deliver OUTSTANDING Corporate Events*, Lulu Publishing, North Carolina

Warwick Conferences (2013) *The Value of Satisfaction: An independent report into how customer satisfaction affects the value of meetings, conferences and event* [online] available from: www.warwickconferences.com/value-satisfaction [Accessed: 1 March 2015]

Destination and venue selection

This chapter reflects the importance of selecting an appropriate destination for an event, which may be a region in the world, a specific country, or a region within a country. The actual location (which may be a town, a city, or a rural locality) is the next priority, followed by choosing the venue for the event. This decision-making process is a vital part, not only of the event-planning process, but also contributes to the delivery and success of the event itself.

The chapter explains the process for selecting a venue and discusses potential issues, with advice on how to resolve problems. Once the venue has been selected, the chapter concludes with a detailed section advising on how to work with the venue team to ensure a smooth event delivery.

This chapter will consider:

- Selecting the destination
- Choosing the venue
- Venue-search options
- The importance of visiting the venues prior to making the decision
- Communicating with event attendees about the venue
- Managing the operational relationship with the venue

The various aspects of the venue selection process, as covered in the chapter, are shown in the diagram (Figure 3.1).

Part of the process of agreeing the venue search brief is to identify the fit between the overall event objectives and 'Must-Haves' and the venue selection 'Must-Haves', which could include:

- Geographical location
- Transportation links
- Image, style, or reputation of the venue or location and fit with corporate culture
- Type of venue
- Venue atmosphere
- Relative size of the venue compared to your event

- Room capacities and layout
- Suitable facilities available onsite or potential to bring them in, including technology and accessibility
- Cost/value for money
- Proximity, quality and cost of accommodation (for the events team and for delegates)

FIGURE 3.1 The venue selection process

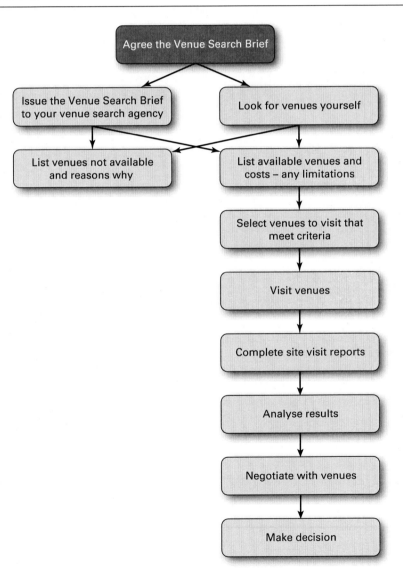

Principles that apply to selecting the destination

When selecting your geographical location there are key aspects to consider.

The image of the location as it relates to the client organization and to the event:

Many event managers spend their time seeking out the most amazing and wonderful locations – yet, perhaps surprisingly, some events are better held in less exotic locations. In this era when corporate governance is increasingly important, there may be valid reasons why you don't want to draw attention to your event, or to your client. Remember the images from the opening ceremony of the London 2012 Olympics – when the corporate guests stayed away from embarrassment about having the best seats in the house? Yet by doing so, they drew attention to themselves, while the person in the street railed at the Olympic organizers because there were visibly empty seats. It's no longer just the public sector that wishes to be seen to be obtaining value for money – the influence of the Freedom of Information Act has its impact here – but more and more companies are considering the views of their stakeholders when selecting event venues and taking decisions that fit with the corporate values they publicly espouse and, increasingly, based on a reaction to: 'What would this look like as a story in the *Daily Mail*?' On the other hand, it may be the *most* important factor to wow your client and attendees with an exciting and unusual location or venue. And it's about what image the location or venue *appears* to have – despite any cost implications. So if it's a five-star luxury hotel, it could be less important that you got it for a bargain, as internal messages about being thrifty can be undermined by the political impact of the image your decision portrays in the media.

Accessibility on public transport and by road

For an event to work, it's important to consider where you want the event to be: easily reached – or out of the way. So if your event is for a global audience that requires an atmosphere of calm and tranquillity, there's no point looking at venues in the area surrounding Heathrow airport, however convenient that seems. Instead, you need to research venues far from traffic and noise, where participants can wander around undisturbed. Understanding the purpose of the event is vital even at this point. Make sure you're clear about that purpose and identify what you want to achieve and what kind of environment and atmosphere you want to create. And here, transport links are vital – especially for one-day events where participants may be travelling for several hours to attend. The last thing you want is for them to arrive frazzled and stressed, so it helps to choose a venue that is easy to reach. Public transport links are also important considerations for event sustainability and you can encourage car-sharing if groups are coming from the same direction.

Travel time for potential participants:

In the UK, a 'central location' for an event is often considered to be London, especially because of the excellent rail and air links into the capital. However, it's important to work out where your event participants are coming from and reconsider any 'southern-centric' views you may have. The time it takes for residents and visitors to travel across London once they have arrived in the capital can often make other locations, such as Birmingham, easier to get to, especially for a larger group of people. Alternatively, if your event attendees are travelling from across a wide area, it may be worthwhile considering holding several smaller events in different geographic regions.

Top Tip

Make sure the choice of location and venue fits with the objectives and style of your event, as well as the image and reputation of the client and their organization.

The next case study explains why Britain is such a popular destination for international events.

CASE STUDY 3.1   Britain: Great for events

Tony Rogers, Managing Director, Tony Rogers Conference & Event Services, website: www.tony-rogers.com, and Visiting Fellow, UK Centre for Events Management

The 2012 Olympic and Paralympic Games illustrated Britain's unrivalled expertise in staging a world-class event, using unique skills in innovation, creativity, logistical planning and presentation. The 2012 Games showed off Britain's array of unique venues, its iconic destinations, its organizational strengths and the ability to fuse a sporting event with opportunities to highlight trade and export opportunities and drive tourism activity.

Britain has one of the best-developed stock of destinations, venues and service suppliers in the world, offering a depth of facility and expertise to ensure the successful staging of events and a guarantee of a memorable experience for those attending them. Servicing business visitors and delivering world-class events also means providing stimulating careers and employment opportunities. The powerful outcomes from the 2012 Games should not be seen as simply a one-off benefit of a once-in-a-lifetime event. Every day, throughout Britain, meetings, conferences, exhibitions, trade fairs, outdoor events, incentive travel programmes, corporate hospitality, cultural and sporting events and festivals are being held. Through the skills of Britain's event organizing companies, some of the highest-profile events in the world – from major industrial, political, commercial, medical, scientific and educational conferences and trade exhibitions to leading-edge motivational, cultural, sporting and music events – are designed and staged. Britain's event businesses are in high demand to deliver more trade and exports, increase knowledge, grow cultural appreciation and enrich the visitor economy.

Festivals, consumer shows, sporting events and other cultural and music events all help to animate destinations which, in turn, encourages more tourism, more business visitors and investors, and students wishing to come to the UK to study.

As an industry, events lead to the employment of some 530,000 people from apprenticeship level upwards. They stimulate thought leadership through the sharing of knowledge, research and intelligence, that progresses scientific and technological understanding and innovation. They also bring communities together, whether united by a common geography, interest, cause or belief.

Finally, events attract international audiences to the UK, who buy British products and services and, in many cases, return with their families, boosting and complementing the UK tourism industry.

The economic dimensions of Britain's events sector

The sector is worth £39.1 billion to the UK economy in terms of direct spend by event delegates, attendees and organizers. A substantially higher figure is achieved once the wider economic impacts (indirect and induced spend plus accompanying persons' spend) are included. Table 3.1 provides 2014's best estimates for the value to the visitor economy of the discrete segments that comprise the overall events sector in respect of their direct spend.

The spend by those accompanying attendees at business events is worth an additional £7.7 billion. It is estimated that, in 2013, 1.25 million business events were held in the UK, attended by some 91 million delegates (source: 'UK Events Market Trends Survey 2014').

Enterprise and employment

There are over 25,000 businesses in the sector including event organizers, venues, destination marketing organizations (DMOs), destination management

TABLE 3.1   The value of Britain's events sector

Conferences and meetings	£19.9 billion*
Exhibitions and trade fairs	£11.0 billion*
Incentive travel and performance improvement	£1.2 billion**
Corporate hospitality and corporate events	£1.2 billion**
Outdoor events	£1.1 billion**
Festivals and cultural events	£1.1 billion**
Music events	£1.3 billion*
Sporting events	£2.3 billion**†
Total	**£39.1 billion**

*   based on new research
**   based on previous research estimates
†   the figure for sporting events is the estimated spend by inbound visitors to Britain to play in and watch sporting events in 2008

companies (DMCs), exhibition contractors, event production companies, and a whole plethora of suppliers: transport operators, telecommunications and IT companies, interpreters and translators, speciality caterers, event insurance specialists, and many others.

Events offer a rich diversity of jobs and employment opportunities, from apprenticeship level upwards, both skilled and less skilled, for the young as well as the more mature, male and female – including many opportunities for volunteering and stewarding.

Business Visits & Events Partnership

The Business Visits & Events Partnership (BVEP) is an umbrella organization representing leading trade and professional organizations, government agencies and other significant influencers in Britain's business visits and events sector.

The BVEP exists to:

- garner the cohesive opinion of these stakeholders and to collectively influence and develop policies, practices and strategies that support and generate growth in the sector

- raise sector awareness through clear communications of the social and economic benefits of the business visits and events sector.

The Partnership seeks to provide a unified point of view for the entire business visits and events sector. The BVEP works with prominent sector leaders including its partners, government departments and agencies to influence and develop policies and practices favourable to the growth of business events, and trade and creative enterprise through business visits and events.

It has the support of the leading trade and professional organizations and government agencies with a shared interest in the economic benefit and growth of conferences, meetings, exhibitions, trade fairs, incentive travel, corporate hospitality, ceremonies, as well as other business, sporting, cultural and festival events.

Read more: **www.businessvisitsandeventspartnership.com**

Different venue types

The range of venues is wider today than ever before, as organizations seek to maximize their income by hiring out their facilities when they are not being used for their primary purpose. So no longer is the only consideration which hotel to use, the world is your oyster; whether you end up holding your event in a field or on a boat, churches, castles, hospitals and aircraft hangars (with built-in aircraft) will all be vying to provide you with event space. The following case study shows how one 'unusual venue' meets that challenge.

CASE STUDY 3.2   An unusual venue – Life Centre Events, Bradford, Yorkshire

Ben Southall, Sales and Event Manager, Life Centre Events, UK Centre for Events Management Graduate

One would not imagine that such a versatile, flexible and unusual venue could be situated in the heart of Bradford, West Yorkshire. Life Centre Events opened in 2000, with the sole purpose of serving the corporate industry by providing a 'blank canvas' venue for events for companies and organizations.

The venue is a modern building with the ability to host a wide range of events, from small training workshops for teachers, to AGMs for 2,000 people, and gala dinners seating up to 850 people. Life Centre Events gives its entire profits to charity. There is a day-care facility on site, where clients can drop their children off should they need to, as well as a Starbucks. The venue has state-of-the-art sound and visual systems and technical equipment, providing excellent support and saving the client hassle and cost. The flat floor means no tiered seating, and no pillars or any other fixed objects to obscure the view and in the four rooms that come complete with stages, three can easily be removed to maximize the space available. The large main auditorium has a fixed, permanent stage, but the hall is constructed in a way that enables easy partitioning, to create a large exhibition space if needed.

Life Centre Events has seven meeting rooms, spread across two buildings, and the site's 280 car-parking spaces are private and add no cost to the client or event participants. These two venues sit parallel to each other, with parking spaces separating them and behind the building as well. Alongside the two buildings there is a grassed area with its own balcony, ideal for hosting informal 'It's a Knockout' events or outdoor dinners, providing an escape from the routine of an all-day meeting.

The venue, which is close to the city's two train stations and the motorway system, is positioned in an enclosed, private campus, that enables attendees to feel secluded from the surrounding areas and able to focus on their purpose.

The benefit of the venue being a blank canvas enables clients to use their creativity and innovation to shape it to meet their specific needs, from room layout to complete décor, whether for the Christmas period or other occasions. This flexibility and the range of rooms provides advantages for client companies who want to book smaller seminar rooms for a one-off training session, or host 70 people for a dinner, but can be used as event production offices for the event team to retreat to, or even do last-minute preparation for their key-note!

As well as corporate meetings and conferences, Life Centre Events has hosted many large gatherings, including, for the past 14 years, the Rocknations Youth Foundation annual conference. The purpose of this event is to empower young people and teach them leadership skills. Attendees' ages range from 11–18, and the campus, with its two venues, allows for a wide range of activities, seminars and even outdoor pursuits, such as skateboarding and football. The event completely takes over the venue for four days with every square foot being used. Participants think it's a great event, and testimony to what such a venue can do. What makes it unusual? On Sundays, it's a church.

Read more: **www.lifecentreevents.com**

Venue selection

When choosing your venue, it is important to start with a series of questions that help you to identify the suitability of a range of possible venues for deeper consideration.

A template of these key questions is provided for you, in Figure 3.2 below, as event managers, to match to your own needs in order to develop a clear venue search brief. This template can be used as a starting point for the venue search, to be tailored to your organization, to your client and to your event. This template is based around a corporate event but could be adapted for any event.

FIGURE 3.2   Venue search brief template

EVENT VENUE SEARCH BRIEF				
To: Venue Search Agency				
Completed by: **Date:**			**Team:**	
Title of event(s):			**Event Owner:**	
Budget holder, team and contact details:				
Budget:	**Total budget:**	**Venue budget:**	**B&B budget (per person):**	**DB&B rate (per person):**
Cost code:				
Event Details				
Number of events: (National, regional or local)				
Proposed date(s): Please provide a number of options				
Event location(s): **NON-HOTEL VENUES ONLY**				
Event timings: Start & finish times – include full programme				
Estimated number of delegates per session:				

FIGURE 3.2 *continued*

Events Requirements			
Main room:	Capacity:		Layout: Cabaret as standard
Breakout rooms:	No. of rooms:	Capacities:	Layout: Cabaret as standard
Exhibition area:	No. of stands (based on 3 x 2m):		

Accommodation
[Please include quote for accommodation with any non-residential conference venues]

All rooms are non-smoking, double rooms for single occupancy

B&B accommodation required befor event(s)	Date:	Qty:
B&B accommodation required during event(s)	Date:	Qty:

- **Please note that if delegates are on a B&B rate, there is a £XX.00 allocation for food & drink (no alcohol). Any additional charges are to be directed to the individual.**
- **If DB&B accommodation is required, dinner and/or breakfast may be taken in restaurant or by room service. Additional charge for room service should go to the main account.**
- **Please ensure all charges are routed correctly prior to delegate arrival at the hotel.**

Catering Requirements
[Please confirm in the response to this brief that these are provided, and the cost]

Breaks:	Normal provision of tea, coffee and biscuits, on arrival, mid-morning and mid-afternoon (3 servings) including:
	  • Selection of decaffeinated drinks, fruit teas, hot water, cold water and orange juice
	  • Fresh fruit (especially bananas)

Menus:	We do **not** have deep fried or fatty foods and the following menus are most appropriate to our events. These are suggested menus and we are open to alternative options from the venue. – Hot meat, fish and vegetarian dishes – Selection of cheeses – Selection of cold meats – Vegetable kebabs – Baked potatoes – Selection of salads including: green leaf, bean, tomato basil & mozzarella, coleslaw and celeriac, pasta and rice salads – Fresh granary rolls / breads – Light dessert including cheese & biscuits and fresh fruit – Tea, coffee, water and fruit juice
Lunch:	Preferred choice eg Packed lunch, hot food, No of courses etc

Dinner:	Date:	Time:	Venue:
	Delegates receive an allowance of £20 for their evening meal and should be charged back to the main account. No alcohol is permitted in this evening meal subsidy.		

Special dietary requirements:	There must be a wide range of choice for vegetarians. Other special dietary requirements will be communicated with the venue with final numbers or as they arise.

Other Requirements
[Please confirm in the response to this brief that these are provided]

Disabled access to all areas used by the event

As a health-aware organization, we require a No Smoking environment. Signage should indicate No Smoking

Car-parking – venue should specify:
- whether car-parking is available on site or nearby
- number of spaces available
- cost
- whether charges can be added to the final invoice

No alcohol to be charged to the main account

Alongside the venue search brief is a list of standard requirements, which you can adapt to those of your organization and its internal processes, policies and regulations (such as the attitude towards paying for alcohol with company money). An example is shown in Figure 3.3 below for a similar corporate event following on from Figure 3.2.

FIGURE 3.3   Sample standard requirements

Standard Requirements	Details

Financial
• Budget Limits
 	
• Bill-back
 	
• Invoices
	Value for money is key
	                  Maximum B&B Accommodation Rate
	London £XX
	Outside London £XX
	             Maximum DDR Average DDR
	London £XX £XX – £XX
	Outside London £XX £XX – £XX
	To include Dinner, B&B for any speakers/events team and all event costs.
	No alcohol to be billed back or paid for with company funds.
	Information required on invoice:
	– Name of event
	– Date of event
	– Contact name (ie Lead Event Manager/Person who made booking)
	– Venue Search Agency used
	– Budget Holder's name and address

Sample policy on **Venue Terms & Conditions**	➢ **Value for money is key** ➢ Request setting up credit accounts between budget holder and venue to agree maximum credit limit for invoicing after event ➢ Terms for payment in advance/deposits Venue terms and conditions need to be approved by Finance Manager
Sample Standard Requirement **Catering**	➢ **Healthy Food** Lunches – sample menu (preferred) **We do not have any deep fried or fatty foods and the following menu is most appropriate for our events.** **NB: this is a suggested menu but we would be open to thoughts and comments from venues.** Selection of cheeses Selection of warm and cold meats A fish option Green leaf salads Bean salads Tomato, basil and mozzarella Vegetable kebabs Baked potatoes Coleslaw and celeriac salads Pasta and rice salads Fresh granary rolls and/or breads A light dessert option Cheese and biscuits Fresh fruit Tea and coffee, water and orange juice

FIGURE 3.3   *continued*

	➢ **With Morning Coffee/Afternoon Tea** – selection of decaffeinated drinks/fruit teas, hot water, water, orange juice, and fresh fruit rather than biscuits. Always have a bowl of fresh fruit available. ➢ **Special Dietary Requirements** – offer plenty of choice for vegetarians. Other special requirements will be communicated to the venue as they arise, by the events team. ➢ **Numbers** – identify date final numbers required. Inform us of: maximum numbers in venue; minimum numbers; final number to be charged.
Sample Standard Requirement **Meeting Rooms**	➢ **Layout** – cabaret style as standard. Please check with Event Manager whether 8/10/12 seats per table are required. ➢ **Ambience** – natural light, internal lighting, air-conditioning controls in room, fresh air, windows that open, temperature. ➢ **Security** – lockable room with key provided. ➢ **Noise** – of AV equipment, external – traffic, internal – works ➢ **Cost** – extras, day rate, 24 hour rate, rack rate or deal ➢ **Rooms** – size of room/s, accessibility, number of rooms required – breakout/main room; flexibility ie splitting rooms in half where possible; shape of room/s, location of rooms and proximity to each other; acoustics, sound equipment required, proximity to catering (meals and refreshments); layout of furniture. ➢ **Audio Visual Equipment** – flipchart and pens that work, equipment included as part of the venue costs, eg sound system, technical support. In the majority of cases we will use an external provider either venue-sourced or sourced by the events team. ➢ **Catering and Refreshments** – flexibility of timings (in advance and on the day); special dietary requirements; location of refreshments/lunch; drinking water provided in room, adequate supplies, replenished at breaks.

Each client will have their own requirements for the style and size of their event. We recommend that these aspects are discussed and agreed with the client when taking the brief, or in the early planning stages. The importance of ensuring that the rooms and facilities used fit the needs of the event as well as the client, cannot be overstated. The following case study considers the specific needs of the pharmaceutical industry, keeping within its own regulatory framework.

CASE STUDY 3.3   Considerations of venue-finding when working with a pharmaceutical client: Ashfield Meetings and Events

Charlotte Exley, Project Executive, DePuy Synthes Events Team and UK Centre for Events Management Graduate 2014

Ashfield Meetings & Events has over 35 years of experience delivering events, with 300 employees located in offices across Europe and the USA. They are leaders in the international pharmaceutical event industry, working with 50+ top healthcare clients. Their expertise in delivering healthcare events enables them to support their clients within this heavily regulated industry.

Why are pharmaceutical clients different?

All events have venue-finding considerations: a specific location, a strict budget, crucial meeting space requirements and so on. Pharmaceutical events encounter all these factors but compliance within the industry mean they experience many more.

Historically there has been a perception of the pharmaceutical industry as being extravagant, non-transparent and providing excessive hospitality to Health Care Professionals (HCPs) in order to secure their business.

To try and change this perception and minimize potential interpretations of bribery through hospitality, individual countries have developed their own compliance guidelines as to how pharmaceutical companies should behave. They want the focus of any HCP-attended events to be on the welfare of the patient and the education of HCPs and so groups were formed to govern this, including the Association of the British Pharmaceutical Industry in the UK and the European Federation of Pharmaceutical Industries and Associations within Europe.

In addition to the regulations imposed by these associations, global pharmaceutical companies have also created their own stricter internal guidelines, often supported by in-house compliance departments.

The compliance process

Compliance guidelines are much stricter when it comes to HCP-attended events, but they still extend to all activities conducted by pharmaceutical companies. Perception is key – how would it look if the press were there and there was no chance for explanations?

Every aspect of a HCP-attended event must meet the compliance guidelines. An initial check examines the medical concept and content of the event; whether there is a scientific or educational need for the event and what will be included. Once this has been approved, the next check encompasses any venues being used throughout the event: hotels, restaurants, meeting venues, etc. There are various details which need to be considered eg hotels cannot be higher than 4-star, cannot be by the sea or a lake, must not have extensive leisure facilities including spa facilities and golf courses or have 'spa' or 'resort' in the name. Restaurants must not have any Michelin stars or be endorsed by celebrities and should not be in a touristic setting. These are just some of the items from an extensive checklist, although exceptions will always be considered for valid reasons such as security concerns.

As well as using these guidelines when venue-sourcing, Fair Market Value (FMV) limits must also be allowed for. These limits determine what is deemed to be an appropriate amount to spend on HCPs attending the events in terms of hospitality eg one particular client states that per delegate accommodation must not exceed €190 per night, dinner can only go up to €60 and the lunch limit is €40.

All these guidelines and considerations take a considerable amount of time and work to be approved by the compliance systems at each stage of the process. Although this often makes the venue-sourcing procedure more intensive than usual, it is important to remember that they have been put in place for a positive reason and the perception of the industry is improving as a result. So much so, that other regulated industries have taken the pharmaceutical compliance model and adapted it to their sectors, eg the FSA – Financial Services Authority.

Overall, event management and the venue-sourcing alongside it cannot take on a 'one size fits all' approach. Insight and understanding are key in being able to adapt knowledge and skill to fit not only the client, but also their industry.

Read more: **www.ashfieldhealthcare.com**

Specific criteria for venue selection

Creating a unique event may involve the use of an iconic venue, a modern, historical, or more traditional venue. It may mean the client has exclusive access, or shares with other groups. But the venue needs to have appropriate facilities and access to technology required by the client, whether these are in place as a matter of course, or whether you need to bring them in. However, it's all too easy to get carried away by your own views and aspirations, rather than looking objectively at criteria. One company had a client who expressed a wish to hold the next event in a castle. The event company researched the options but they soon concluded that a castle really wasn't a suitable venue for this event; and they realized that the organizer just wanted to spend some time in a castle. So they arranged a trip for the client to stay in a castle, and booked the event into a more appropriate venue. (Consider the ethical aspects of such actions!) But two-way communication with the client is key to understanding their event requirements and developing an accurate and realistic brief to enable you to find the venue of their dreams.

Top Tip

Don't get carried away by your own fantasies of hosting an event
somewhere you've always dreamed of – save the exotic for your holidays;
keep both feet planted firmly on the ground when it comes to making your
choice for the perfect event venue!

Venue search options

Destination Management Organizations (DMOs) and venue search agencies
are on hand to help in the search for a venue. DMOs may operate on behalf
of a country, region or city, to promote the benefits of a specific geographic
area, and may provide resources to support you in bringing your event to
that destination, including a list of venues from within their membership.

However, venue search agencies vary hugely in terms of the services
they provide, their knowledge of and relationships with venues, the quality
of their advice, and the amount they charge. This section will unveil the
mysteries of how such services are paid for, and what to look out for when
selecting an agency to assist you. Alternatively, you may choose to search for
a venue yourself, which, despite the obvious benefits of the internet and the
many web-based venue-finder sites, can still prove to be a lengthy, tricky and
costly process.

Venue search agencies operate on the basis of commission, which is
charged to the successful venue. In theory this means that it doesn't cost you
(or the client) anything, and a good venue search agency will benefit your
client with their knowledge of venues and negotiating clout, which more
than covers the cost of finding a venue yourself. Commission can range from
8 per cent to 15 per cent, but venue search agencies can be quite secretive
about this aspect of their income. It has to be said that there are some agencies that have negotiated a varying rate with different venues – and it is
surprising how much more often those paying the higher 'Gold' rate find
themselves on a shortlist of potential venues than those willing to promise a
lower 'Bronze' rate. It is also interesting to find that there are some venues
who will not countenance working with certain organizations – and it's
always worthwhile asking if there are any venues or hotel chains a venue
search agency does not have a relationship with.

The process of using a venue search agency requires you to agree a thorough brief to enable them to search on your behalf. (The previous section of
this chapter explains how to develop a detailed brief.) What you should
NOT do, is to brief more than one agency at the same time, as this leads to
confusion and annoys the venues no end. There are different types of venue
search agencies, and some are more useful and effective than others. Some
agencies have benefited from advances in technology and used the internet

to develop a database of venues that can be interrogated to find properties that match a given list of requirements. However, these may be little more than glorified call-centres, whose staff have little actual knowledge of the venues themselves, almost certainly have never visited them, and have no backing or experience to be able to negotiate on your behalf. Finding a good venue search agency is like finding a pearl of great price; they will be experienced negotiators who know not only the venues but have, over the years, built up good working relationships with venue managers and directors. A key advantage of using a venue search agency is that they will be able to negotiate on your behalf – and working for multiple clients, their purchasing power is likely to outstrip your own.

This case study examines the work of Pineapple Events, a Yorkshire-based venue search agency.

CASE STUDY 3.4 Venue search company, Pineapple Events

Ruth Dowson, Senior Lecturer, UK Centre for Events Management

Business partners Lauretthe McClellan and Wendy Ashton-Evans founded their boutique venue search agency, Pineapple Events, in 2006, having started their collaboration in 1998. Both women already had extensive experience working in the hotel industry for many years, and so started off with great contacts not only across the UK but around the world. They recognized that they each had different skills and strengths, and that their different personalities enabled them to combine their forces to become a dynamic team, with in-depth knowledge and experience of many venues. 'The Pineapple is a symbol of hospitality' explains Lauretthe McClellan, 'and this was really important to us as it reflected our values.' The company has grown organically through a small client base, initially mainly in the public sector, but they have found that as their client contacts moved on to new jobs elsewhere, they took Pineapple with them, as well as introducing them to new colleagues in their respective organizations. In contrast with many venue search agencies, which often consist of a database and telephone sales staff with little direct knowledge of venues, Pineapple Events not only know the venue sites, they have built up strong working relationships with the venue managers, and they are passionate about what they do. Weekends are often taken up with site visits, trade shows and 'fam trips' where they will inspect a range of up to 18 new or existing venues in a day, or they may accompany a client on site visits to assist in the selection of a suitable venue.

Venue search agencies are there not only to source a selection of venues that meet your criteria, but they should also negotiate and troubleshoot on your behalf. In contrast to the office hours kept by bigger agencies, Wendy Ashton-Evans notes, 'We're here 24/7 to support our clients, so if there's a problem, we're on hand to resolve it, and always contactable, to give the client peace of mind.' The service is free of charge to the client, which is covered by the usual commission paid from the venue direct to the agency. So if no business is placed, they don't earn anything. However, they will book venues that don't pay commission, if it's the right venue for their client's event.

The process starts with a brief from the client, often in a quick email – where the event might be held (this could be as little detail as 'North'), when (dates), how many delegates are expected, and sometimes a little more information. 'Very often,' says Lauretthe McClellan, 'we're able to interpret the client's view of venue style and affordability, because we have got to know their organization so well – we think about where would suit the client and their delegates.' Transport links are of key importance to the location of potential venues, and they're usually in cities because they provide transport hubs, with rail, road and sometimes air travel required. Many of their UK clients' events are held in London (so popular now, it's not the buyer's market it once was) or Birmingham or Manchester, and even looking beyond London to Brighton or Reading.

One of the frustrations occurs when organizations send requests to multiple venue search agencies all at the same time, so everyone is scrabbling for space, with a low probability of conversion. It's preferable for clients to pick one agency and send them their requirements, then if they can't find what you're looking for, try a different agency. Pineapple Events have found that it's more effective to work with a client with whom they have good access and clear communication, which in turn helps Pineapple Events to gain the trust of venues, who are more likely to offer a first option, which then benefits the venues, as they are more likely to convert enquiries into business. Pineapple Events source venues for some 300–400 events a year, of sizes ranging from 10 to 1000 attendees. They may have six or seven events on a day, placing business of around £2 million–£3 million a year.

Read more: **www.pineappleevents.com**

Issuing the venue search brief

Once you have issued your brief to the venue search agency, they will undertake research to find venues that potentially meet your requirements, and provide you with a list of possible venues for your event, along with initial prices. These venues should be placed by the agency 'on hold' provisionally on your behalf (on first or second option: second option means that another company has a first option ahead of you), for the dates needed, until you have either rejected or accepted them. It is useful (at least for the purpose of corporate governance, procurement requirements and transparent decision-making), to also keep a list of those venues that do *not* meet your criteria, for example because they are not available on the dates you require. Flexibility of dates can be a blessing or not, as the agency may randomly pick dates for you rather than providing a whole range but once dates are firmed up, it may be worthwhile revisiting the list. A useful way of managing this process, which could take from one or two days to several weeks for a complex enquiry, is to use a spreadsheet to track the responses as they come in. This process will also enable you to decide whether a venue meets your criteria or not, list any limitations and support your decisions; a sample layout of the spreadsheet is provided in Table 3.2. At this stage the venue search agency will set up site visits for you at the shortlisted venues.

TABLE 3.2 Venue selection decision matrix

Venue	Venue A	Venue B	Venue C
Location			
Days			
Dates Required			
DDR			
24hr Rate			
Dinner – non-residential			
Explanation			
Room Hire			
Total Cost	£0.00	£0.00	£0.00
Notes			
Meets Criteria			
Savings			
Venue Known			
Min Nos			
Comments			

Venue site visits

Many venues offer familiarization or 'fam' trips, and these may be co-ordinated by a DMO; however, such visits are usually made on the basis of building a general awareness, rather than having a specific event in mind. In contrast, once you have an actual event, undertaking site visits of potential venues is vital, even if you have been to the venue before on a fam trip. This is because you will see the venue with new eyes and be able to walk through the event as you inspect the venue.

Figure 3.4 provides a form with a template for undertaking a site visit, which has been developed mainly for conferences and has been used for hundreds of venue.

FIGURE 3.4   Site visit template

SITE VISIT CHECKLIST	
Venue:	**Date of visit:**
Event title:	**Event date:**
Site visited by:	**Contact:**
Address:	**Tel:** **Fax:** **Email:** **Web:**
Location	
Proximity to motorway network:	Proximity to rail network:
Nearest tube station: Taxi:____mins Walk: ____mins Bus: ____mins	Nearest rail station: Taxi:____mins Walk:____mins Bus: ____mins
Main Room	
Location and proximity from main room: ➢ Registration: ➢ Catering area:	Maximum capacities / layouts
	Theatre style:____ / Cabaret: – Based on 6 around each table: ____ – Based on 8 around each table: ____ – Based on 10 around each table: ____
Number of Syndicate Rooms: Comments:	Maximum capacities: / Syndicate 1: Theatre:____ Cabaret:____ Syndicate 2: Theatre:____ Cabaret:____ Syndicate 3: Theatre:____ Cabaret:____ Syndicate 4: Theatre:____ Cabaret:____
Remember to request a copy of the venue's capacity chart in electronic format if not available online ☐	
Stage included in venue hire? ☐ Yes, already installed Cost of hire: £ ____ ☐ Yes, can be installed Cost of hire: £ ____ ☐ No	Basic AV included in venue hire? ☐ Yes, already installed Cost of hire: £ ☐ Yes, can be installed Cost of hire: £ ☐ No If included, please list items:

FIGURE 3.4 *continued*

Does room have good acoustics? Yes ☐ No ☐
Does room require PA system? Yes ☐ No ☐
PA included in venue hire?
  ☐ Yes, already installed Cost of hire: £____
  ☐ Yes, can be installed Cost of hire: £____
  ☐ No
	Is the room soundproof? ☐
	Noise levels:
	➢ Air-conditioning: Noisy ☐
	  Acceptable ☐ None ☐
	➢ Roads: Noisy ☐ Acceptable ☐
	  None☐
	➢ Interconnecting doors: Noisy ☐
	  Acceptable ☐ None ☐
	➢ Kitchen: Noisy ☐ Acceptable ☐
	  None☐
	➢ Comments:

Temperature controls located in room? Yes ☐ No ☐ Comments:	Natural light in rooms? Yes ☐ No ☐ Comments:
Is the room lockable? Yes ☐ No ☐ Comments:	Cloakroom available? Yes ☐ No ☐ If so, cost of hire: £____

Bedrooms

On-site accommodation: Yes ☐ No ☐ Nearest hotel if not on-site:	No of Bedrooms:
Viewed standard double bedroom? Yes ☐ No ☐	Comments:
Free upgrades to organisers? Yes ☐ No ☐	If so, how many?

Disabled Facilities

Disabled access throughout venue? Yes ☐ No ☐	Number of disabled bedrooms:____

Hearing loops provided?
  ☐ Yes, already installed Cost of hire: £____
  ☐ Yes, can be installed Cost of hire: £____
  ☐ No
	Disabled toilets: Yes ☐ No ☐
	Disabled car-parking: Yes ☐ No ☐

Catering

Dietary requirements – can venue cater for special dietary requirements such as:
  Halal ☐   Kosher ☐   Diabetes ☐   Other ☐ Comments:

Remember to request a copy of the venue's menus and check regarding healthy food ☐

Car-Parking

On-site ☐ Off-site ☐	Number of spaces available:
Name of external car park:	Location:
Proximity to venue:	Cost to delegates:
If public parking, does venue receive preferential rates: Yes ☐ No ☐	If cost, is bill back available:

Health & Safety

What day is the fire alarm test?

Non-smoking site
Yes ☐   No ☐   All ash trays should be removed and signage should indicate
                     'No Smoking'

The format can be adapted to fit different events and includes a question about fire alarm frequency after one experience in a hotel when the night-time fire alarm turned out to be a regular occurrence, due to a faulty boiler. This form should be completed for every site visit and provides a valuable source of information for future use, as well as providing a rationale for venue selection decisions.

Top Tip

There's no substitute for a physical inspection of the venue to identify the constraints and opportunities it holds for your event: and one note about toilets – always inspect them!

Analysing venue search results and negotiations

Having undertaken site visits and completed the report for each venue, this information is combined with the previous data gathered to enable you to reduce your shortlist, ask any outstanding questions and have the venue search agency negotiate any specific requirements, special rates or terms and conditions on your behalf. You may wish to include a request for references from a client with similar needs to your own. Once you have made your decision – with or without further input from the venue search agency – the agency will ensure you receive contracts and manage any problems or additional requests you might have with your selected venue.

Communicating with event attendees about the venue

Once you have chosen your venue remember event attendees will require directions. The type of information you will need to provide is found in the template in Figure 3.5 below.

FIGURE 3.5   Venue information template

Venue Name		
Image of venue		
Full address including postcode:		
Telephone number:		
Fax number:		
Email address:		
Web address:		
Facilities:		
Disabled access:		
Directions:	**Air**	
	Rail	
	Underground Metro	
	Road	
Route planner:		
Helpful hints:		
Parking:	**Number of spaces**	
	Charges	
Local taxi number:		
Please note that the above information has been taken directly from the venue. While we have checked this and provided additional information where available, we are not responsible for errors on the part of the venue or online route planners.		
Maps:		
Additional Information:		

Working with venue operations

Once you have agreed on your chosen venue, the hard work begins. Having a structured approach to informing the venue of your needs as they change (they will, inevitably), will help you to control the budget and keep your client happy. In Figure 3.6 there is a draft for an event function sheet which can be used to inform the venue of specific and detailed requirements for your event. The following chapters provide more detail about developing the content and structure of the event.

FIGURE 3.6   Function sheet template

EVENT FUNCTION SHEET						
<<EVENT TITLE>> <<DATE>> <<VENUE, LOCATION>>						
Pre-event contact (Events Team):			**On-site contact (Events Team):**			
Tel: **Mobile:** **Fax:** **Email:**			**Mobile:**			
Venue event co-ordinator pre-event: **Tel:** **Mobile:** **Fax:** **Email:**			**Venue operational manager on-site:** **Mobile:**			
Signage:			**Meeting room name:**			

Pre-event set-up

Activity	Timings	Location / Room(s)	Set-up and venue responsibilities	Numbers	
				Confirmed	Set

Venue AV Requirements

Equipment	Location / Room(s)	Set-up and venue responsibilities	Number	Agreed Cost
LCD Projector				
Flip Chart				
Overhead Projector				
Screen				

Event

Activity	Timings	Location / Room(s)	Set-up and venue responsibilities	Numbers	
				Confirmed	Set
Registration					
Morning sessions					
Mid-morning refreshments					
Sessions					
Lunch					
Sessions					
Mid-afternoon refreshments					
Sessions					
Close					

FIGURE 3.6 *continued*

DIETARY AND SPECIAL REQUIREMENTS	
Dietary Requirements	
Option	**Number**
Vegetarian:	
Vegan:	
Halal:	
Kosher:	
Other:	
Special Requirements:	
Requirement	**Number**
ROOMING LIST	
Name	**Special Requirement**
Other Requirements:	
Billing Instructions:	
Authorized Signatory for main account:	
No. of Bedrooms Contracted/Required:	
Minimum Numbers:	

Chapter summary

- The event site and location should be chosen to match the corporate image and culture of your client, as well as meeting your client's event criteria.
- While event organizers are often attracted by a perceived opportunity to create a unique 'WOW' factor for their event, subtlety can sometimes be a more appropriate tool. It's unlikely that any venue will be perfect, as all sites have constraints – but they will also provide opportunities.
- The best way to check that a venue is right for your event is to undertake a physical inspection yourself – armed with structured checklists so you can ask the right questions.
- Ensure you have all the information possible to enable you to make the most of your choice of location and venue.

Developing the programme and content

04

Creating a programme or developing the content or for an event is often relegated to the back burner for event managers, who may be more focused on the practical logistics and marketing. There is a key difference between developing the structure, style and content of an event programme, and then communicating the key messages, which more naturally falls within the remit of event promotion (see Chapter 7). The new concept of curating an event is beginning to emerge through the museum sector, in which the programme or content is crafted to meet the needs of stakeholders, including attendees and the client organization. Far more than developing a simple schedule or writing an agenda, this can be an exciting and creative process.

This chapter returns to the all-important objectives (for the Five Es – see Chapter 2) and identifies the components that make an event successful, from Plenary Sessions to Workshops and Seminars, Exhibition and Market stalls, to facilitating networking. Even then, the content has to be created, and this chapter draws on the expertise of 30 years in the events industry, making the most of experiences that work, and learning from those that don't, with internal and external resources to support a range of budgets. Examples demonstrate the importance of providing different kinds of refreshments, and using structured and unstructured breaks and sessions that enable event participants to network, as well as developing a practical time space for reviving the brain and re-energizing the body. Events for PR purposes may be themed explicitly to promote the client organization, or be more subtle, perhaps engaging with a third party – and here the importance of shared values and brand identity is highlighted.

Napoleon's observation that 'an army marches on its stomach' can be applied to events, and evidence suggests that one of the most important factors for corporate delegates is that they think with their stomach (Renneisen, nd). Social activities, hospitality and entertainment options are discussed, with Food and Beverage (F&B) options that cover a range of service styles, and costs, and we even discuss the pros and cons of drinks.

This chapter will include:

- Aligning the event content with objectives
- Event programme options
- Creating engaging content for attendees
- Developing event objectives

Strategic considerations

There is a range of preliminary strategic considerations that are vital when beginning the process of thinking about creating a new event, and these are discussed in the following sections. They include the level of congruence between the values and aspirations of the client and the supplier (eg the PR agency), and the choices available in terms of the types of events and their purpose.

Organizational fit

There are many different types of event that PR professionals may be involved with on behalf of their clients. Whatever the event, it is vital to begin with a consideration of connections that already exist or could be created, between the client organization and the event selected. There needs to be a 'fit' between the two, which is communicable and explicit, in terms of the values held and the message that will be promoted by the activity. So, for example, you obviously wouldn't expect to see a cigarette company sponsoring an event that is raising funds for a cancer charity. Perhaps that's a little too obvious as an example but the point is one that cannot be overstated. A recent example was a cigarette company sponsoring a competition in Asia for a trip to Europe; when searching for appropriately qualified tour leaders, it is important to ensure that the individuals concerned are open to the use of tobacco. How this message is portrayed is vital; if I am personally opposed to tobacco advertising or its use, I may not be the best person to ask for recommendations. When considering the content of an event for your client, the same concept applies: you wouldn't expect to present participants, or staff working on the event, with any activity or message that offended their sensibilities, beliefs or values. So it's worthwhile considering throughout the process of constructing your event and its content, how others might view the offering. But not only are you trying *not* to offend, even more, your aim is to develop and deliver an event that sits in harmony with the target group of attendees and any organizations they might represent, as well as with your client, and with your own staff working on the event. When researching the different types of event, it is important to keep this in mind.

DIY or existing events?

Another important consideration, before you start thinking about the type of event, is whether to participate in a pre-organized corporate hospitality function (where your client might be one of many, but less work would be involved, and it might possibly cost more money), rather than a programme individually tailored just for your client (giving more choice, more control and a more customized feel to the experience). And in the era of The Bribery Act (2010), it is important to consider the financial value of what you are providing and how it will be interpreted, not only within legal restrictions and guidelines, but also in the light of the client's policies on corporate social responsibility, and the potential response if it were to appear in the press. How will the connection between the event and your client be communicated to those attending the event?

Before you start thinking about what type of event, there are some preliminary decisions you need to make.

Work out some important strategic aspects – such as how this event will fit with the culture and style of your client's organization, as well as meeting their objectives.

Secondly, are you going to take an off-the-shelf product and make it your own, or build an event from scratch?

And thirdly – where are the resources coming from, and how much budget have you got?

Event programme options

The following is a (non-exhaustive) list of the different event options that might be considered for PR purposes; these may be stand-alone events in their own right, or contribute towards a multi-faceted event held over a longer period of time. The groupings below are discussed in the following section:

- Corporate hospitality at existing events
- Parties, including celebrity guests, visiting notables, dinners with or without guest speakers, private viewings and art exhibition launches
- Press briefings, new product launches, speaking opportunities for key individuals at external events
- Charity events and sponsorship, community events
- Seminars, workshops, conferences, roadshows, exhibitions, team-building
- Social activities and refreshments (F&B).

The use of **corporate hospitality** at existing events, and particularly sporting events such as tennis at Wimbledon, or Formula 1 at Silverstone, provide a common, traditional way for PR companies to support their client's event needs. There are options to consider, such as which sport (football, rugby, horse-racing, or events with a range of sports such as the Olympics) would be best, and then which specific event. In today's environment there is a wide range from which to choose, including VIP status at festivals, music concerts, ballet, theatre and the arts – at international, national, regional or local levels. Would your client prefer to take their customers to a VIP box at Henley Regatta, or to a local performing arts group?

Parties also provide a more traditional way for clients to entertain their staff, their customers (or potential customers), or those who can influence their businesses ('introducers', such as lawyers and accountants, for example). Is there a 'hook' or theme to the party that links with the client's business, or a seasonal tie-up (such as Christmas)? Is it an evening event (adults only), or held during the day (with families)? Is there a time limit on the duration of the event ('cocktail hour' or 'till late')? Is it held with or without food? Is alcohol provided? Will there be limits or restrictions on alcohol consumption? How will these be monitored? Are guests invited alone or with a 'plus one'? Are there restrictions on who the 'plus one' is?

Celebrity parties are held so that clients and their customers have an opportunity to mingle with one or more celebrities; this depends very much on your budget and who the celebrity is. Is it your client's goal to be featured in *Hello* magazine, or the *Tatler* (or to be singled out by one of the red-top newspapers)? Are you participating in a party at which there will be celebrities, or holding your own party, and paying them to attend? What kind of celebrity does your client want (footballer, musician, an actor – from stage, cinema or TV)? What is the role of the celebrity at your event? How can they help you to communicate your client's message?

Costs of **after-dinner speakers** can be tens of thousands of pounds and more, for a short period of time. Like celebrity events, the question is – why? Why a specific person? Do they add value to your message? Formal dinners reduce the amount of time available to meet and network with others, and many of us will have spent hours at dinners, sitting next to people discussing a topic of no interest to us, or about which we feel we have little knowledge, so cannot contribute. Placing an internal client on each table can help if their role is to facilitate conversation, but this can seem too orchestrated. Consider how you can add time for informal networking, such as a pre-dinner drinks reception or post-dinner open bar.

With **visiting notables**, whether royalty, media or company chiefs, visits to the client's site often involve a lot of tidying-up – and for royalty this can mean that toilets are specially painted 'just in case'! If your VIP requires particular security arrangements, these can take place in advance as well as on the day, and may include liaison with police and security services, as well as restricting access to certain parts of the site for long periods of time. If the site is expected to carry on working while the visit happens, a walk-through of the route is vital to ensure that staff have access to areas as needed, with special identification if necessary. Consider the provision of appropriate food and drink, not just for the guest and their entourage, and recognize that timing of the event may be crucial to fit in with the guest's programme for the day.

Whether concurrent with other events, such as VIP visits, or opportunities for the client's management to meet and respond to media questions on a specific topic, media briefings on-site should take place in a secure, quiet environment where the participants will not be disturbed by external noises or interruptions. For launches of new products or new site facilities, on-site considerations are similar to those for visiting VIPs and press briefings, described above. What parts of the site will guests be allowed to enter?

Will the site continue to work, and how will that impact on the event/working plant? What security measures will be required to contain access? For off-site events, consider how you will communicate the experience of the new facilities, machinery or products in an external venue. For example, if launching a new car, can you get access to take the car into the venue itself?

Inviting your client's customers to an exclusive **launch** of a new art exhibition or to a private viewing can provide a relatively relaxed environment for an evening's networking while perusing the artwork. Again, in addition to the type of art being shown, consider food and drinks, time limits on the event, and what to do when an important client suggests you take the party on elsewhere. (If nothing else, have your credit card ready...).

When seeking to raise the profile of an individual from your client's organization, identify target groups and **external** events for the person to speak at. (Check first that they can speak!) Find a contact within the organization you have chosen and agree dates. It sounds so simple! But it's all too easy to book your busy client in to speak at an event that wastes their time, so advance in-depth research is vital.

A major factor when working with **charities** is to ensure and agree the level of consensus between the values and brand of your client's organization and that of the charity. This is more than a photo opportunity; you need to consider the links with the client's corporate social responsibility policies, as well as the long-term relationship with the charitable organization. Some organizations choose a different charity each year, often linked to a longer-term relationship with a staff member, while others prefer to maintain one long-term charity relationship. Yet others put aside a specific amount of funding for charity activities and invite bids (from staff or direct from charities). Another important factor is the cost of the event when compared to the amount that will be donated; but charities may not want only money, they may wish to recruit volunteers, or raise awareness through your client and its direct or indirect contacts. This is a two-way relationship, not just about giving some money, taking a picture and walking away. Today, the pictures will be taken by all, and posted online with appreciative or withering comments alongside. The following case study gives an example of the use of technology to support fundraising events with leading charities.

CASE STUDY 4.1   Interactive live fundraising technology – tablets or texting: which wins the transatlantic debate?

Antje Strietholt, Marketing Manager, iBid Events & UK Centre for Events Management Graduate (BA (Hons) Events Management, 2014)

Event organizers are watching an international debate with interest – the effectiveness of mobile versus tablet technology at fundraising events. Pen and paper are fast becoming a thing of the past. The last five years have changed events beyond recognition and even in 2014, we have seen technology come a long way. Organizers are looking for maximum income, but often with enhanced branding and guest loyalty or interaction. In today's technology-led event business, these developments are measurable aspects of success.

The US market has leant increasingly towards mobile giving at charity events in the recent past. Guests often register with their cell-phone on entry to an event, so they can easily 'check out' at the end for items won or donations made. All seemingly straightforward. Mobile bidding also means everyone has access to their own device, so high-volume bidding can be achieved within a very short space of time – perfect also for events that aren't the traditional sit-down galas, where guests are able to flow freely between rooms and different entertainment options.

However, from a European perspective, the use of mobile technology can raise problems. Fundamentally, mobile usage relies on connectivity as well as on internet access, which can be unreliable. In addition, even online 'checking in' to an event can lead to queues as guests arrive; not the first impression organizers would prefer.

It is also important to consider the effect that using a mobile has on the atmosphere of an event. Guests can become distracted, and who wants to sit next to someone who is texting, emailing and checking Facebook every five minutes? This certainly goes against the European sense of occasion. The key to maximizing fundraising therefore, is to keep the technology simple, visual and interactive. Keeping guests engaged is what leads any brief for technology and in fundraising, is this achieved more effectively with tablets?

Tablet technology allows guests to bid quickly and simply, often pre-loading guest names so no registration is needed. Tablets offer bespoke branding and sponsorship opportunities, keeping the event focused on the reason it is being held. They are also often set up using a system's own internal wireless network, meaning no reliance on mobile coverage, which can open up potential new venues.

Other aspects of mobile bidding can be added to the tablet platform, such as pre-event online bidding, and text notifications to winning bidders, once the auction is closed. The professional view is that there is only so far you can take bidding technology before it gets too complex for guests and therefore has an adverse effect on the funds raised.

Here's an example of why fundraising and technology are an ideal partnership:

Up to 2013, The Prince's Trust Head Office used a range of solutions to support their silent auctions and pledging. In 2014, they used iBid, with:

- 360 people at the event

- two tablets per table of 10

- The tablets (Kindle Fires) were synched with guest data per table, event information, menu options, the evening schedule and a library of all the lot items available

- Auction items included luxury holidays, VIP experiences and signed memorabilia

- two free-standing bidding stations at the cocktail reception

- Guests bid in the silent auction directly from their tablets at their tables in real time

- Incoming bids were displayed on two large leaderboard screens on stage which also showed a totalizer filling up towards the charity's target

- If a guest was outbid they were informed via the tablets

- The silent auction saw a total of 226 bids coming through the system.

Here's what Catriona Mason, Event Manager for The Prince's Trust, had to say about her experience with iBid:

iBid have delivered a consistently great service across all our events, and as a result our auctions have helped us raise more vital funds to help disadvantaged young people in the UK. Their staff are fantastic and always go above and beyond our expectations, even when delivering three large events for us in three weeks!

The Prince's Trust found that there were significant increases in funds raised compared to 2013:

- Event 1: The Leadership Dinner: 191 per cent increase

- Event 2: Handbags & Gladrags: 17 per cent increase

- Event 3: Invest in Futures: 16 per cent increase – raising £146,000 in the first seven minutes

As a result, The Prince's Trust recommend iBid to other charities and plan to increase the number of regions using iBid throughout their organization. While this is only one example, iBid's client list continues to grow, having supported events for each of the UK's top 10 charities. iBid are proud of their deep partnerships with leading UK charities, and take great pride in every event they support, no matter the size of event or organization.

Read more:

Community events or activities that engage with the wider community may be an option because your client is based in a specific locality and wishes to 'befriend' its neighbours, or because their customers are the general public. From fun, outdoor summer events (beware of rain), to 'listening' events that encourage feedback, these can be a relatively effective way of making inroads to community opinions. But beware of the damage that can be done by those who mistrust your intentions – especially online.

Seminars and **workshops** provide a business-like networking space for actually getting to know people, combined with providing a (theoretically) useful activity. Collaborating with other organizations or companies that provide connected services can be a useful way of developing new relationships and strengthening existing relationships for your client, as well as providing a valued input. Regular series of seminars can cover a range of themes with content delivered by speakers from different fields (eg lawyers, accountants, HR advisers, consultancy firms) and can encourage the development of a 'community' of attendees. Breakfast meetings or early evenings are more popular than lunchtimes or half-day sessions, which can end up taking most of the day out of busy working lives. Holding smaller sessions on the client's site can provide a more intimate atmosphere than paying to hire larger rooms at the local hotel, and enables conversation with more of the attendees, which can then be followed up after the event. If your client doesn't have the space, perhaps one of their collaborative partners does?

Top Tip

Consider working collaboratively with another organization who has a similar client base, where you each invite your own contacts and you share the cost of resources as well as the event organization. They might be great at throwing parties but you might have some excellent key speaker contacts. Together you could develop a fantastic event and build new contacts at the same time.

There are no excuses today for holding a (boring) traditional **conference** where the audience sits and listens. The average attention span lasts for as little as 10 minutes, so why would you seat 100 or 500 or 1000 people for an hour or more (or even for a whole day), when all that will happen is that they will get itchy bums and squirm in their seats – and mostly turn to Facebooking or reading their emails, instead of listening to your (probably expensive) guest speakers? The emergence of the TED event (Technology, Entertainment and Design), although structured and passive (for the audience), is at least time-limited to 15 minutes per speaker. The opportunity to co-create an event engages attendees and their interest well in advance, and can be combined with a structure that encourages and facilitates engagement and participation. Learning is another key function of conferences, and this can be a two-way process. What better result for your client, as well as delivering a message, than to gain an understanding of their customers, and of the customers' responses to that message? The **'UnConference'** is emerging as a preferred route to enable such conversations.

How about including sessions that adapt the **'speed-dating'** structure, where small groups are seated around tables, with one guest speaker or facilitator at each table? The guest explains their relevance or proposes a discussion topic, which the group discusses and asks questions about for a set period of time – 10–15 minutes or even up to an hour. Then all the groups move so everyone is sitting at different tables. This works with groups moving from one table to another, either together as a group, or offering a choice to individuals to move to any other table. There might be themes, or multiple tables with the same topic – but each time there will be a different conversation, with different people meeting each other. This can be done successfully with over 500 people in a flat-floored room, all seated around numbered tables, with plenty of space for ease of movement – and is much more enjoyable, useful and appreciated than sitting and listening to a speaker drone on for an hour, but it takes simple logistical planning, which can be easily done on the day, or in advance.

The type of speaker invited is another key aspect that traditional conferences often get wrong. Politicians, well-known personalities or corporate big-wigs need to be briefed – and there are too many examples of big-name speakers who refuse to be briefed, and get it wrong, or who trot out the same speech every time, however irrelevant to the audience. What most conference attendees want to hear are what we call 'war stories' that address the following themes:

- 'this is what happened to me when I was in this/a similar situation'
- 'this is what went wrong'
- 'this is what I learned'

And there's nothing wrong with having several speakers contributing at the same time, just don't have a panel taking questions from the floor. We have probably all witnessed the times when the same person (you know who they are), gets up and asks the same question – or worse, makes the same point as always. Having a room layout (such as seated around tables) that facilitates small group discussion, means people can ask their own questions, and discuss the answers, rather than being told the 'expert's answer', which they may not agree with, or which may not be relevant to their situation; this reduces the problem of the questioner who dominates the session with unwanted questions. This case study shows how technology can support a group feedback process, using interactive media to invite questions or submit summaries of small group discussions.

CASE STUDY 4.2   Technology and events: The Live Group

Rosie Ford, Business Development Manager, The Live Group

The Live Group, a full service events agency, has 26 years' experience of delivering conferences and events for the UK and Welsh Governments. It counts amongst its clients, major arm's-length bodies, third sector organizations, membership associations and blue chip companies. Since the economic downturn and the huge cuts in public sector spending, the digital event tools it has developed have not only ensured its survival but its pre-eminence. The Live Group has run linked multi-venue regional staff events for Natural England, and internal roadshows for the Home Office (64 events in two to three months), and webinars for the Pensions Regulator and Financial Conduct Authority, where audiences up and down the UK could gain clear insights into complex legislative changes from the comfort of their own PC.

The technological tools were devised specifically by The Live Group to enable clients to continue to communicate effectively with their audiences, at a lower cost and often without employees even having to leave their workplace. These tools have been developed after decades of observing the behaviour of conference audiences, and understanding how they learn to become fully engaged. When The Live Group's clients want to use these next generation tools, they are provided with a multi-skilled team giving sound, practical advice, not just on the technical aspects, but also on constructing agendas, a range of facilitation methods, and detailed 'How To' guides that walk them through the event process.

The Live Group has found that the key to using technology is not to have it merely as a tool on the event day, but to build it into the entire delegate journey. The Live Group has won a clutch of industry awards for its development of a suite of integrated, delegate tools that increase the impact and depth of engagement with content, from online registration to on-site interaction, to final evaluation and materials download.

The company's specially designed registration sites enable delegates to post questions in advance, join forums, vote on specific issues, suggest topics for discussion, see who else is coming, and learn much more about the day. This early investment gains crucial buy-in to the content, and indeed occasionally even drives it, encouraging delegates to commit to attend and to arrive better prepared and more eager to participate.

So when the event opens with presentations containing answers to their questions, the results of polls they've participated in or their chosen topics they really sit up and listen. They're all on the same page. Using a web app on attendees' own devices (smartphones and tablets) means that further voting and feedback on these same topics happens more efficiently and effectively and lets them dive deeper into the subject matter. Results are instantaneous. Broken down into audience demographics. Everyone included.

When an interactive webcast using the Greengage platform takes place alongside an event, as it did at the government's Disability Confident Summit, or the launch of consumer health champion Healthwatch, the audience size increases further, for little extra financial cost. After the event, audience interaction continues online, with questions continuing to be answered and materials uploaded for later review and dissemination. Just as important, the quality and depth of the event evaluation is huge. No more indecipherable flipcharts. No more results skewed by the loudest voices. Instead, superb evidence is available of how content has been received, by whom, and any shifts in audience perception, knowledge and understanding over the lifetime of that event.

Read more: **www.livegroup.co.uk**

Whether **exhibiting** at an existing externally-organized exhibition or developing and running your own, exhibitions offer great potential for engaging with stakeholders. If you take a stand at an established exhibition, consider the benefits of using the existing shell scheme (usually cheaper but less flexible) or creating your own stand in a way that reflects your client and their offering in the marketplace. You might wish to hire a separate room or use the space in your stand to hold an invitation-only event for your client's guests. This could be in the form of a seminar-style presentation, or an informal drinks reception, or a formal meal. Holding such an event at an exhibition that the target market is likely to attend might encourage potential guests to combine the two, but beware that any specific time may not be convenient for all. The greatest weakness in exhibition participation is not following up with contacts made and conversations held with clients and potential clients. Deciding which externally-organized exhibitions are most appropriate should be part of your core marketing strategy discussions. Organizing an exhibition on your own takes more effort, but you won't have to compete with other exhibitors for the attention of your contacts. You would also need a significant amount to display. A **'market stall'** approach can be useful here, where different sections of the client organization each have space (say, a table, or display panels) and perhaps associated activities, to make it worthwhile for guests to attend. As with other event types, consider the location – in-house or external venues, and what you would expect the attendees to do during their visit. Exhibitions are a fantastic way to meet up with your existing and potential clients or customers, because the communication is face to face, and this is where building a relationship really starts in earnest. It's much easier (and more effective) to call or email someone once you have already met them, and attending an exhibition gives the attendee more control over who they interact with, which exhibitor's stands they stop at, and how long they visit.

Roadshows are usually short events that move around a geographical area (say, England, or Europe) on a rolling basis, delivering the same messages and content on each occasion. They may use a seminar format, include market stall exhibits and networking opportunities. The limitations include burn-out by those delivering the roadshows – the first 10 times might be exciting, but after 50 it can get monotonous. The events delivery team will often develop a 'family' mentality out on the road, and closer working relationships – but beware that when things go wrong, relationships can easily sour.

CASE STUDY 4.3 Bluehat Group

Holly Glover, Event Consultant Support, Bluehat Group & UK Centre for Events Management Graduate 2014 Winner, The Eventice, 2014; MPI Young Achievers Award Winner, 2013

Established in 2001, Bluehat Group is a multi-award-winning team-building organization, based in London and Hertfordshire, that is made up of five strong core brands: 'Bluehat', 'Catalyst', 'Guinness World Records', 'Go Team' and 'The Big Event Company'. These partnerships mean that Bluehat has an extensive portfolio of over 100 team-building activities; in 2013, Bluehat delivered 490 events. Despite being a relatively small company, Bluehat is rapidly expanding, with some 35 full-time employees and a pool of freelancers who work on events, making it a more flexible organization. Bluehat's team-building activities are designed by an in-house creative team and range from 10-minute conference energizers to full-day events and away-days. What helps Bluehat Group stand apart from other team-building organizations is the ability to use its creative division to design and deliver unique experiences that support clients' key messages, brand, culture and identity, while ensuring that their objectives are met. When organizing an event that involves elements of team-building, it is important to know what outcomes you would like to achieve as a result of the activity, and what skills or messages you would like your attendees to take away from the event.

Tim Shepley, Bluehat's Managing Director, recognizes that Bluehat's clients understand the importance of team-building and that a successful team-building event has a positive impact on a company's objectives. In order to ensure that the event is a success and that the objectives are met, when taking the enquiry, the Account Managers and Directors at Bluehat will establish the event's key themes and endeavour to suggest relevant activities. Sarah Turner, an Account Director at Bluehat, says that clients often want activities that either incorporate 'team-building' or 'team-bonding'. Corinne Tatham, an Account Manager at Bluehat, explains that team-building exercises are chosen when organizers want to 'build better teams while achieving learning objectives', whereas 'bonding' can include 'just for fun elements'. Tatham and Turner both identify collaboration, communication, negotiation and networking as some of the most popular learning objectives.

Two of Bluehat's most popular events, 'Go Team' and 'Guinness World Records Team Challenge', successfully integrate 'just for fun elements' with 'learning objectives'. 'Go Team' is a high-tech GPS treasure trail, that turns any area into an exhilarating journey, full of interaction and adventure. Teams use tablets to navigate their way to various checkpoints where they then need to work together to complete sets of challenges. 'Go Team' is the perfect activity to end a conference, as it encourages planning, communication and collaboration. While the activity is fun, the challenges can include event-specific questions that can be tailored to any meeting or event. This can allow the client to establish whether delegates understood the key themes of the conference. 'Guinness World Record Team Challenge' is another of Bluehat's most popular events, because it gives participants the chance to come together as one to achieve a shared goal and the opportunity to break a Guinness World Record. The activity encourages interaction and engagement, and can be used to reward high-performing teams or to create collaboration amongst a new team.

Learning and Development workshops are also one of Bluehat's best sellers, with 18 events delivered in September 2014 alone to some of Bluehat's biggest clients, including Tesco and HSBC. These workshops can be delivered as stand-alone events or combined with another team-building activity. Using facilitation helps to draw out the learning points from a team event and enables delegates to realize how the activity will benefit them once they are back in the office. A facilitator will engage with the group and ask appropriate questions in order to encourage honest and open discussion and check the delegates' understanding.

In order to get the most out of a team-building event you need to have the following points in mind:

- Who is taking part? Do they already know each other or is it a group of new starters?

- Is it an even distribution of men and women? Is there anyone with a health issue, pregnant or disabled?

- What are their interests? Do they work in HR, Finance? Are they all from one department or is it the whole company taking part?

- When and where is the activity taking place? Indoors or outdoors? Is it a 10-minute energizer, or a day-long activity?

- Lastly, what are your event objectives? Is it about having fun or developing new skills to take back to the office?

With so many activities, it's important that the client knows what they want to achieve, and have confidence that their needs are fully assessed so the Account Manager can recommend relevant activities, to meet agreed objectives and fulfil the brief, because Bluehat knows team-building and the relevant products, inside out.

Read more: **www.bluehatgroup.co.uk**

Top Tip

Whether using an existing event or developing your own event, ensure that the structure, style and content of the event fits with your client's ethos and values, as well as their specific objectives for the event, and consider the relevance to the target market of potential attendees.

'F&B'

Key activities within any event, that participants might complain about or sing the praises of, are those that involve eating and drinking. Hertzberg (Hertzberg, Mausner, and Snyderman, 1959) was known for studies that identified two different types of factors that influence behaviour and mood at work – the motivating factors, such as recognition, achievement and personal growth, and what he called 'hygiene' factors that had the potential to demotivate and dissatisfy. In an events context, it's really important to get these hygiene factors right, otherwise guests will not even recognize the existence of any positive motivators. Hertzberg was talking about pay and working conditions – but the basic events equivalents include toilets, parking, queues, cleanliness, temperature – and food and drink! It's important to get these right, before the content has its impact, because if you get them wrong, no one will notice the effort you put in to get the most exciting guest speakers.

Having the appropriate type of food does not just rely on the type of event – it also relates to the diversity of the people who attend. Dietary requirements might be due to religious reasons. (For example, halal food for Muslims, or kosher food for Jewish event participants. Many Hindus follow a lactovegetarian diet, which means no meat, poultry or fish, and no eggs, although milk products are allowed. Beef is especially prohibited as the cow is considered sacred.). But it's also important to know that there are different types of kosher, for example. Some people whose religion dictates what they can or cannot eat, may be strongly guided by such dietary regulations, while others will ignore them completely. And how are you to know if someone abides by these regulations or not, or the extent to which they will deem that the provision you have made is acceptable? And there are other reasons, such as medical – allergies, for example, or those with diabetes or high blood pressure – as well as individual choices made on the basis of non-faith principles, such as vegetarianism or veganism. Asking participants if they have any special dietary requirements is a good first step. Making sure that the food that you present is what they can eat is another good step, and provided in a way that they can eat it. But you don't want to pay £100 for a special meal to be brought in for a Glatt Kosher guest, only to have the person who is delivering the meal to the guest's room remove the protective film covering the meal, making it inedible to the guest, as a result. But hospitality is a more subtle consideration than that – there are times when it's worthwhile rethinking the hog roast, out of consideration for your guests who can't or won't eat pork, for whatever reason.

Some organizations always choose to promote healthy eating at their events and would, therefore, provide no deep-fried or fatty foods. Using the venue search brief to outline what catering is expected is a good place to start, and the example below gives an idea of a healthy lunch menu from which guests can choose:

- A selection of hot meat, fish and vegetarian dishes
- Selection of cheeses
- Selection of cold meats
- Vegetable kebabs
- Baked potatoes
- Selection of salads including: green leaf; bean, tomato, basil & mozzarella, coleslaw and celeriac, pasta and rice salads
- Fresh granary rolls / breads
- Light dessert including cheese & biscuits and fresh fruit
- Tea, coffee, water and fruit juice, including decaffeinated and fruity hot drinks

A menu such as this will ensure that many dietary requirements will be catered for with little need to provide lots of options, without causing embarrassment. The post-lunch session has traditionally been thought of as a time when participants are prone to a dip in energy levels – usually brought on by a high-carbohydrate lunch, and often worsened by alcohol. At the start of the day, you could provide a pre-event healthy snack, to ensure that those who missed breakfast can survive, and then offering a 'brain-friendly' menu for lunch. Serve fresh fruit rather than biscuits, locally-sourced organic produce, (look for the Red Tractor and Fair Trade logos), decaffeinated hot drinks, and a choice of cold drinks including tap water. Have regular breaks, especially in a long all-day event.

Food and dietary restrictions might also depend on the timing of your event, for example, during the month of Ramadan, practising Muslims will fast during the hours of daylight, even from water. Other religions have stated fasting times, which should be noted when planning your event, while the increasingly popular 5:2 fasting diet might also be recognized. One of the authors was once invited to the launch of an interfaith organization that took place on a Friday evening in Ramadan – which meant no attendance from the Jewish or Muslim communities!

Alcohol is another issue that demands attention. Increasingly, care should be taken not only of those who follow religious guidelines that restrict or prohibit the consumption of alcoholic drinks (or its use in cooking), but also for those who have chosen not to drink alcohol or who have been advised for medical reasons not to partake. Stories of the effects of binge drinking are widely known but consideration should also be made of the impact of alcohol on physical and mental states, as well as on behaviour. Corporate entertainment should also take account of appropriate spending restrictions to ensure that legal limits are not infringed – and recognizing that a free bar usually means that somebody will over-indulge.

Finally, do the taste test – make sure that you have eaten what your guests will eat – make sure that at least you see the menu beforehand, rather than simply agreeing to what the chef selects on the day. And if your event lasts for more than a day, make sure you check that the menus are coordinated – so you don't end up having chicken twice, or that you overfeed guests so much they go home weighing more than when they arrived.

Social activities

As with any part of your event, social activities should fit with and be relevant to the purpose of the event, as well as linking (perhaps explicitly) to the values of the client organization and the messages it wishes to promote through the event. Also consider the event attendees from your target market – what type of activities will they enjoy or be unhappy about? Health factors and physical fitness can impact on participation in events but, equally, so does the cost – or perceived cost – of the activity, in relation to the event. While value for money is vital, there are times when a good deal can be too good, such as using a five-star hotel. No matter how good a deal has been struck with the supplier, always consider how it will look in the press if word gets out. In these days of social media, photographs and comments made in all innocence can be identified and picked up by press outlets (or go viral on YouTube) with no control – instantly, while you're busy running the event, or weeks later, when news is slow. Social activities can make amazing memories for participants and offer opportunities for fantastic creativity, so they may be viewed as the icing on the cake by some event managers – and some clients, but the real content is often about change or learning.

Objectives – going deeper?

Having addressed the different types of events and their limitations, in addition to the need for any event to fit with the client organization's brand image, values and target markets, every event needs to have objectives. This process is discussed in Chapter 2. For those wishing to develop a deeper understanding of more complex event-content design, the second part of this chapter provides in-depth processes and thinking about good practice and curating event content from a process-driven perspective, in contrast to the off-the-shelf approach earlier in the chapter.

Such objectives go beyond Judy Allen's five event design principles; these are the '5 E's' that she recommends for consideration when visualising an event (Allen, J, 2009: 8):

1 The elements – all the parts that make up the event

2 The essentials – must-haves

3 The environment – venue and style

4 The energy – creating a mood

5 The emotion – feelings

At the start of any event-planning process, the team developing the event needs to agree the objectives with the client. Sometimes the client isn't always clear about what their objectives are, so they may need assistance in this aspect. But before you start to organize an event, consider the following:

- Is there timely information that you need to disseminate to or receive from a specific audience?

- Can this information be gathered via an existing planned event, or is the subject matter 'stand-alone'?

- Can the information be distributed by a cheaper communication channel, such as a brochure or webmail report, rather than a live event?

- How will you include delegate participation as part of the event – for example, through structured approaches such as workshops, or by using interactive technology?

- Do you have access to speakers who represent a range of information, perspectives or views, to include in your programme?

Ideally the objectives for any event should be viewed within the context of the client organization's overall strategy, as support activities with specific deliverables within specific projects.

Detailed example of good practice developing content

A detailed example of a process linking an event aim to its objectives is shown in the following pages, focused on a training event for a professional events team:

Event aim

To develop a process, along with the appropriate tools, skills and techniques to produce clear event briefs that will enable the events team to play their part in ensuring that all events that they support deliver the best possible value for their organization, for those leading the event (clients), and for participants.

Suggested outcomes/objectives

The team will:

1 Have developed a clearer understanding of the wide range and differing nature of events that they are called on to support and how to adjust their support and develop a brief accordingly.

2 Have developed confidence in supporting a wide range of clients in developing their thinking about an event to ensure clarity of purpose, outcomes and subsequent processes that will deliver those outcomes.

3 Have developed their judgement in assessing where additional support or expertise is needed to ensure that an event is successful.

4 Be able to apply a few basic tools to support the above.

Such objectives would then be developed into evaluation criteria, which can be addressed using a format as below in Table 4.1:

TABLE 4.1   Evaluation criteria format

What is being evaluated	What content this covers	Source/s of information

The following figures present sample documents that support this process of developing a clear rationale for the event, its programme and content, as well as its costs and benefits.

FIGURE 4.1   Project proposal

Section 1 : Project Proposal To be completed by Project/Programme Manager					
Client:	Name of Client	Client Lead:	Name of Client Lead Contact	Approved as part of business plan:	YES / NO
Client Manager:	Name	Event Manager:	Name	Management Control Level:	High-Low
Event Project Name:	Roadshow				
Project description:					
The Roadshow Project seeks to deliver 40 events for local client stakeholders to run alongside the public-facing customer Roadshow scheduled for October – December. The project will require working closely with the client's Regional Managers and will need to be communicated via the Communications Team. • Describe the explicit need, eg in response to an external report, and how it relates to the client and its regional management staff, and to its customers.					
Project objectives:					
The objectives of the project are: By:					
Strategic goals:					
How does the project help to achieve the client organization's strategic goals as defined in the client's business plan?					
Business case:					
Business benefits:					
The benefits to the wider client organization are:					
Business options:					
Options available:	The delivery of this project would draw on in-house resource as follows:				
Recommended options:	It would be inappropriate for this project to be delivered by an external organization on behalf of the client as the skill sets for all elements are already employed within the company.				
Risks:					
Describes any risks that are known at this time, how they are being dealt with and who is responsible for owning and resolving the risk.					

An Approval Form or document could also include the following aspects, to support the rationale for the development of the content and programme template:

TABLE 4.2   Event approval details

Event name	Title of event
Event date/s	Day, date, time
Event type	Workshop/conference, etc
Location	Geographic area, eg London, Birmingham
Client	Client name
Fit with business plan	The workshop supports:
Strategic objectives	The workshop supports:
Budget, Cost centre	Costs for this event include: 1 The event speakers. Estimate: 2 The venue: room hire, equipment and refreshments; these will be confirmed by (date). Estimate: 3 The delegate travel costs, which will be met from the client travel expenses budget. Estimate: 4 Event management costs. Estimate:
Audience type	Description of relevant stakeholders/target market. The event will be by invitation only.
Cost to delegates	None
Audience number	Maximum and minimum numbers
Roles	Event owner: Name Content development and delivery: Name Communication & logistics: Name Event management: Events team

Table 4.3 below outlines the categories required for deciding event content:

TABLE 4.3   Content details

Requested speaker(s)	List name, organization, contact details
Aim or theme of the event/s	State aim
Objectives	State and discuss objectives of the event
Benefits	State benefits of running the event
Date approval required by	State date and relevant information eg venue search and contacting potential attendees
Comments	Any other information

Table 4.4 below provides the content aspects that need to be considered for the event planning document, for the team event.

TABLE 4.4   Event planning document: content

Background, context setting & event rationale	Background to the event, brief explanation of the context – eg previous events held and their outcomes Rationale for the event Proposed title Accreditation
Audience	Anticipated size of the audience – potential target audience and estimated numbers attending Constraints to participant attendance eg specific requirements or qualifications How communication with potential participants will be delivered – advertising, specific websites, social media, cascading invitations through existing networks or contacts
Messages	The specific messages which the event aims to leave the delegates with are: (list)

TABLE 4.4   *continued*

Conference themes	The over-arching theme of the event is: Discussed with: Approved by: On (date): Agreed outputs: (eg report)
Event details	The planned date for this event is:
Overview of event	Over-arching theme and benefits to client company (list)
Venue	Name and location of venue/s selected and any important information (eg meeting specific criteria)
Budget	State full amount, break down into specific cost areas and approval details Residential or one-day event – rationale
Resources	Roles required: • Event owner – Name • Content development – Name • Project Manager – Name • Communications – Name • Event logistics – Name
Press conference	Will a press conference be necessary for this event? If so, state details.
Outline itinerary	The event is structured into three main sections: Evening Day 1: Setting the context Morning Day 2: Exploring the reality from recent projects in this and related industries Afternoon Day 2: How can XX role influence the future?
Outline agenda	*Day 1* 6pm Welcome and introduction – Event Chair 6.15pm Key note address either: Option A – title and speaker Or Option B – title and speaker 8.00pm Evening meal and discussion

TABLE 4.4   *continued*

	Day 2	
	8.30am	Run previous evening's unused option session
	10.15am	Coffee
	10.35am	Plenary session
	12.35am	Lunch
	1.35pm	Plenary session
	2.35pm	Tea
	2.50pm	Plenary session
	3.50pm	Chair's summary and closing remarks
	4.05pm	Event close

Detailed itinerary breakdown	*Registration* Registration will take place on arrival and will be managed internally by the Project Team. *Opening:* The Chair's opening welcome will include an overview of the activities and achievements of the past year, including the achievements, progress, the current environment and context of the conference, the aims and objectives of the conference *Plenary Session/s:* The format for the event is based around five main plenary sessions all of which lead into a workshop activity, the feedback from which is summarized in plenary. *Refreshment Break:* Refreshments and networking opportunities. *Workshops/Audience interaction:* The workshops will take place within the main auditorium. Feedback from each of the plenary sessions will be summarized within a final discussion document for use within the client organization. *Lunch:* This will be a chance for delegates to network and learn more about the client organization through meeting its members. *Q&A Panel Session:* There will be no formal Q&A Panel. However, each of the five main items on the conference agenda close with a plenary Q&A session with the lead speaker. *Close:* Delegates will begin to leave the conference ensuring all associated delegate packs are taken. *Exhibition Stands:* There will be no exhibition stand other than a formal client stand to promote the business and future direction of the organization.

TABLE 4.4 *continued*

Supporting Literature/Materials: Literature/Information packs will be made available for delegates:

- Agenda/programme for the day
- Profile of the Faculty
- Speaker biographies
- Company brochure
- Event publications

Supporting Technology/Stationery: It is not anticipated that stationery and other technology will be required for this event. All publicity material will be produced in-house and all outputs from the event will be posted onto the company website.

Dependencies: The following is an outline of dependencies that the conference team have on others: (list)

Funding and expenses: The conference/accommodation will be free to attendees. The rationale for this is: (list) No travel expenses will be reimbursed.

Additional Items for consideration and guidance: None currently identified.

Contact details:

Progress on conference planning to date: To date, the following actions have been undertaken: (list, with dates)

Top Tip

Use the examples given as templates for reviewing and planning your own events, rather than start with a blank sheet of paper.

Event content

At this stage there is still the need to develop and deliver the programme or content of the event. This may include guest speakers, topics for discussions, entertainment, activities, food and refreshments. The concept of event curation has developed from a museum exhibition function and now relates to finding and presenting content on websites. But curating an event – for example, a conference – uses the same skills, and involves the crafting of input and activities to meet complex multiple stakeholder needs. It's not only the client who might want to input into the event content – but also attendees and the organizations they represent, media and shareholders, to name but a few. The power of working with these stakeholder groups to develop an event will craft stronger and more successful outcomes, which would include piloting the event, to building in constant improvements. Events that work are interactive, in which participants can add their own thoughts, meet with others, as well as meeting organizational requirements and objectives. Any guest speaker or facilitator should be fully briefed (both face to face and in writing) on the event, the client organization and its values, and care should be taken to ensure that content is appropriate to the audience and the client.

Having a separate team responsible for the development of event content also means they have to talk to the team responsible for logistics, such as the room layout, because even the layout of the room can impact positively or adversely on the success of your event. The layout of chairs and tables you choose will depend on the type of event, or the environment you wish to create, as follows:

Cabaret style (round tables, enabling interaction between delegates)

- Best suited to an informal or interactive event
- Between 7–10 people per table

Theatre style (rows of chairs facing front/stage)

- Best suited to a formal event or very large event

Classroom style (rows of tables with three or four chairs at each facing the front/stage)

- Best suited to a smaller event where delegates have to do work

Boardroom style (oblong/square table with delegates seated around the outer edges)

- Best suited to smaller meetings/events

It's also possible to have a *Flowing layout,* where you start off theatre style, and as participants move into different activities (eg sharing in threes, then in sixes, then in small discussion groups), the layout of the furniture around the room changes, as participants move their chairs to meet in groups of different sizes. Making this style of event work requires a more flexible and interactive atmosphere and activities.

There are a number of companies that specialize in working with organizations to develop the content for events – including supporting you in specifying event objectives and facilitating delivery of the event. While individuals within any company might work together to come up with an interactive programme, the use of specialists to develop the content using tailored interventions and activities to bring people together, or experienced facilitators to guide the event to a successful conclusion may be costly, but worthwhile. The case study below demonstrates the approach of one successful company that works with a range of public and private sector organizations.

CASE STUDY 4.4   Design team

Phil Hadridge, IDENK

I work planning many conferences – from the small to the large, from one day to longer, in the UK and around the world. However, the process I go through is always the same – and can be presented visually (see the diagram in Figure 4.2 below) and the 13P checklist I draw on (see p108 below).

However the key ingredient for a successful event is engaging with the hopes, wishes (and fears, dreads) of those coming – maybe through a survey or canvassing ideas in regular staff meetings, though more often via a design team.

FIGURE 4.2   The design process

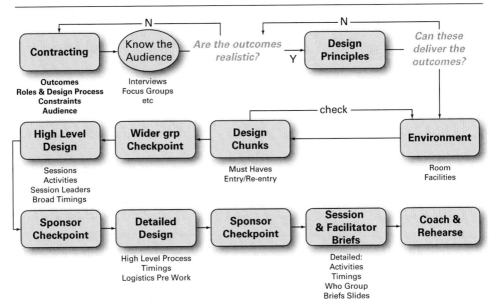

Bellis and Hadridge (2003)

So, in a range of sectors from fashion to conservation, health to education, I work with clients to harness their ideas and imagination in the design process.

At the time of writing this (as dawn is just arriving in Cambridge) I am about to head off to work with the first session with a design team for a cross-sector conference on economic growth. I find design groups invaluable for shaping important sessions – especially when they represent a diversity of perspectives: senior, junior, different functions, enthusiasts... and also cynics. Their role is to work with what is 'preordained' by the sponsoring leader and make the best recommendations or decisions to improve the experience of the group that will meet in the venue (or online space) that has often already been chosen.

A great way I find to start the planning process with this sort of 'max mix' group is to ask: what are the best meetings we have ever been to and why; if this meeting goes well what will happen; if it fails miserably why might that be? When planning an event for a group that has regular meetings, it is worth reviewing the last or previous meetings with an After Action Review or the De Bono 'six thinking hats', for example.

One particular story comes to mind when I think about the power of the design team in the planning process. The Exchange Event, grew from an engaged and iterative exchange of ideas...

Just after the millennium I was planning a conference with a group of colleagues. In those days I called it 'producing' an event if I wanted to sound 'hip'. Now I might say curating an experience! (Both are probably a bit naff, but let's leave that for another time).

Anyhow, I expected about 150 people. But we started differently and that created a whole chain of events that led to a conference format unlike any of the others I had become well-known for delivering during the 1990s.

What was the first step? The letter (email actually) that went out to invite participants to apply to come was far from a typical one. Firstly, it asked people to come only if they were really enthusiastic and ready to share their interest and create further excitement with others. Places were not limited to a few per organization, which was normal, with the expectation of director-level attendance. So secondly, in those days before social media, those who received the letter were asked to pass it on to others who might be interested, whatever their role. Thirdly, as the 'price' of entry, those registering were asked to note their offers and requests on a registration form: they had to clearly state what they wanted to get (learn) and give (as ideas to share in the coffee queue or a table-top discussion or a poster presentation).

The result? Over 650 applied. Fortunately we had to stop there as we had just bust the capacity for the venue, as usually configured. We didn't even send one chasing-up invite – again the norm for that sector at that time.

So, we then shifted gear to discover a way to make it work and came up with a format I still call Exchange. We focused on answering a question: 'What if we could redesign the traditional conference: taking out the boring bits and the need for everyone to sit together at the same time?'

The Exchange method evolved and involves:

- A blend of more familiar conference formats: Open Space, trade fair and academic conference

- Ensuring things are creatively captured – with artists, video – so those not there (and no one can attend everything), can get a sense of the whole, the proceedings

- Making use of music and media to create the right mood – including humour consistency

- Promoting responsibility for finding your way – making good choices about what to go to, and how long to stay... so the meeting is self-organizing within a clear framework and set of written briefings

- Simplifying catering – going continuous, brown bag...

- Using overflow spaces if necessary – a barn and a marquee in this instance (sometimes linked by video)

- And largely designing out plenary sessions (a couple of optional 'magazine style' fringe sessions in the round where most came, gathered round, sat on the floor)

Subsequent innovations over the other Exchange events I helped with over the next five-plus years led to:

- Electronic systems to register, share ideas and pick and mix your own agenda

- Café sessions as an option – world, knowledge

- TED style punchy presentations (in the days before TED!)

- Innovation with voting methods

- Motivational inputs with speakers, actors, music

- Introductory and 'Masterclass' level training – plus learning sets, co-consultancy

- Visits and 'raids' to nearby places

- Use of the emerging technologies and social media to link in colleagues and site remotely

While these days the technology for this sort of process is getting easier (especially with Twitter, etc), all of these improvements arose from engagement with a classic design team. There are other things that more recent 'Exchange' conversation with design groups are raising: how to add in a simulation or some of the ideas from this resource.

So the key for success?

- Inviting passion, questions and contribution in those coming

- A Design Team to imagine what might be and to challenge assumptions – iterating and developing the ideas as they go

- A bespoke approach – cherry picking the best and most useful of other tools and methods

Fundamentally, the overall lesson in the success of this story is the innovation that invented a new format. And at the heart of this innovation was deep curiosity about:

- How could we say yes to all – we did build it and they did come! So, we spent time imagining ways to host all (including an option that involved a trek outside for some – a walk and talk with a task that connected to the overall theme).

- How to make it a memorable (yet recognizable) meeting by copying and reusing elements from other formats – it was fresh and familiar at the same time. Tried and trusted methods were combined in new ways.

So, the open and respectful exchange of ideas in the design process led to The Exchange.

Read more: **www.idenk.com**

The checklist below details the IDENK structure for planning meetings.

CHECKLIST: Phil's 13Ps for planning perfect meetings

The 13Ps to help you perfect the planning for important meetings and events. You can approach them in any order, though 4 and 10 are key to get right early on (as my diagram illustrates too), coming to the agenda later (really!):

1   Personal skills: what can you do (and what can't you manage)... fill this self-assessment in on the basis of events you have led.

2 Personal preferences: think of great large events you have been to (from festivals and weddings to work ones)... what made them special?

3 Past: What is the context, history and story so far for this meeting?

4 Purpose: questions, aims, outcomes... what is the unique purpose?

5 Potential risks: what possible problems might there be... where might it go horribly wrong?

6 Preordained: What is given by any leaders... what is non-negotiable? What must you do (or not do)? What is your freedom to decide?

7 People: Thinking of participants, who is coming (or who would you like to come)?

8 Place: What is the venue, date, day of the week... what are the logistical options, costs and fixed points? How can you work around what you have, if not ideal? See this for seating and other options.

9 Pre-work: what sort of survey, interviews or vox pop would research the range of opinion efficiently and clearly? Do you need to do more work searching for speakers, consultants, a better venue and thinking of how you use social media as a design team?

10 Principles: What is the style of the event you (or if working with others, the design team or leaders) want? How much of the meeting should be familiar – and how fresh would you like the experience to be? What is the degree of fixed structure and/or open flexibility you are looking to provide?

11 Process: Only now come to the agenda including online elements and connections – resist the urge to jump to here at the start!

12 Practise: what new elements are important to rehearse; are there any speakers to prep?

13 Post-event: What sort of record, gift or keeping-in-touch strategy do you want... plan this from the start (like how the best hospitals plan discharge – from the moment someone knows they will need to be admitted!).

www.idenk.com/blog/the-13-ps-for-perfect-meetings/

The risks to an organization of outsourcing key events functions include:

- Blurred lines of accountability. A specific in-house delivery model ensures transparent lines of internal organizational accountability and enables the building of consistent processes within established procurement guidelines.
- Tracking and management of event deliverables – both past and future – become more difficult if events are delivered by external suppliers not operating within mandated internal corporate guidelines and policies.
- Governance issues – each organization holds detailed knowledge in-house, and the use of an external company adds a level of complexity that risks any existing accountability and robustness. (It may, however, provide professional events management expertise that is not otherwise available within your own organization).
- Supplier relationships require close management that take up time as well as financial costs.
- Recognition that the challenging nature of some client organizations or the high profile nature of their organization impacts on every aspect of communication, including events.
- In-house events management systems can only be used by trained personnel within the organization. As a result of outsourcing, reporting functions would not cover events run by external suppliers; the provision of real time details of every event enables immediate responses to requests for information from senior management, that would not otherwise be provided.
- Explicit costs incurred in employing an external resource (compared to the often hidden costs of using in-house resources).

For further information on finance and procurement see Chapter 8.

Chapter summary

- In planning and developing any event, you don't start with a blank sheet of paper. You start with a team of people, an organization that has views, values and a purpose to its activity.
- The more people involved in event-content development the better – though this can make it more complex and more challenging.
- Learn from your previous experience: with this group – with any group; with this client – with any client; with this type of event – with any type of event.
- Review what works well and how you can improve it. Review what didn't go so well and how you can learn from it. Review what new ideas the activity has given you. Review content, activities and processes, style and structure.
- But more than anything, know what you are going to do, and why, before you do it.

Site planning and logistics

05

A wide range of sites (both indoor and outdoor) are used to host events. The appearance and layout of the site depends on the type of event as well as the nature of the activities taking place. At an outdoor music festival, one is likely to find stages, tents, mobile bars and catering units, whereas at a gala dinner dance you're more likely to find round tables, a dance floor, decorative displays and props. But no matter what event is taking place, it's important to think carefully about the layout of the event and produce an accurate plan (or map) of the site.

A poorly planned site can have a detrimental effect on the enjoyment of the event attendees. Take, for example, our gala dinner guests: they're unlikely to be impressed if there isn't enough space for them to sit comfortably to enjoy their meal and the evening's entertainment. On the other hand, music festival-goers may enjoy the buzz of a crowded festival site, adding to the festival atmosphere and experience. However, a busy atmospheric festival site is one thing, but an overcrowded festival site can become unsafe, with potential risks to public safety. While there are many things to consider when planning the layout of the event site, there is nothing more important than the safety of everyone on-site: attendees, staff, volunteers, contractors, suppliers and so on.

To ensure the smooth running of an event, it is important to develop a thorough plan for managing on-site logistics. The purpose of site logistics planning is to ensure that all the right elements (people, equipment and goods) are at the right place and at the right time. The tell-tale sign of poor logistics planning is when delays and disruptions occur at the event. For example, people stuck in traffic waiting to park their vehicles, standing in long queues to enter the site, to collect their tickets, to be served food and drinks or waiting around because of delays to the event schedule. Most event attendees will be able to relate to many of these examples and it's likely that delays or disruptions experienced were influenced by poor planning.

This chapter will look at the following topics:

- Planning the site layout
- Planning a safe event site
- Logistics planning for events.

> ## A caveat
>
> This chapter has been written with planning and managing a large event site (eg conference and exhibition, outdoor festival or sporting tournament) in mind. However, the same basic principles of site planning, site safety and site logistics are relevant to a smaller event.

Planning the site layout

Whatever the type of event, the nature of activities, the chosen location or venue, it is always necessary to think carefully about the layout and create some sort of site plan. For smaller events, planning the event layout is unlikely to be an onerous task. For example, if a family birthday party is being held at a local restaurant, a simple hand-drawn sketch of the desired layout is all that is needed to show how the tables will be set out, who is sitting where and if any decorations or props are needed (eg a cake table). As a general rule, however, the larger and more complex the event, then the more important it is to plan the layout of the site.

There is no exact science involved with planning the site layout (indeed it is often referred to as the *art* of site planning) but the following three stages are recommended:

1 Determine the space and resource requirements
2 Carefully design the site layout
3 Produce a map of the site.

Stage 1: Space and resource requirements

Before designing the layout of the site, it is first essential to determine both the space and resource requirements for the event.

Space requirements

Regardless of the type of event you are planning, it's important to understand how much space will be required for the type of activities that are planned. Specific types of events inevitably have different space requirements. If you're planning a business conference then space must be allowed for meeting rooms and hospitality areas, whereas if you're planning an outdoor festival site then allocating sufficient space for camping and car parking is essential.

As well as allocating space for public areas, it is necessary to allocate space for 'back of house' areas, including:

- Administration/offices
- Changing facilities
- Crew catering
- Equipment storage
- Green room
- Media facilities
- Staff rooms

Resource requirements

Determining the physical resource requirements involves creating a list of all the equipment, facilities and infrastructure needed to ensure that the event runs smoothly. Thinking about our earlier example, the family birthday party at a local restaurant: a few balloons, decorations, birthday banners, place cards and a cake stand may be all that is needed. But for larger, more complex events the list of equipment, facilities and infrastructure required will inevitably be much more comprehensive.

The checklist shown below has been designed to help you to determine the physical resource requirements for an event. It provides a list of the most important resources that should be considered. The checklist is intended to act as a good guide but it is essential that a specific list of the equipment, facilities and infrastructure is drawn up for each event.

CHECKLIST: event equipment, facilities and infrastructure

Temporary structures

☐ Staging

☐ Stage backdrop

☐ Towers

☐ Temporary seating

☐ Hospitality marquees/tents

☐ Grandstands

☐ Canopies and coverings

☐ Stalls

☐ Cabins

Crowd management

- ☐ Crowd barriers
- ☐ Temporary fencing
- ☐ Ropes and stakes
- ☐ Floor coverings
- ☐ Temporary walkways
- ☐ Entranceway features
- ☐ Directional signage
- ☐ Information points

Furniture

- ☐ Reception and registration desks
- ☐ Dining tables
- ☐ Chairs
- ☐ Sofas
- ☐ Cocktail tables

Hospitality and catering

- ☐ Catering units
- ☐ Mobile bars
- ☐ Catering equipment
- ☐ Catering storage

Administration

- ☐ Computer
- ☐ Printer
- ☐ Photocopier
- ☐ Telephones
- ☐ Phone lines
- ☐ Communications equipment

Health, safety and welfare

- ☐ first-aid tent
- ☐ medical supplies
- ☐ drinking water
- ☐ meeting points
- ☐ lost and found tents
- ☐ fire fighting equipment
- ☐ health and safety signage

Technical equipment

- ☐ lighting
- ☐ speakers
- ☐ special effects
- ☐ video projection
- ☐ lighting rigs
- ☐ public address system
- ☐ power supply
- ☐ mixing/control desks

Transport and vehicles

- ☐ forklift
- ☐ cherry picker
- ☐ crane
- ☐ off-road vehicles
- ☐ vans
- ☐ cars
- ☐ buggies

Public facilities

☐ Toilets

☐ Hand-washing

☐ Showers

☐ Disabled facilities

☐ Recycling points

☐ Waste bins

Decorative

☐ Scenery

☐ Theming props

☐ Decoration and dressing

☐ Floral and landscaping

Determining space and resource requirements

Three factors to consider that will have a direct bearing on the space and resource requirements for each event:

- Event programme and content: This will vary depending on the type of event. Having a clear idea of the different elements of the programme is essential in order to allocate space requirements as well as drawing up a list of the physical resources required (ie equipment, facilities and infrastructure).

- Profile of the attendees: The people attending will also be a factor in determining both space and resource requirements. Take, for example, an international conference where several delegates have travelled from overseas to attend. After a long journey, a comfortable environment for them to sit, relax and unwind and have a cup of tea, before the conference gets under way is sure to be appreciated along with a secure facility to store their luggage until they can check in to their hotel.

- Nature of the event site: The site itself is an important factor in determining what additional equipment, facilities and infrastructure are needed. If a conference is taking place at a large convention centre, for example, then it can be expected that the venue already has staging, seating, sound and lighting as well as facilities such as public cafés and toilets.

The following case studies about the Yorkshire Event Centre and Honourable Artillery Companies show that some event sites are better equipped than others to host a wide range of events.

CASE STUDY 5.1 Yorkshire Event Centre (YEC)

Sophie Bunker, Sales Executive, Yorkshire Event Centre. UK Centre for Event Management Graduate, 2014

Situated on the outskirts of Harrogate, with 6 million people living within an hour's drive and 10 per cent of the UK's population living in Yorkshire, the Yorkshire Event Centre (YEC) is well placed to welcome large events who want to attract big audiences. It has all the space and support you need to run all kinds of events from exhibitions, conferences, dinners, weddings and concerts – along with pretty much anything else you can think of! If you've got the vision, they've got the venue.

The YEC currently hosts 5,372 m² of indoor space provided by two halls – Hall 1 which is 3,422m² and Hall 2 which is 1,950m². These halls are linked by The Yorkshire Café so everything is on one level, which means the venue is easily accessible for visitors and exhibitors. Wifi is also available throughout the exhibition halls.

In 2015 the YEC will be building a new Hall 1 to replace the current building. This will provide 4,320m² of modern clear-span space, representing a significant investment and a huge vote of confidence in Harrogate as an events destination. The new hall is set to open in summer 2016 and will increase the total floor space available to 6,270m². This build will help YEC develop the solid foundation it has in consumer exhibitions and expand further into trade shows and large scale corporate events and conferences.

The Tandem Tops are two distinctive, large open-span buildings that are perfect for fun days and sales. They offer 5,458m² of covered event space surrounded by grassed areas, giving organizers a world of opportunities and making visitors feel as if they are outside.

Furthermore the venue sits on 250 acres of land providing a variety of flexible outdoor event spaces ideal for film location shoots, concerts, scout camps, team-building events and car rallies. In addition to all that space, seven miles of roadway, lots of quirky buildings plus a disused viaduct means the venue really can cater for all events while ensuring an abundance of free parking space.

Managing Director of YEC, Heather Parry, commented: 'We are incredibly proud of the great and varied facility we offer in the heart of Yorkshire. It is fantastic that our great county is recognized as an events destination, one which we can only hope will develop even further over time.

'Having started originally for the Great Yorkshire Show we have developed the site continually over many years to maximize the space and facilities that we have, and are now celebrating the benefits not just for us but for Harrogate and Yorkshire as a whole.'

Read more: **http://eventcentre.co.uk/**

CASE STUDY 5.2   The Honourable Artillery Company: an exceptionally versatile London City venue

Rowan Bennett, Head of Marketing and Events at The Honourable Artillery Company, UK Centre for Events Management Graduate, 2005

The Honourable Artillery Company (HAC) is a unique, historic London venue offering a variety of event spaces for conferences, meetings, awards dinners, summer and Christmas parties, fun days and wedding receptions. It offers a secure, stylish and very flexible canvas for up to 400 guests for a dinner or conference or up to 700 for an informal stand-up party. Located just a stone's throw from Moorgate and hidden away in a quiet location unseen from City Road, the HAC, with its five-acre garden, is an oasis of green in a City of glass and steel.

The largest events we host tend to include the outdoor space, which, with its five acres, adds a huge benefit to central London events. The flexibility of the venue means that sporting events can be hosted to high professional levels while offering hospitality options within either the main House or the Prince Consort Rooms without the added cost of temporary structures that many greenfield sites incur. London Marathon's City Sprint Race sees 3,000 runners setting off from the HAC each July, while Saracens recreate their home stadium offering, twice yearly, for 2,000 spectators watching international rugby right in the heart of the City.

Marilyn Allen, Senior Sales Co-Ordinator comments: 'One key benefit of having both an outdoor and indoor space is the ability to offer a wet-weather contingency. The HAC is one of the most popular summer party venues in the City, not only due to its stunning location, but should the weather turn we have the perfect indoor space to move under cover, meaning no risk of cancellation fees for the client.'

Invariably, as with many event venues, the variety of equipment needed to meet the differing requirements of client events means large levels of apparatus can build up. We already have amongst our inventory some 710 conference chairs, 131 tables and 298 table centres for the Prince Consort Rooms alone, so storage is always a challenge. Our strategy is to hold the highest levels of essentials for delivery of our regular events such as conferences, dinners and weddings, and then allow the client to contract their own suppliers directly for more specific elements such as AV, as each event typically has its own specification to meet. And as the outdoor space is very much a blank canvas and every event invariably has a different brief, we only hold the essential sporting equipment on-site.

The safety of our venue is paramount for delivering events and remains at the forefront of our planning and delivery at all times. Not only within the indoor spaces, but also on our grounds. We work closely with our clients to advise on barriers, fencing and trackway required when large temporary structures are installed to ensure minimum damage to the grounds is caused and maximum efficiency and safe practice is achieved. Communication is key, as is control of contractors and often, to ensure the best delivery, it takes a pretty hands-on approach from our operations team!

There are many aspects to event-delivery, whether this be indoors or out. The key to success is planning, preparation, communication and care. By care I mean passion, and taking pride in what we do – working together in partnership with clients and suppliers to deliver high-quality events.

Read more: **www.hac.org**

Stage 2: Design the site layout

Having determined the space and resource requirements, the next task is to design the layout of the event site. It's important to think carefully about the design of the site in order to ensure 'optimum space usage' (making best use of the space available).

The following three steps are recommended:

Step 1: obtain a detailed plan of the site

This is the first thing to do and is easy enough to achieve for most indoor venues. The venue team will be able to provide a detailed map (eg dimensions, capacities, entrances/exits, fixed points) or you can usually find a map on the website. For instance, the venue plan for Hall 2 at the Yorkshire Event Centre is available for event organizers to download from their website, should it be needed.

It can be more difficult to obtain a plan for an outdoor site. For a site that is frequently used for events, we recommend contacting previous event organizers, the land owners or local authorities, to find out if a detailed plan of the site is already available to help design the layout of your event.

Step 2: determine the layout of the event

This brings us to one of the most difficult tasks for an event organizer, especially for larger, more elaborate events with a wide range of activities taking place. Determining the layout of the event involves deciding where best to position all the activities and attractions as well as the facilities, services, equipment and infrastructure.

Top Tip

A good technique for designing the event layout is to print off a large map of the site and cut out icons, or use 'Post-its' to represent the various activities as well as the equipment, facilities and infrastructure needed on-site (the old fashioned methods are sometimes still the best!). Keeping it all to the same scale will enable you to move around different icons on the map.

Each event will have its own requirements, but the following points should be considered – although even the order that you follow may change, according to the specific type, nature and location of the event:

- **Determine the best position for the central feature of the event.** Once you've decided on the best location for the main activity or attraction then the other activities and attractions can be positioned around this. Be prepared to move things around – it's an iterative process, so consider using cut-out icons or Post-its so you can make alterations.

- **Situate complementary activities and attractions next to one another:** eg food and drink stalls generally work well alongside one another, whereas food stalls and toilets don't go so well together!

- **Avoid concentrating too many popular activities in one area.** This will inevitably lead to crowd build-up and congestion and the associated risks to public safety.

- **Ensure a safe distance between high- and low-risk activities:** eg careful consideration needs to be given to the location and allocated space for potentially dangerous activities, such as archery and shooting.

- **Site medical and welfare facilities in a prominent position.** First-aid tents and 'lost and found' meeting points need to be positioned where they can be easily located.

- **Allocate prime space for VIPs, corporate guests and media partners.** VIP tickets and hospitality packages are sold at a premium to ensure the best views of the action. Journalists and media organizations require a good view of proceedings as they unfold.

- **Ensure the correct and safe positioning of any technical equipment.** Sound and lighting equipment must be positioned appropriately in order for people to hear and see what is happening at the event.

- **Maintain a visibility distance between front and back of house areas.** Equipment storage, staff offices and crew catering should be kept out of sight and out of reach.

- **Make the event accessible to everyone.** The layout should be designed to allow people with mobility problems, sight or hearing impairments or other special needs to enjoy the activities and attractions.

Note: the above list was compiled to assist with planning the layout of an outdoor event such as a food and drink or music festival. However, the same basic principles can be applied to other types of events (including indoor events).

Top Tip

Free online tools such as **www.floorplanner.com/** and **www.planner.roomsketcher.com/** are typically used to design the floor plan of your home but are perfectly adequate for designing the layout of a smaller event site.

Step 3: Seek feedback on the proposed layout

Once you've created a proposed layout for the event it is a good idea to share this with other key stakeholders. The venue manager will have first-hand experience of what works and what doesn't in the venue; similarly, suppliers and contractors (particularly those with previous experience of having worked at the event site) can help you avoid any obvious pitfalls. It's always a sensible idea to share the proposed layout with your client (or whoever is footing the bill) to ensure it meets their expectations.

Stage 3: Produce a map of the site

Much like a street map, the purpose of a site map is to help people to find their way around. It's easy to think about a site map being only for the event attendees, but staff, suppliers and contractors will also need a map of the site to find their way. Indeed, the first people to use their map will be the staff, suppliers and contractors who need to know where to install temporary structures, locate technical equipment and deliver supplies. Only once the doors open and the attendees arrive on-site, will they then refer to their maps to find their way to the various activities and attractions, as well as locating catering areas, toilet facilities and so on.

Trying to fit too much detail on a single site map will only serve to confuse anyone trying to use the map to find their way. It is preferable to have a master map and separate maps for attendees and staff (including suppliers and contractors). For an event taking place over a large site or even multiple sites and venues, it will be necessary to produce a series of smaller maps.

The following checklist provides a list of what should be included on the site map for attendees and staff; note that this detail may not necessarily be the same for each grouping. This is not an exhaustive list but the most common items to include on a map of the site are listed here.

CHECKLIST: what should be included in the venue/site map

Attendees:

☐ Main entrance and exits

☐ Access roads

☐ Car parking

☐ Public transport

☐ Taxis

☐ Information points

☐ First-aid areas

☐ Meeting points

☐ Toilets

☐ Catering stalls

☐ Hospitality areas

☐ Cash machines

Staff:

☐ Staff entrances and exits

☐ Load-in /Load-out areas

☐ Delivery bays

☐ Equipment storage

☐ Administration/offices

☐ Crew catering

☐ Changing facilities

☐ Power supply

☐ Water supply

☐ Off-limits areas

☐ Emergency access

☐ Fire equipment

Top Tip

As a general rule a site map should always include a comprehensive list of the symbols used on the map. Using universal symbols helps to make it easier for people to read the map and find their way.

Producing a site map also involves choosing the right size and the correct material for the map. For a small indoor event, such as a village fete, a hand-drawn map will be perfectly adequate. This can be photocopied and given to the stallholders, volunteers, attendees and anybody else who may need a copy. However, if it is decided that the event will take place on a larger scale and is moved outdoors then this type of map will no longer be fit for purpose. An outdoor site could well mean wet weather, so the map would need to be made waterproof (eg laminated). If the event is taking place on a larger scale, the level of detail on a hand-drawn map will not be sufficient, in which case it needs to be created electronically and enlarged. Table 5.1 gives an idea of the different types of site maps that would be used by a delegate attending a large conference and exhibition.

TABLE 5.1   Examples of site maps needed at a large conference and exhibition

Format	Purpose
Downloadable location map available online	Help delegates to plan their journey, eg • How to find the venue • How to access car parking • Where to enter the building
A4 size colour-coded plan in the conference brochure, displaying the agenda and exhibitor locations	Allow delegates to plan their personal itinerary, eg • Which speakers and exhibitors to see • Where they will be located
Large waterproof display board in the car park	Enable delegates to find their way to the venue, eg • Locate the entrance • Decide if it is within walking distance • Locate the shuttle bus or transport links
Large display board inside the entrance	Ensure a smooth arrival for the delegates, eg • Where to register or collect their badge • Where to find the cloakroom, refreshments and toilet facilities
A5 size colour map in the conference programme	Help delegates to find their way around the venue, eg • Which way to go • Where to find key note sessions • Where to find specific exhibitors

Planning a safe event site

There is nothing more important than ensuring the safety of everyone at the event. This includes attendees, the event staff and volunteers, the wider event team (contractors and suppliers), as well as anybody else in close proximity to the event (eg people living and working nearby). Under the Health and Safety at Work Act 1974 (HASWA), event organizers are required to take 'reasonable' precautions to ensure the health and safety of everyone involved in an event. It is good practice and strongly recommended to undertake risk assessments to help you decide which risks are specific to your event, and what measures are needed to control potential risks. See the later section on Risk Management.

Sadly, the following examples of tragedies occurring at concerts and festivals since 2000 serve as a stark reminder of the risk to public safety at large events.

Fatal incidents occurring at concerts and music festivals since 2000

2014 – K-Pop Concert, South Korea

16 people watching an outdoor pop concert fell 20 metres into a concrete shaft, to their deaths.

2011 – Pukkelpop Music Festival, Belgium

Severe storms caused multiple stages to collapse at the festival, leaving four people dead.

2010 – The Love Parade Festival, Germany

This unticketed free festival drew more than 1 million people to an area that had capacity for roughly 250,000. More than 500 people were injured and 21 people died.

2003 – Great White in Rhode Island, USA

A pyrotechnics display ignited soundproof insulation, causing a fire that killed 100 people, including the band's guitarist, Ty Longley.

2000 – Pearl Jam at The Roskilde Festival, Denmark

Nine people died, killed as fans rushed the stage.

SOURCES:
Billboard (2014) Many fall to their deaths at K-Pop Concert in South Korea
 http://m.billboard.com/entry/view/id/103720 (Last accessed 6 February 2015)
Warlaw, M (nd), *10 Worst Concert Tragedies: Ultimate Classic Rock*. Available at:
 http://ultimateclassicrock.com/worst-concert-mishaps-and-tragedies/?trackback=tsmclip
 (Last accessed 9 September 2014)

Safety concerns

Events vary tremendously and it is therefore very difficult to provide a definitive list of specific safety concerns. Event planners are advised to seek specialist guidance when it comes to health and safety at events. There is more detail about where to find further information and receive guidance and assistance, at the end of this chapter.

Below we set out the broad safety considerations that are applicable to most event sites:

Crowds

For any-sized event it is important to determine the number of people the event can safely hold. The profile (or dynamics) of the event attendees must be taken into consideration. The earlier examples show the potential dangers associated with a 'high-spirited' concert or festival crowd.

Effective crowd management techniques at a concert or festival include the use of crowd barriers as well as positioning stewarding and security personnel.

All event sites must allow people to safely enter/exit the site and also move around the site safely. Careful attention is needed to ensure public walkways are sufficiently wide and clear from obstruction (eg blocked by stalls or equipment). If an event is being held outdoors, then footpaths that are suitable for use in adverse weather conditions must be used. It is also important to make sure that there is appropriate directional signage throughout and, where necessary, suitable lighting for people to find their way (particularly if the event takes place at night).

Traffic management

Allowing any vehicle on to a busy event site is fraught with danger. It is best practice to only permit vehicular access at specific times and not during the event itself. There should always be a traffic marshal on hand to guide vehicles on- and off-site (maintaining a safe speed). A well-designed site layout will help to reduce the necessity for vehicles to access the site. It will help to situate car parks and loading bays for exhibitors and stall holders within walking distance of stalls as well as positioning staff and volunteers nearby to assist with unloading equipment and goods.

It may also be necessary to control traffic outside the event site (eg temporary road closures, designated routes, directional signage) and a comprehensive traffic-management plan should be drawn up and agreed with the relevant authorities (eg Highways department).

Temporary structures

Many events (particularly those held outdoors) require temporary structures such as staging, tents, marquees and stalls. If this is the case then the siting/location of such structures needs to be carefully considered. It may be necessary to maintain a safe distance between each of the structures as well as maintaining a safe distance from the crowd (eg to reduce the risk of items falling from stages and towers). It is important to think about arrangements to stop unauthorized persons gaining access to temporary structures such as stages and towers. Furthermore, it is extremely important that any temporary structures are not positioned in such a way that they obstruct any of the public walkways/routes or site entrances/exits.

Electrical safety

Electricity and water can cause death or serious injury – fact! For any event taking place outdoors it is recommended that, whatever the weather forecast, any electrical equipment is properly covered. Even with events being held indoors, it is still important to be mindful of electrical safety. For example, electrical equipment needs to be properly enclosed, warning signs should be clearly displayed and electrical cabling properly secured. An indoor or outdoor event could be cast into darkness with a sudden loss of power (and light) and so emergency lighting, as well as backup power, may be needed on-site.

Adverse weather

The onset of adverse weather conditions can pose an instant danger for anybody attending or working at an outdoor event. Temporary structures, such as stages, fencing and tents are extremely vulnerable to high winds. Extreme wet weather will create slippery conditions under foot and make driving in muddy conditions potentially dangerous. Contingency plans should be in place (pre-event) to deal with the implications of extreme weather conditions. For example – in wet-weather conditions the event could be moved to an alternative indoor venue or specialist matting could be used to stop people from slipping.

Medical and welfare

The nature of the event, the age of the attendees, the size of audience and the duration of the event will all influence the level of medical and welfare provision needed on-site. The provision of adequate numbers and types of resource (eg first aid, ambulances and paramedics) should be based upon published guidance such as the Event Safety Guide (more commonly known as the 'Purple' Guide). Adequate provision should also be made for lost persons, lost and found children and lost property, and special arrangements should be made to ensure disabled visitors have adequate facilities and services.

Indoor venues may already provide many of the required facilities but an outdoor site is a very different environment. In this case, it is important to seek appropriate support from an established provider of medical and welfare services for outdoor events (eg St John's Ambulance, Samaritans). Medical provision for the event should not rely upon the normal provision made by the statutory NHS Ambulance Service for use by the General Public (ie '999').

Cleanliness and hygiene

Adequate toilet and hand-washing facilities are required for attendees to maintain personal hygiene. The number of toilets needed will depend upon the anticipated attendee crowd numbers as well as the gender of attendees (women require more toilets than men). Adequate provision must also be made for attendees with disabilities. Indoor venues may already have adequate facilities but additional portaloos may need to be hired for larger events. Toilets, hand-washing, baby-changing and possibly shower facilities (eg festival campsite) will all need to be hired for an outdoor event. Anybody who has attended an outdoor event knows that maintaining the cleanliness of these facilities can be difficult and so they need to be located to make cleaning them straightforward.

Any catering outlets should be located in areas where there is minimal risk of contamination of food, so ideally they need to be kept well away from toilets as well as waste/refuse areas. Caterers need to be provided with sufficient food waste disposal, washing facilities and clean water. A power supply for catering equipment (eg refrigeration) is also important in order to keep food fresh and edible.

Fire safety

Basic fire prevention begins with separating flammable and combustible materials (including liquids and gases) from a naked flame or spark. Take, for example, a small fire breaking out on a catering stall at an event. Storing gas bottles elsewhere when not in use minimizes the risk of the fire spreading. If a small fire does occur, then fire safety equipment should be available for putting it out (eg fire extinguishers and fire blankets). Catering staff should be trained how to use this equipment. In this example, providing appropriate distance between catering stalls would also help to prevent the spread of fire. If, however, the fire does develop then everyone on the event site must be able to escape easily to a place of safety.

Security

Security generally becomes more of a concern when VIPs are in attendance at an event. Consider, for a moment, the heightened levels of security at any location/venue hosting major political events such as the G20 Summits. Event organizers must work closely with the police force and specialist security firms to determine whether security measures, such as the use of protective barriers to guard against unauthorized access, security searches on entry as well as the siting of surveillance cameras is needed. It is important, however, to be mindful that there is a fine line between stringent security at an event and actually creating a heightened sense of fear amongst attendees. An event site littered with security check points, surveillance cameras and security personnel will ultimately make many attendees feel less safe at the event.

Major incidents

For larger events, there should always be a plan in place for dealing with major incidents and emergencies, including terrorism or force majeure. This is known as a Major Incident Plan and covers aspects such as crowd control (eg crowd evacuation), traffic management (eg access for emergency vehicles), communications (eg raising the alarm) and staffing (eg what staff should do in the event of an emergency); the emergency services will take over control of all activities in such a situation.

Risk assessment

There will always be risks associated with events (just as there is an element of risk every day when you walk out of your front door). What is important is to put the risk into some sort of context. For example, setting up temporary structures at a large outdoor event site brings a higher degree of risk than setting out tables and chairs at a wedding.

Carrying out a risk assessment will enable you to identify potential risks and take steps to minimize or reduce the impact of these risks and decide what measures need to be put in place or what actions need to be taken to reduce the risk.

The three basic steps involved in carrying out a risk assessment are as follows:

1 Look for the hazards ie anything that can cause harm.
2 Decide who might be harmed and how.
3 Evaluate the risks and decide what needs to be done first (if anything).

Step 1: look for hazards

The first step of your risk assessment is accurately identifying the potential hazards at the event. A good starting point is to take a tour of the event site to look for any hazards. For large events it will probably help to divide the site into smaller sectors. An outdoor festival site, for example, could easily be divided into the following sectors:

- ticket office;
- wristband exchange;
- car parking;
- main stage;
- main arena;
- arena entrance;
- individual marquees;
- camping field.

Figure 5.1 shows an example of risk assessment for the wristband exchange at the entrance to an outdoor music festival. As can be seen from the first column, the potential hazards identified included electric shock, overcrowding, violence, tripping and adverse weather.

FIGURE 5.1 Sample risk assessment

Wristband Exchange

The wristband exchange procedure takes place under a temporary light weight structure offering protection from the weather, but the structure is open on both sides, providing an easy and highly visible entrance and exit to the main arena.

Risk Level [R]	S1	S2	S3	S4
P1	O	O	O	C
P2	O	O	C	B
P3	O	C	B	A
P4	O	B	A	A

Probability [P]	Severity [S]
1 = Improbable	1 = Negligible
2 = Remote	2 = Minor
3 = Possible	3 = Severe
4 = Probable	4 = Extreme

Consequences
A = Hazard **must** be eliminated or avoided, work **not** to proceed.
B = Risk **must** be controlled by physical safeguards.
C = Risk **must** be controlled so far as is reasonably practicable.
O = Risk is adequately controlled/insignificant.

Hazard	Hazard description	Safety Precautions (details of preventative or control measure for hazards)	Risk Evaluation (without controls)			Residual Risk Evaluation (with controls)		
			P	S	R	P	S	R
Electric shock		All electrical equipment and wiring to be checked by electrical contractor.	2	4	B	1	4	C
Overcrowding		Fencing to control numbers of visitors entering site. Security guards and stewards assisting in the direction and flow of visitors into site. Effective signage detailing waiting areas and ticket to wristband procedure.	2	2	O	1	2	O
Violence	Confrontation	Security shall be sited in this area with two roaming guards available for back-up if required.	3	2	C	2	2	O
Tripping	Hazards posed to pedestrians in this area (eg boggy or slippery areas, other trip obstacles, etc)	Boggy or slippery areas to be cordoned off with tape and/or repaired with wood mulch or gravel. Monitor and remove all trip hazards wherever possible. All wiring to be flown over head or buried.	3	2	C	1	2	O
Weather	Hypothermia, trench foot, sunstroke, dehydration.	Visitors to be informed (via website, tickets, festival documentation) of the importance of bringing appropriate footwear and clothing. Welfare tent to offer free sun cream and water. A limited supply of warm clothing and blankets on site if required.	3	3	B	2	3	C

Step 2: decide who might be harmed

The second step involves identifying groups or people at risk of harm. Examples of people at risk on a festival site would include:

- festival-goers;
- employees;
- temporary workers;
- volunteers;
- members of the public;
- contractors;
- suppliers.

You should always pay particular attention to vulnerable people, such as young children, people with disabilities or inexperienced staff.

Examples of how people could be harmed on a festival site include:

- cuts and bruises;
- sprains and strains;
- broken and dislocated bones;
- absorbing substances;
- noise injuries;
- burns and scalds;
- crushing or trapping injuries;
- flying or falling objects.

Step 3: evaluating the risk

To help evaluate the risks, a scoring system can be used. Numerical scores are given to the Probability (P) and Severity (S) of risks and these scores are multiplied to get a rating for the risk.

Risk = Probability × Severity

The amount of risk is usually categorized into a small number of levels because neither the Probability (P) nor harm Severity (S) can typically be estimated with accuracy and precision. An example is shown in Table 5.2:

TABLE 5.2   Risk scoring system

Probability (P)	Severity (S)
1 = Remote Possibility	1 = Nil
2 = Unlikely	2 = Slight
3 = Possible	3 = Moderate
4 = Highly Likely	4 = High
5 = Inevitable	5 = Very High

By multiplying the scores for the Probability (P) and Severity (S), the risk is given a rating ranging from 1 (no severity and unlikely to happen) to 25 (just waiting to happen with disastrous and widespread results). This is not intended to be a scientific process but helps to determine the level of risks, priority of risks and the urgency to act on them. An example is shown in Table 5.3:

TABLE 5.3   Risk rating system

Risk Score	Risk Rating	Action
1 – 4	Acceptable	No action required
5 – 9	Moderate	Reduce risks if reasonably practicable
10 – 15	High risk	Priority action to be undertaken
16 – 25	Unacceptable	Action must be taken immediately

For further information see the very useful Risk Management section of the Health and Safety Executive (HSE) website at **www.hse.gov.uk/risk/index.htm**

Logistics planning for events

Logistics is considered to have originated in the military where the ability to supply troops with weapons, ammunition and rations, before and during the battle, can make the difference between victory and defeat. As Sun Tzu, the Chinese military strategist of 2,500 years ago famously said: 'Every battle is won before it is even fought.' In other words, you must win the battle through superior logistics planning. More recently logistics planning has been applied to other specialisms, such as business and event logistics. The essence still holds true – in order to succeed in business or put on a successful event, a sound logistical plan is essential.

Logistics planning for events requires you to ensure that all the people, equipment and goods (rather than weapons!) are moved to the right place at the right time. Think about a live concert performance; it's no good having the staging, sound and lighting equipment, musical instruments, special effects, camera crews and even the crowd in place, if the star performers are nowhere to be seen.

What happens at an event means there are always going to be logistical challenges for event managers to contend with. Certainly for larger, more complex events which take place over multiple sites (venues or stages), multiple

FIGURE 5.2   Phases of event logistics

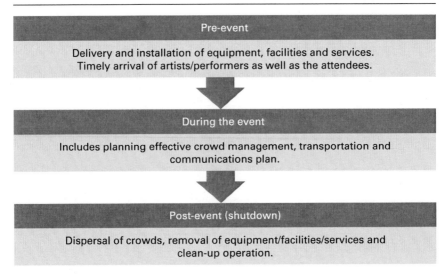

Adapted from Bowdin *et al* (2011)

days and involving multiple roles (staff, volunteers and participants, as well as attendees), then dealing with the logistical challenges is a key part of the job. Unlike a logistics manager in a generic business operation, there is no second chance for an event manager to get it right. Hence the need for a sound logistical plan.

Many people regard event logistics as what happens during the event but ignore what happens pre-event (supply of equipment and arrival of the performers/artists), and post-event (eg dismantling of the site and clean-up operation). Logistical planning should concern the whole operation including what happens pre- and post-event, as shown in Figure 5.2.

Pre-event

Sound logistical planning should ensure that all resources are in place for the start of the event, including delivery and installation of equipment, facilities and services; timely arrival of artists and performers; and smooth arrival of attendees.

Delivery and installation of equipment, facilities and services

The delivery and installation of any temporary structures (eg staging) is known as the 'Build-up' which is followed by the 'Load-in' of any equipment, services and goods. Different events involve very different timescales for

'Build-up and Load-in' – some a matter of hours, some days and others weeks. Indoor venues are likely to include an extra charge for any time needed to set up (which needs to be factored into the budget) so sound logistical planning will help minimize costs.

The general rule is that 'bulky' items (eg large temporary structures such as staging and backdrops) are delivered and installed first. Any extensive structural installations will usually arrive on large trucks and trailers and, if an event is being held at a venue close to a built-up area, could cause traffic congestion on nearby roads. In order to avoid this, 'Build-up' may take place during the early hours of the morning. Whatever time of day 'Build-up and Load-in' occur, it is essential to ensure clear routes for large vehicles to access the site (indoor or outdoor) and also to provide adequate parking, and ensure that local residents are not inconvenienced by noise or other disruptions.

Once the 'bulky' structural installations are in place, then the medium-sized items (eg tents/marquees and catering outlets on an outdoor site) will be set up, and technical equipment such as sound and lighting can be installed. Finally, smaller items such as furniture (eg tables and chairs) and decorative items can be put in place.

The case study below provides an overview of the typical sequence of the 'Build-up' and 'Load-in' for a large exhibition venue.

CASE STUDY 5.3   Earls Court and Olympia – 'build-up' for a large exhibition

---

Philippa Hallam, Conference Producer at Forum Business Media Ltd. UK Centre for Events Management Graduate, 2014. Placement Student at EC&O 2011–2012

Earls Court and Olympia London (EC&O) holds a vast amount of history within their exhibition and conference spaces, with the venue hosting some of the UK's biggest trade and consumer shows for more than a century. Olympia was opened in 1884 by the National Agricultural Hall Company, to form the country's largest covered show centre. It has since gone on to hold large annual events such as the International Horse Show and the London Book Fair, with 42,910m^2 of event space. Earls Court One opened in 1937 with Earls Court Two opening in 1991; together they have an impressive 60,000m^2 of event space, hosting events such as the Ideal Home Show, the Great British Beer Festival and the British Military Tournament.

For large exhibitions, there are many facilities and services that have to be installed prior to the event. Many different companies are involved in the 'build-up' phase ahead of the doors opening to the event attendees. The following outline is provided as an overview of the typical sequence of the 'build-up' for a large exhibition held at EC&O:

–4–5 days: The show floor has to be marked out, to identify where exhibition stands will be built, where stages will be constructed and where aisles will be placed for attendees. This forms the basis for all contractors to follow throughout the build of the event.

–4 days: Electrics will be installed. Floor plans are essential here to ensure electrics (based underneath the flooring) are pulled through at correct points to correspond with exhibitor stands.

–3 days: Stages are then usually built by the in-house AV specialists at EC&O. They have to ensure stages are placed correctly so other contractors can work around them. It is useful to have stages in place fairly early so it becomes clearer where to place furniture.

–2–3 days: The next service to be installed is the shell scheme, which makes up exhibition stands and forms the main structure for the exhibition floor. This may be built by a contractor brought in by the organizer. Some exhibitors have space-only stands, where they build their own structure – sign-off by an independent structural engineer (if height breaches four metres) may be required before the event is allowed to open.

–2–3 days: To assist with lighting/speakers/signs above ground at Olympia, a rigging company is used to attach items to trusses, making certain they are safe and secure once in place. It is important to earth all cables attached to trussing, to ensure electrical safety while cables are live.

–2 days: Catering units will usually be put in place once all temporary infrastructures are installed. There are some permanent cafés within some Olympia halls as well.

–1–2 days: It is now time to lay carpets/flooring on exhibitor stands and aisles. The company used may recycle the carpets post-event, following their own recycling guide and EC&O's sustainability policy. Exhibitors may also be allowed on-site at this point to start dressing their stands.

Throughout build-up: Cleaners are provided to keep the venue clean and hazard-free during build-up, as well as remaining vigilant for suspicious behaviour/packages.

It is also worth noting that a lot of hard work goes on outside the exhibition halls in order to manage the traffic impact generated by a large event. Traffic management for contractors/deliveries/exhibitors is conducted to ensure the correct people enter the relevant hall for each event. This can also be managed by security.

Read more: **www.eco.co.uk/**

Timely arrival of artists and performers

As we discussed in Chapter 4, an event is often made up of a series of activities with a variety of performers, artists, entertainers, speakers, trainers, facilitators and others participating in the event programme. All of these need to arrive on-site prior to the event getting under way or in good time ahead of their participation.

In order to ensure the timely arrival of artists and performers (we will refer to the plethora of participants as artists and performers for simplicity) it may be necessary to make travel arrangements, to arrange airport transfers, to book accommodation and schedule accommodation pickups on the day of the event. On arrival at the event site, artists and performers may require assistance with unloading, moving and storing equipment and it will also be necessary to organize accreditation passes (eg back stage passes) for them. Don't forget the artists and performers are the 'stars of the show' and it's very important to ensure they arrive in peak mental and physical condition to put on a great performance.

Top Tip

Situating the Event Organizer Office in a prominent position close to the site entrance makes it easy for everybody arriving on-site (contractors, suppliers, staff, artists and performers) to report to the office. That way you know exactly who has arrived on-site and, perhaps more importantly, who hasn't!

Arrival of attendees

The larger the event in terms of the number of attendees then the bigger the logistical challenge to have everyone arrive at the event on time and safely. For an event manager, there are two main challenges:

Dealing with the large number of attendees

It is not only dealing with the large number of attendees but also the fact that most of them will probably arrive at a similar time (known as a 'dump' of attendees). For example, at a football match, the stadium is often largely empty until 10–15 minutes before kick-off with the majority of fans arriving in this small window of time. In this case, having the appropriate number of turnstiles (entrances), ticket sales booths, clear signage as well as a sufficient number of stewards on hand is important to ensure the safe entry of fans (attendees) into the stadium.

It is also advisable to encourage attendees to arrive at different times to ensure a steady flow of attendees (known as a 'trickle'). For instance, at a football match, offering entertainment before kick-off (eg dance or musical performance) or offering promotions on food and beverage (eg cheap drinks before kick-off) will help to encourage people to come earlier.

Dealing with the extra traffic generated by the event

For attendees travelling in their own vehicles, good directional information and signage (including information available pre-event) as well as adequate car parking (preferably close by to the event) is needed to ensure their timely arrival. By encouraging attendees to use public transport, you will help to cut down on the number of vehicles on the road. Some events managers negotiate reduced fares with local public transport operators, increased bus services, the installation of temporary bus stops close to the event or they provide free shuttle buses from local rail stations.

Certainly for events generating a large volume of additional vehicles on the roads, a traffic-management plan is essential. This will be drawn up in advance in consultation with the Highways Department and the police and will include measures such as temporary road closures and diversions. This will help to avoid delays for attendees and also disruption for the normal day-to-day traffic.

During the event

The movement of people (eg attendees, staff, artists and performers) and equipment/goods from one place to another during the event, is referred to as 'on-site' logistics and involves Crowd management, Transportation and Communications.

Crowd management

Crowd-management measures that would typically be implemented during an event include:

- Well positioned and clearly signed entrances and exits to enable easy access to/from the site.
- Additional exits to use in case of an emergency.
- Use of crowd barriers and fencing to direct crowds and to encourage orderly queues.

- Walkways and routes should be wide enough for all persons including wheelchair users.
- Transportation may be required on-site for anybody with mobility issues.
- Site maps are displayed in a suitable format (eg on a large display board or on a small leaflet) for attendees to find their way around the event.
- Good directional signage both inside and outside the venue.
- Appropriate information on signage, eg the event programme (timing and location of activities).

Top Tip

Most indoor venues already have appropriate signage in place but this isn't always the case with outdoor sites where it is advisable to create a plan especially for event signage. The plan should clearly identify what types of signs are needed (eg directional, informational, emergency), where these will be positioned, how signs will be mounted, whether multilingual signs are needed as well as the use of logos, symbols and colour on signage.

Transportation

On a large event site it may be necessary to put in place a transportation system (eg shuttle buses, pick-up and drop-off points) to allow attendees to move around the site. Special arrangements will be needed for any attendees with mobility issues (eg very young, elderly, pregnant or disabled) as well as those attendees who are to be given the 'VIP' treatment (eg chauffeured buggy service).

The artists and performers may require on-site transportation to move equipment during set-up as well as transportation to/from rehearsal areas to changing rooms and performance areas. Media personnel, particularly those with large equipment (eg camera crews), may also need transportation to get where they need to be to view proceedings or meet with VIPs, performers and artists.

The staff and volunteers working at the event may also require the use of transportation on-site. For example, transport may be needed to help with the restocking of supplies at catering or merchandising stalls, as well as for waste collection and disposal during the event. However, on a busy festival site, large vehicles should not be allowed on-site at certain times of the day.

Communications

An effective communications plan will ensure that appropriate systems are in place to provide information to the attendees as well as for members of the event team to communicate both routinely and in an emergency situation.

Event attendees

There are several ways of communicating important information to the attendees during an event. Traditional methods include the use of a public address system as well as information boards situated around the event site. New technology has seen the increasing use of digital communications on-site such as video boards and mobile apps. As a general rule, the more information that can be given to attendees in advance of the event (eg a detailed programme of activities as well as an accurate map) the more this will reduce the need for communication during the event.

Event team

Effective on-site communications between members of the event team is essential in order to ensure the event runs smoothly. It is important to determine the best communication equipment to use and also to establish an effective procedure for communication between team members. The most suitable communications equipment to use will depend on the size of the site as well as the number of individuals who will be using the apparatus. Each type of equipment has its advantages and disadvantages, eg walkie-talkie radios may seem a little outdated but mobile phones can encounter challenges with busy networks and poor signal reception in both indoor and outdoor venues, so checks should always be made, rather than relying on the word of the venue managers.

Establishing effective communications procedures will help to ensure all team members are clear about who is the right person to contact in certain situations. For instance, if a problem arises with the projection equipment during a conference then it is important to contact the technical team, or if one of the catering outlets is running short of supplies then the catering manager should be contacted as soon as possible. An effective communications plan will clearly identify who is the right person to contact in order to ensure decisions are made quickly on-site. This is especially important when it comes to dealing with medical and emergency situations.

Top Tip

Just prior to the event, a walk-round inspection of the site is often carried out to check everything is in place and to spot any potential safety risks or logistical problems. During this walk-round it is also advisable to test that all communications equipment is working properly.

Post-event

Once the event is over, the task of shutting down the site begins. There is a tendency to think that the hard work is done when the event is over but there is still much to do. Any delay in closing down the event could mean a delay for the next event coming in (this is certainly the case with popular indoor event spaces) and this will most likely result in a penalty cost. To a large extent what takes place post-event will happen in reverse order to what takes place pre-event.

The first logistical challenge is to ensure the smooth dispersal of the event attendees which can be particularly problematic if all attendees leave en masse (eg at the end of a sporting match or concert performance). In this case, event stewards and security personnel will be on hand to assist with the moving crowd. For some events, it may be possible to encourage a staggered dispersal of crowds (in much the same way as a staggered arrival). For example, providing a late bar at an entertainment event or a post-event networking room at a conference is likely to mean some attendees don't leave right away. The journey home is often the lasting impression of an event for the attendees and too often for the wrong reasons – sitting in a long traffic jam, waiting for a long time to board public transport or finding an available taxi. Sound logistical planning involves thinking carefully about how traffic will exit the site (eg opening additional exits) as well as making arrangements for an orderly system for anyone travelling by public transport or taxi.

Once the event attendees have dispersed, the 'load-out' of equipment and goods begins. Smaller items must be packed up and moved off-site before the 'break-down' of the larger items (eg temporary staging and seating). It is important to ensure supplier and contractor vehicles can access the site easily and it may also be necessary to store some equipment until it can be collected, eg secure overnight storage may be required for an event finishing late at night. When the 'load-out' and 'break-down' of the site is taking place late at night, it is likely that staff and volunteers are tired, and when people are tired more mistakes happen. Tiredness can pose a risk to personal safety and the safety of others, so it is important to factor this in to any risk assessment.

Finally, the clean-up operation can get under way. The site should be left as it was found; penalty charges will be incurred for any damages and unwanted mess (eg posters stuck on walls, balloons on the ceiling). It is vital to ensure sufficient staff are allocated for the close-down and tidy-up operation to ensure this all happens smoothly without too many disruptions and delays. By this point in most events, the staff are exhausted, so bringing new staff on-site at this point, where possible, is advisable.

The following case study demonstrates the intense time pressures faced when transforming the London 2012 Olympic Stadium after the Opening Ceremony into an athletics stadium.

CASE STUDY 5.4   Gold medal for fast-turnaround at London 2012

Olivia Pole-Evans, Operations Team at London 2012 Ceremonies Ltd. UK Centre for Events Management Graduate and Student of the Year Award for Contribution to the Course, 2014

During the summer of 2012, the eyes of the world were on London for the Olympic and Paralympic Games for what proved to be an unforgettable summer of sport.

The 'Greatest Show on Earth' officially began with a spectacular opening ceremony created by Oscar-winning, British director, Danny Boyle. Up to 1 billion people worldwide watched the Opening Ceremony on television along with 80,000 inside the Olympic Stadium.

The London Organizing Committee of the Olympic and Paralympic Games (LOCOG) formed London 2012 Ceremonies Ltd (L2012C) for the sole purpose of producing the opening and closing ceremonies for the Games.

On the evening of Friday 27 July in the Olympic Stadium, the L2012C delivered an unforgettable showpiece to officially open the Games, with a cast including 15,000 volunteers, 10,000+ athletes from 205 teams, 40 sheep, 10 chickens and three sheepdogs as well as a surprise appearance from Her Majesty The Queen.

The spectacular set for the opening ceremony was to remain a secret even though it took more than three months to build. Yet after the ceremony had finished, the team had only seven days to dismantle the set in time for the first athletics events to begin.

This short timescale presented a huge challenge and the team could not afford any delays even though they faced many restrictions such as vehicle access, restricted delivery hours and driver screening processes.

Owing to the size of this challenge, a specialist department, MDS (Master Delivery Schedule) Storage and Freight, was formed to manage the on-site logistics to ensure that the venue was ready in time. From the moment the opening ceremony finished, the MDS team took responsibility for coordinating the transition from a spectacular show stage to the track and field arena needed for the first athletics event to begin. This was a remarkably busy and time-pressured period for the MDS team, despite it being a time when other departments could relax and celebrate the success of the opening ceremony.

The MDS team continued to be responsible for managing the post-event transition which occurred following every day of events throughout the entire Olympic and Paralympic Games. While the remaining events were not on the same scale or under the same pressures as the opening ceremony, effective logistical planning and management remained essential for the success of the Games.

Despite working exceptionally long hours and dealing with many challenges, the prestige and high profile of the event helped to keep the team motivated. Event planning and management can involve extremely diverse experiences but few as challenging and exciting as the Olympic Games!

Read more:

BBC News (2012), London 2012: Olympics Opening Ceremony Details Revealed, [Online], available from: **www.bbc.co.uk/news/uk-18392025** [Accessed: 21st September 2014]

Buchanan, S, Kiely, A and Young, R (2012) *London 2012 Ceremonies – sustainability achievements and lessons learned.* Sustainability Report: London Organizing Committee of the Olympic and Paralympic Games, LOCOG2012, London

Milmo, C (2012) *London 2012: Danny Boyle's opening ceremony set dismantled ahead of athletics events in Olympic Stadium,* [Online], available from: **www.independent.co.uk/sport/olympics/news/london-2012-danny-boyles-opening-ceremony-set-dismantled-ahead-of-athletics-events-in-olympic-stadium-7987725.html** [Accessed: 21 September 2014]

Reuters (2014) *Factbox: Statistics for Olympic Opening Ceremony* [Online] Reuters, available from: **www.reuters.com/article/2012/06/12/us-olympics-opening-factbox-idUSBRE85B00820120612** [Accessed: 21 September 2014]

A final word on safety...

It is extremely important to emphasize that this book provides only a general overview of the broad safety concerns at events. For anybody involved in planning a larger event or any event involving what might be considered 'risky' activities (eg fire walk or fireworks display) it is essential to seek more specific, detailed guidance and assistance as early as possible.

The organizations below will be able to offer specific, detailed guidance on areas such as crowd management, transport and traffic management, medical provision and major incident planning.

Emergency Services: Police, Fire and Rescue, Ambulance Service

Local Authority: Highways Authority (Roads), Health and Safety, Environmental Health

Private Organizations: Health and Safety Consultants, Licensed Security and Traffic-Management Firms

It is good practice when organizing large outdoor events (eg music festivals, open-air concerts, firework displays and street parties), to meet regularly with members from the emergency services, local authority departments and appropriate private organizations (eg licensed security firms). Together the individual members of staff from the various organizations will form what is known as the Event Safety Group (ESG) and will meet to give advice to help ensure the safety and welfare of anyone at the event.

The Health and Safety Executive (HSE) is responsible for the regulation of almost all risks to health and safety arising from work in the UK. The HSE website is an excellent source of advice and there are numerous publications, guides and leaflets available to download (the majority freely available) **www.hse.gov.uk/event-safety/publications.htm**

Guidance:

Managing crowds safely: A guide for organizers at events and venues
Electricity at work: Safe working practices
The safe use of vehicles on construction sites

Health and safety regulations:

Management of health and safety at work. Management of Health and Safety at Work Regulations 1999.
Approved Code of Practice and guidance
Memorandum of guidance on the Electricity at Work Regulations 1989. Guidance on Regulations HSR25
Noise at work: A brief guide to controlling the risks

Leaflets:

Health and safety made simple. The basics for your business INDG449
Five steps to risk assessment INDG163
Working at heights in the broadcasting and entertainment industries ETIS6
Electrical safety at places of entertainment GS50
Workplace health, safety and welfare. A short guide for employers
Theatrical and stage effects (including guidance on the planning and management of special effects)

Other publications:

Guide to safety at sports grounds (Green Guide) Sports Ground Safety
 Authority (SGSA)
Temporary demountable structures. Guidance on design, procurement and
 use (3rd edn) Institution of Structural Engineers
*Safe use and operation of marquees and temporary demountable fabric
 structures* (Revised March 2011)
Fire safety risk assessment: Open-air events and venues

Chapter summary

- A wide range of sites (both indoor and outdoor) are used for
 different types of events but, whatever the event, it is always
 necessary to think carefully about the layout and create some
 sort of site plan.

- There is no exact science to planning the site layout but the following
 three stages are recommended: 1) produce a list of the equipment,
 facilities and services needed; 2) design the layout of the site
 carefully; 3) produce a map of the site.

- The nature and size of the event, as well as the attendees and the site
 itself, will all have a bearing on the equipment, facilities and services
 required to put on the event.

- A good technique for designing the event layout is to print off a large
 map of the site and cut out icons representing the various activities as
 well as equipment, facilities and services. Keeping it all to scale will
 enable you to move the icons around on the map.

- Trying to fit too much detail on a single site map will only confuse
 people and it may be a better idea (particularly for larger events
 taking place across multiple locations) to produce several smaller
 maps. It is also sensible to produce different site maps for those
 attending the event and those working at the event.

- There is nothing more important than ensuring the safety of
 everybody attending or working at an event and it is extremely
 important to seek specialist guidance when it comes to health and
 safety at an event.

- There is always the chance of something going wrong at an event,
 but carrying out a risk assessment will enable an event manager to
 put measures in place to minimize the risks to public safety.

- The very nature of large events means there are always going to be logistical challenges involved with moving all the people, equipment and goods to where they are needed. A sound logistics plan is needed which should consider the whole operation including what happens pre- and post-event.

Reference list

Billboard (2014) Many fall to their deaths at K-Pop Concert in South Korea. Available at http://m.billboard.com/entry/view/id/103720 [Last accessed 6 February 2015]

Bowdin, G, Allen, J, Harris, R, McDonnell, I and O'Toole, W (2011) *Events Management: Third Edition*, Butterworth Heinemann, Oxford

Warlaw, M (ND) 10 Worst Concert Tragedies. Ultimate Classic Rock. Available at: http://ultimateclassicrock.com/worst-concert-mishaps-and-tragedies/?trackback=tsmclip [Last accessed 9 September 2014]

Building the event team – collaboration and relationships

06

Event delivery is a complex process, requiring a range of roles and activities to be integrated and well managed for a successful event outcome. This complex reality of event delivery combines with the pulsating nature of the events industry, which requires a much larger group of people to install and deliver an event on-site than it does to plan. As a result, many event organizations have developed a flexibility that includes the capacity to increase in size for on-site delivery of events.

The limitations and benefits of working as a wider team, alongside those outside your own organization are explored in this chapter, covering models that have proved their worth, and identifying drawbacks and opportunities in an industry where groups of individuals, previously unknown to each other, come together to deliver an outstanding event. Understanding individual communication preferences, and developing processes for managing partners, clients and suppliers, we explore a range of approaches, and develop the concept of collaborative working as it applies in the events industry. We also detail some of the partnerships that exist between event organizations and universities or colleges through 'Ambassador' programmes.

This chapter is divided into three main sections which address the core people-related issues facing those who are involved in developing and delivering events:

1 **Complexity:** the first aspect we cover is the overall complexity of events, the interconnectedness that events professionals recognize, and for which they need to develop plans and processes. The pulsating nature of organizations in the events industry combines the event's core team with a wide variety of contractors, suppliers, freelancers and, often, volunteers, part-time and full-time, who have to work together effectively within a team structure, from a standing start. This makes events very different from many other industries, as events organizations are not made up of standard full-time jobs.

2 **Developing your operational events team:** the second aspect of this chapter details the processes for recruiting and training events staff, providing a range of role descriptions and suggesting useful tools such as EMBOK (Events Management Body of Knowledge), personality instrument MBTI® (Myers Briggs Type Indicator) and Belbin's team role-assessment, that provide benefits to a range of events organizations.

3 **The wider events team:** Running an event requires the collaborative efforts of a 'team-of-teams approach', often in a short time period. This section considers how teams can function more effectively, not only within the team but across teams – because if they don't, the event, and the organization, are in danger of failing. But when it comes to working successfully with a client or suppliers, some people forget that there's no 'I' in Team.

This content includes:

- Complex event delivery
- Complex events team structures
- The pulsating nature of the events workforce
- Staffing levels
- Diversity
- The Event Management Body of Knowledge
- Role descriptions
- Communication
- Working together, as individuals and organizations
- Collaborative working and developing strategic partnerships

Events complexity

The complexity of events should not be underestimated. The larger the event, the more complex its delivery. The nature of the events organization, or that of the client, impacts upon this complexity, adding layers of internal influence and external regulation. On top of this, the type of event selected can again add to the mix that has to be kept in balance, and the type of attendee (such as VIPs) can also add to the mix. Despite the fact that most people think anyone can run an event, experience shows that most events could be managed more effectively and efficiently if the complex people-aspects of the process are acknowledged and taken account of, in planning and delivering the event.

Complex team structures

Within an event, there is a 'team of teams', some of whom are permanent staff, others are suppliers, contractors and volunteers, not necessarily under

FIGURE 6.1   Complex stakeholder relationships

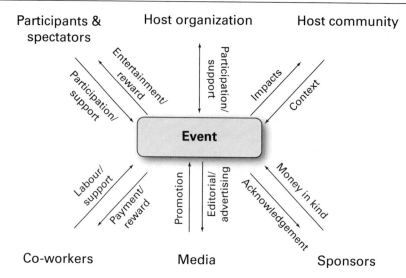

SOURCE: Dr Wolfgang Georg Arlt, http://www.arlt-lectures.com/8398wise10-040.htm

the direct command of the event manager – a complex mix. And in events, just about everything is for hire, and the 'White Book' (**www.whitebook.co.uk/**) shows the wide range of potential support services available, which need to be integrated within the event delivery team.

The complexity of stakeholder relationships within events management, and particularly where that function is outsourced to a third party, underlines the need for structure in planning and delivering an event.

Figure 6.1 demonstrates the multiplicity of stakeholder relationships that emerge in an events context. All these stakeholders have their own team, and together comprise the team of teams that deliver a successful event.

The following section provides an in-depth study to demonstrate the complexity of the 'team-of-teams' structures that deliver an event, looking at the 2014 Yorkshire Grand Départ of the Tour de France (**http://letour.yorkshire.com/**), and the impact on the on-site teams on the day of the event. For this event, detailed transport and travel plans were compiled by staff in the local authorities. This task was undertaken in consultation with the main event organizers, and the final document provided specific information for each location on the route, for those travelling by public transport, as well as cyclists and car drivers, with specific parking restrictions and road closures. Some road closures were in place for over 24 hours, requiring some of those members of the public whose access was blocked, to have to decamp to alternative accommodation, while others had more overnight guests than usual! On the night prior to the first stage of 'Le Tour', the 22 teams with almost 200 cyclists were welcomed to Yorkshire, along with a crowd of 10,000 paying guests at Leeds First Direct Arena, for the Opening Ceremony.

This initial event was produced and delivered by a separate organizing team, led by Martin Green, who had previously been responsible for producing the opening ceremony of the London 2012 Olympic Games.

During the event itself, dealing with increased numbers of event attendees on-site will require greater numbers of staff, whether paid or voluntary, working within a structure that not only enables the event to take place but also provides for responses to unforeseen circumstances and emergencies of any kind.

The scale of recruiting and training large numbers of event staff adds to the complexity of the team structures. For the English *Grand Départ* stages of the Tour de France, an online process was developed for individuals applying to volunteer at the event. Recruitment, selection and initial training all took place using online resources, supported and sponsored by Asda, while volunteers were informed by email and encouraged to join social media groups on Facebook, as well as joining the specialist Tour social networking website, Rendezvous. In the weeks before the event, multiple face-to-face training sessions were held, (events in themselves), as the 12,000 volunteers gained an understanding of the importance and scope of their own roles, those of paid security and stewards, and how to respond in a range of emergency scenarios. Finally, once trained, they were able to collect their uniforms.

The day of the first stage dawned and by 7am there were on-site briefings led by local authority staff, gathering volunteers and staff in hubs along the route, where the teams met each other and their supervisor, found out their individual location for the day, and received two-way radios with headsets to aid communication and responses to any problems. The reporting structure on the day is shown in Figure 6.2 below. Each local area reported in to a Bronze Command that co-ordinated the event organizers, security and emergency services in every designated local area across the race routes of up to 200km per day.

During the induction and training process, due to the sheer numbers involved, volunteers were unlikely to meet with their fellow team members but there was an hour or so prior to the start of their shift to get to know each other face to face. The online social media resources provided another opportunity pre-event for making contact, for those with access. In fact, the online groups on Facebook continued to develop a sense of community in the months following the Tour, and serve as information sources for other volunteering opportunities.

In an ideal world, there would have been an opportunity for each team to spend time together, developing a working relationship and deepening their local knowledge to enable them to respond to event attendees' questions and situations that might arise during the day. In reality, the volunteer teams of TourMakers and Wayfinders were spread out geographically along the race route and in areas on the way to the route, and on the ground, they worked closely with the security and stewarding teams based in the same location.

FIGURE 6.2 Tour de France on-site organizational structure

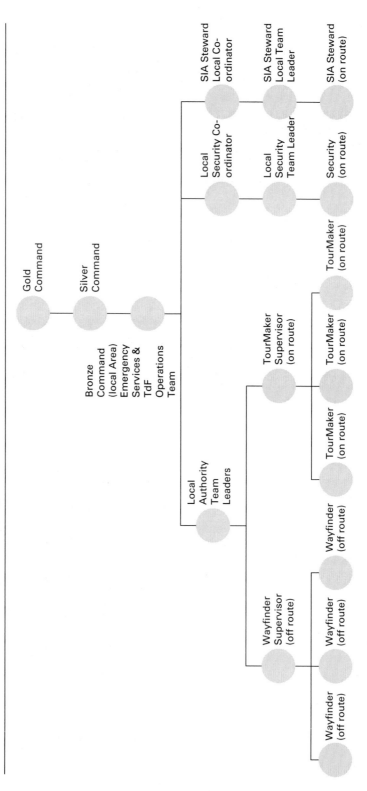

Event complexity therefore emerges from a combination of factors, including the event type, size and attendees, as well as the role of sponsors, the impacts on the community in which the event takes place, and the range of suppliers involved. Ensuring that you're aware of the full range of stakeholders is key to delivering a successful event and minimizing issues that might arise.

Complex event delivery

In addition to the complexity of event organizational and team structures, events agencies and PR companies may be called upon by their clients to roll out a series of events or multiple events in a specific time period. Such requirements can pose particular strains on people within the event-planning and delivery teams and may also cause problems with processes for event management.

One key problem in event planning is that it is difficult to anticipate the number of participants who will attend, although when making venue bookings and catering arrangements, as well as staffing the events, the event manager will have to make an accurate estimate for numbers attending. While event marketing and communications play their part, there will always be other factors that complicate the process. As an example of this complex event delivery, we examine the actions of a large national organization planning delivery of nine residential events for training or information-delivery purposes taking place over a six-week period. These events were attended by over 1,750 participants, all key local leaders and managers in the organization. All were required to attend an event to learn about and give feedback on an important new initiative that would fundamentally change the way their organization and their industry worked. Table 6.1 below shows the variations between expected and actual attendees.

For this event series, there was a core events team (of six), so they sent at least two experienced event managers to each event, with additional on-site support provided by freelancers with whom they worked regularly, and who were regarded as part of the team. In addition, the AV supplier was present at every event, providing equipment and technical support as required. Although new to the organization, this AV supplier quickly became part of the team, increasingly valued by some speakers for being 'in the room' and able to recall and clarify content issues and questions. The call by delegates and speakers on the event manager's time peaks during the periods in between sessions, so for a conference or training event such as this, event managers are unlikely to be 'in the room', unless needed for a specific task. For multiple parallel sessions, the event would require someone in each separate session, to keep the session to time and be available to sort out any problems that arise. However, this role does not have to be undertaken by the event manager, as long as they are contactable immediately (eg by mobile phone).

The complexity of the programme that needs to be managed on-site is shown below in Figure 6.3, with three parallel sessions and 15 different speakers. As part of a series of events, it is important to ensure that speakers,

TABLE 6.1   Event series statistics

Geographic Area	Event timing	Anticipated number of delegates	Actual number of delegates	Delegates' Event Rating: Excellent / Good
East	Week 1 Weds Thurs	190	195	95.4%
West Midlands	Week 2 Tues Weds	180	177	85.3%
North West	Week 2 Thurs Fri	245	237	74.2%
London	Week 3 Weds Thurs	200	201	95.0%
Yorkshire & Humber	Week 4 Tues Weds	235	226	92.9%
North East	Week 4 Thurs Fri	130	111	96.0%
East Midlands	Week 5 Tues Weds	175	178	85.5%
South West	Week 5 Thurs Fri	175	172	92.1%
South East	Week 6 Weds Thurs	220	256	86.1%

as well as event managers, do not experience burnout, so planning in 'time out' is also important for all the different teams: the events team, the freelance support, suppliers and speakers.

With 15 different speakers presenting, there were plenary sessions, with some workshops to address additional questions arising from the plenaries, and some stand-alone workshops, so managing this event is complex. But repeating the event nine times around the country, with some continuing speakers and some new speakers, requires thorough advance planning, as well as the ability to adapt the content and the structure of the event, within a changing delivery team. As with many events, attendees booked places at the last minute, and there were some sessions in overcrowded rooms, with not enough seats. This was at its worst on the final date, when attendance finally became urgent for those managers who had not attended an earlier (and probably geographically closer) event.

Ensuring that the meeting rooms are refreshed in between sessions, that speakers and delegates are in the right place and that each session in the event runs to time, demands a team of event managers who work well together, communicate clearly, and support each other, taking immediate action to resolve issues as they arise, without adherence to hierarchy or rank.

FIGURE 6.3   Example of complex programme

Learning Exchange: Programme **Location – Venue**				
DAY	**TIME**	**MAIN ROOM** **Suite A**	**BREAKOUT 1** **Suite B**	**BREAKOUT 2** **Suite C**
Day 1	14.00 – 14.30	*REGISTRATION*		
Day 1	14.30 – 14.45	**Welcome / Aims – Plenary: Chair Speaker A**		
Day 1	14.45 – 15.05	**Vision – Plenary: Speaker B**		
Day 1	15.05 – 16.30	**Services – Plenary: Speaker C**		
Day 1	16.30 – 16.45	**BREAK – COFFEE**		
Day 1	16.45 – 18.15	Finance – Plenary **Speaker D**	Services – Follow- up Workshop **Speaker C**	Health – Workshop **Speaker E** (17.45 finish)
Day 1	18.20 – 19.15	Nursing – Workshop **Speaker F**	Hours – Plenary & Workshop **Speaker G**	Finance – Workshop **Speaker D**
Day 1	– 19.50		(19.50 finish)	(19.50 finish)
Day 1	20.00 for 20.30	**DINNER / NETWORKING**		
Day 2	08.00 – 08.50	Welcome / Implementing to meet the Strategic Tests – Plenary **Speaker A**	Organizational support – Workshop **Speaker H**	IM&T – Plenary **Speaker I**
Day 2	09.00 – 10.30	Framework – Plenary **Speaker J**	New Innovations – Plenary **Speaker K**	Finance – Workshop **Speaker D**
Day 2	10.30 – 11.00	**BREAK – COFFEE**		
Day 2	11.00 – 11.55	Contracting – Plenary **Speaker C**	Framework – Follow-up Workshop **Speaker J**	Role and good practice – Workshop **Speaker L**
Day 2	12.05 – 13.00	Permanence & Quality – Plenary **Speaker K**	Contracting – Follow-up Workshop **Speaker C**	IM&T – Plenary Style **Speaker M**
Day 2	13.00 – 13.45	**LUNCH**		
Day 2	13.45 – 14.30	**Action Planning**	**Action Planning**	**Action Planning**
Day 2	14.40 – 15.40 (Coffee/Tea outside rooms from 15.15)	Premises – Workshop **Speaker N**	Framework – Follow-up Workshop **Speaker J**	Workforce Development – Workshop/ Discussion **Speaker F /** **Speaker O**
Day 2	15.45	*SUMMARY & CLOSE – CHAIR Speaker A*		

The events team encouraged feedback from attendees and speakers and, after the first event, adjusted the format to provide a shorter and simpler programme, giving delegates more choice in attending specialist workshops, and implementing learning from the delivery of each event. Residential events generally mean early starts and late finishes – especially where there is a bar open until all hours, and morning sessions begin early. Event managers are the first up and the last to bed, so again, burnout can be a real issue.

It is vital to be able to pass on learning from each event to those who are managing the next one. One option is to have at least one member of the events team at the last event travelling to the next, communicating any changes, developments and requirements, and for members of the team taking it in turns to have a rest day (though likely spent in the office). Technology today enables faster communication, and constant access to online resources and emails, and facilitates a more structured approach.

In the post-event evaluation, these intensive 28-hour events were recognized as demanding for delegates, speakers and event organizers, but drew very positive feedback from those taking part. Delegates particularly valued the direct access to speakers (within and outside event sessions), the interactive style, opportunities for networking and sharing information, and the connections being made between the practicalities of implementation and the wider purpose of modernising their industry.

Despite a gruelling schedule for the events team, AV supplier and speakers, the recognition of these complexities involved enabled a successful delivery of this vital event series.

The pulsating events workforce

The build-up to events and post-event break-down require fewer workers than at the event itself, and this is reflected in Alvin Toffler's 1990 concept of the 'pulsating organization' that changes in size, in response to circumstances. Large sports events provide good examples of this feature, such as the London 2012 Olympics, which recruited and trained some 70,000 volunteers; in 2014, for the *Grand Départ* and three initial stages of the Tour de France, held in Yorkshire and South East England, 12,000 volunteers were needed; and the 2014 Glasgow Commonwealth Games required 15,000 volunteers. However, the Commonwealth Games organizers were inundated with over 50,000 applications.

As indicated in the earlier example of the Tour de France *Grand Départ*, the reality of managing an event on the ground requires a much larger workforce than in the planning stages. This pulsating nature of organizations in the events industry combines the event's core team with a wide variety of contractors, suppliers, freelancers and volunteers, part-time and full-time, who have to work together effectively within a team structure, from a standing start. This makes events very different from many other industries, as events organizations are not made up of standard full-time jobs.

Organizations that deliver events are usually working on a number of events at any one time. This requires accurate planning and the development of processes that are adhered to by all event managers for a consistent approach. Chapter 2 explains the development of such processes, but a team approach is vital, to gain agreement and consistency in applying such processes. (The last thing you need when you have a shared way of delivering events, is for one person to go their own way and not abide by the process. That's not to say that the process cannot be changed – indeed it would be inappropriate to insist on that, but when a change is agreed by the team, everyone implements it.)

In managing a team of people to deliver a series of events, the complexity becomes clear. Not only are people required on-site, but others will be needed back at base to prepare for forthcoming events, and to manage communications.

Prior to an event, a small, 'core' team develops, plans and coordinates the structure, style and content of the event, outsources and procures any support services that are required. These outsourced services may include: security and stewarding, temporary demountable structures (eg marquees), furniture, toilets, catering, hospitality and bars, technical teams (eg audio-visuals – sound and lighting) and may include the use of a venue search agency to source the event location (see Chapter 3). Chapter 1 gives a range of suppliers and support services. Such coordination teams will also liaise with emergency services and local authorities to ensure appropriate cover and planning for emergencies, and develop and deliver marketing, sales and communication plans for the event (see Chapter 5 on event site planning and logistics and Chapter 7 on promotion and publicity), although these functions may in reality be delivered by separate teams, depending on the size and complexity of the event and the structure of your organization.

Top Tip

Events require a much larger team to deliver on-site than is needed to plan the event. Communication is vital within the team and between those who have different responsibilities and with any suppliers providing outsourced services for the event. Prior to the event, make sure you include the wider team in event briefings.

The following case study was developed by a team of volunteers working together, and demonstrates the power of learning from experience and implementing changes as a result of that learning. The complex nature of events teams is highlighted here, as events producers struggle within the constraints imposed by an event sponsor, rather than working together as a team of teams.

CASE STUDY 6.1   Ideas worth spreading: TED and the TEDx community

Imran Ali and **Linda Broughton**, Co-founders of LSx Living Lab

The annual TED conference has become synonymous with thought-leadership in the internet age. For innovators in arts, science, technology and design, TED provides a platform unrivalled in reach and prestige by TV broadcasters and print media. Though its mid-1980s Silicon Valley origins predate the proliferation of internet culture, the conference blossomed with the widespread adoption of internet video: TED's library of 1,700 talks has been watched more than a billion times across the planet.

TED is a highly curated, invitation-only affair, costing several thousand dollars in attendance fees. Reacting to rising accusations of elitism, TED launched the TEDx programme in 2009, allowing communities and cities to curate and host their own smaller scale, independently organized editions of TED. In essence, TED began licensing and franchising its conference, with both commercial and creative motivations:

- Expanding the reach of the TED brand to new audiences and territories.

- Incrementally increasing demand for its core conferences.

- Widening the audience for TED's video archive and thus interest from advertisers and sponsors.

- Using the community of TEDx organizers to scout for new speakers at the TED conference itself.

Bringing TEDx to Leeds

As business partners, we were approached by the founder of the Thinking Digital Conference in 2009, to work with peers to develop TEDx events across the North of England: specifically Leeds, Liverpool, Newcastle, Manchester and Sheffield.

Taking responsibility for Leeds, we thought this would be a great opportunity to provide a platform for innovative voices from within Leeds, position the city itself as a destination for thought leaders and expand our own reach beyond technologists.

Prior to this we had both worked on events where content was largely directed by attendees in 'unconference' formats, leaving us to simply provide logistics and infrastructure. Working on the first TEDxLeeds would allow us to hone our curatorial desires, define and explore themes as well as situate the content in a larger narrative context and purpose.

Beginning in September 2009 and concluding in March 2014, we went on to curate and produce over a dozen TEDx events in both Leeds and Bradford, as well as assisting the Huddersfield one with two editions.

The curatorial process

We wanted to bind the content of each edition to the city's concerns. In Leeds we explored the evolving nature of cities as platforms for innovation, as a preamble to lobbying local government to consider open data and open governance policies. In later editions we built on the city's financial legacy to explore the future of money, launching a local currency to illustrate where money could be bound to localism and invited innovators from the BitCoin to consider global contexts. As the smart cities movement became increasingly corporatized, we took a countercultural position, curating speakers on smart citizenship and communities. In Bradford, the city was keen to use TED to amplify the launch of the Internet Galley at the city's National Media Museum and in 2014 we worked with graduating students from Bradford University to understand emerging mechanisms for progress and change in a city with deep challenges to its prosperity.

In both cities we also worked with guest curators to bring particular perspectives, followings and tastes to bear on issues such as modern feminism and the role of women across society. Broadly, our approach was to locate emerging 'weak signals' in society, follow interesting people over a period of time, cultivating a relationship before inviting them to speak or recommend others.

Logistics – venues, catering and volunteers

Our ongoing motivation wasn't simply to showcase our host city's innovators to wider audiences, but also to allow attendees to experience venues and vendors' institutions that they would not otherwise encounter. Everything from gourmet hot-dog vendors and awardwinning Gujarati chefs to locations such as old corn exchanges, disused office blocks and galleries became part of the language of TEDx in West Yorkshire. Nurturing relationships with the city's institutions, including universities and local government provided us with a wealth of inkind resources and volunteers for media production, promotion and access to venues.

Working with the TED organization

We've gained much in 'borrowing' and aligning with a trending and growing global brand over a number of years. However, the proliferation of TEDx events around the world has diluted the brand; weak TEDx events have meant that the organization has reacted by policing more closely how TEDx events can be produced. Support is limited, we believe, particularly with access to TED's sponsors. What communication there is with the organization, is mainly about rules.

On reflection:

- The work required in producing a TEDx event, or developing our own is about the same. While TED afforded us gravitas, with hindsight this time may have been better spent building our own brand.

- Having developed a strong curatorial capability, thanks to the use of the TEDx brand, the constraints imposed by the TED organization now seem too restrictive.

- It's interesting to contrast TED's approach to franchising and the relationship it offers to event producers with other conference organizations which permit use of their brand. O'Reilly Media for example, maintain a light touch and promote the development of shared value, rather than the transfer of value from one party to another.

For the future, we'll take what we've learned and continue to develop our own brands, particularly for the audiences we've developed around gender issues.

Read more: **www.lsx.co**

Developing an operational events team

This section focuses on the operational aspects of professional events-management teams, and outlines the range of events roles, with examples of job descriptions and person specifications that might prove useful. We briefly outline operational processes for recruiting and training events staff, and share international models such as EMBOK (Events Management Body of Knowledge) that can provide benefits to a range of events organizations.

Events roles

In addition to the core event-management team (working alongside any freelancers), a wide range of roles will be required on-site. These additional roles are influenced by the range of support services required, so suppliers of security and stewarding would provide security people and stewards; suppliers of temporary demountable structures, furniture and toilets would need to provide staff to deliver, set up, manage, maintain and break down the equipment provided; suppliers of catering, hospitality, bars and technical teams would need to provide staff to deliver, set up, manage, maintain and break down the equipment, as well as providing trained and qualified technical teams, including staff to serve food and drinks. Event production roles might also include: stage production management and crew; sponsorship management; artist liaison; photography; media liaison; decor and signage; venue team managers, team leaders and team members; event production; event licensing; health and safety; campsite or accommodation management; security management; box office and wristbanding; film crews, including directors, producers, camera operators, researchers and editors; sound engineers, DJ station crews including DJ station managers, technical supervisors, and team members.

Developing role descriptions

When planning an event, you will need to develop role descriptions for each level of position in an events team. At the end of this chapter, generic role descriptions are provided that can be used as a basis for this process. They will need to be tailored to the organization, client and event. A specific job description for a temporary role at a festival may not be as detailed as might be expected. Sample role descriptions for core events-management team members are provided at the end of this chapter, that can be used as they stand, or adapted for your own use, including a role description from a volunteering project that Leeds Beckett University runs for its students working in the events and creative industries, collaborating with major festivals and events in the UK and beyond.

Diversity and teams

Many event teams will include people from a diverse range of backgrounds, whether in nationality, ethnicity, gender, sexuality, disability and beliefs. Such differences benefit the team, bringing a range of perspectives and ideas, that contribute to the success of the event, but some may also involve the need for employing organizations to meet specific requirements. It should be noted that event participants may also share these requirements. (Also see Chapter 3 on accessibility for all, and Chapter 4 in the section on dietary requirements and alcohol.)

Recruitment and training

Recruiting and training large numbers of on-site events staff adds to the complexity of team structures but it is also important to ensure that you recruit the right people for the core team as well. With recruitment for large-scale events that require many volunteers, mainly online methods are used to advertise vacancies and for recruiting, supported by email, social media and online resources for selection and training processes. In addition, multiple face-to-face training sessions might also be held in different geographical locations to enable volunteers to understand their own roles and those of professional paid staff, such as security and stewards, as well as how to respond to specific scenarios.

Increasingly, core events teams require professional skills – specifically, those of events management. As a key supplier of qualified events professionals, the UK Centre for Events Management, which was established at Leeds Beckett University in 1996, has an international team with over 30 events academics and practitioners. While events management education is now offered at some 70 higher educational establishments, the UK Centre for Events Management was the first to offer pure events-management degree-level qualifications, and is widely recognized for its innovations in teaching and in placing employability at the heart of its provision. Such educational institutions have strong links with their alumni, and events sector vacancies are often circulated by graduates through their alma mater, whether in addition to or outside of publicly-advertised means. As the first provider of degree-level events management education, the UK Centre for Events Management has the largest network of several thousand graduates working around the world, from the UK to Australia, China and the USA.

Online social media sites such as LinkedIn provide useful contacts with educational and professional events networks; in addition, there are professional industry associations and networks, including the following, that may be useful for recruiting events professionals:

- Association of British Professional Conference Organizers **www.abpco.org/**
- Association for Conference & Events **www.ace-international.co.uk/**
- Association of Event Organizers **www.aeo.org.uk/**
- Association for Events Management Education **www.aeme.org/**
- Association of Event Venues **www.aev.org.uk/**
- Association of Independent Festivals **http://aiforg.com/**
- Event Hire Association **www.eha.org.uk/**
- Event & Visual Communication Association **www.evcom.org.uk/**
- Eventia **www.eventia.org.uk**
- Events Industry Alliance **www.eventsindustryalliance.com/**
- International Association of Exhibitions and Events **www.iaee.com**
- International Congress & Convention Association **www.iccaworld.com/**
- International Special Events Society **www.isesuk.org/**
- Meetings Industry Association **www.confpeople.co.uk/about-us/mia**
- Meetpie.com **www.meetpie.com**
- National Outdoor Events Association **www.noea.org.uk/**

- Scottish Events & Festivals Association **http://sefa.org.uk/**
- Society of Event Organizers **www.seoevent.co.uk**
- Society for Incentive Travel Excellence **www.siteglobal.com/**
- The Association for Conferences and Events **www.exhibitions.co.uk**
- The Association of Festival Organizers **www.festivalorganizers.org/**
- The Event Services Association **www.ace-international.co.uk/**
- The Professional Speaking Association **www.thepsa.co.uk/**
- World of Events **www.worldofevents.net**

For smaller core teams, recruitment may be through formal associations or more informal networks, such as events educational establishments or personal contacts.

The Events Management Body of Knowledge (EMBOK)

In the past, as practitioners, we would have found a tool such as EMBOK extremely valuable, particularly in the area of human resources, covering fundamental HR practices such as training and recruitment, performance management, staffing and organizational structure. The EMBOK is a descriptive summary of the scope and processes of event management, a framework for future development of the event-management profession, and a flexible tool for all industry stakeholders.

EMBOK's purpose is:

'To create a framework of the knowledge and processes used in event management that may be customized to meet the needs of various cultures, governments, education programmes and organizations.' (**www.embok.org/index.php/downloads/documents/detail**)

The HR section can be found on the following link: **www.juliasilvers.com/ embok/Guide/ADM/HRMgmt/HumanResources.htm**

The HR section of the EMBOK website gives details of the major functions and performance elements of relevant human resources aspects of events management.

Further useful online sources of information and support on EMBOK include:

www.embok.org/

www.juliasilvers.com/embok.htm

www.juliasilvers.com/embok/EMBOK_structure_update.htm

www.ulviyaman.com/data/TheEventManagementBodyOfKnowledge.pdf

Practical implications: staffing levels

If an events team was only delivering one event at a time, or even an event series, that can be challenging enough, but – as is common in the events industry – there may be new events being planned and developed through-out the delivery period, and the example in Figure 6.4 shows the complex programme of events delivered by a team of five event managers, an events assistant and six freelancers over a five-month period.

In order to provide adequate on-site staffing for managing regular events like this, a rule of thumb is to provide at least one experienced event man-ager for smaller events up to 100–150 attendees.

However, it should be noted that if some of these events are repeated at different locations around the country, as the team becomes comfortable with the structure and content, it is much easier to leave on-site work to one person. Once numbers go above 150, the number of events staff increases, thereby underlining the concept of the pulsating event workforce. Thus, for 500 delegates, 8–10 staff are needed, but this also depends on the complexity of the event.

It must be said that the number of events staff depends on the event – and that size is by no means the only factor to consider. Additional staff might be required depending on the type of event and its complexity, as well as whether there are any logistical or security considerations, such as the at-tendance of VIPs.

So, imagine how many staff are needed to run a much larger event, such as a festival. At the annual Beatherder Festival (**http://beatherder.co.uk/**) held on the Yorkshire/Lancashire border, there are 10 staff working in the box office alone, dealing solely with accreditation for approximately 2,000 artists and performers, on-site staff such as stewards, stage technical crews and operations managers, commercial traders, press and media and VIP guests – as well the wristband exchange for the 10,000 paying attendees.

To summarize: when developing a team to work on your event, selection processes may range from online, to word-of-mouth and personal recom-mendation, but care must be taken to verify that recruits have the required experience – and increasingly, relevant (events) qualifications. Training should include: the event and its background, the role, attendees and their needs, processes to be followed during the event, communication channels, working as a team and activities that enable the team members to get to know each other.

Wider team of teams: individuals working together

From an outsider's perspective – such as that of an event attendee – the individual does not care whether your team is made up of core members, freelancers or suppliers. To illustrate this, imagine that you visit a super-market where you're unfamiliar with the layout. You see a young man in a uniform, kneeling down nearby, so you ask him for directions to find a specific item. 'Sorry', he replies, 'I'm on the cleaning team.' You hadn't noticed that his uniform was orange instead of the familiar blue, but what

FIGURE 6.4 Complex planning and delivery programme of conferences and roadshows

Month	Event types	Locations	Delegate numbers	Event team days
November	Workshop 1	London	50	1
December	Learning Exchange Events Part 1	London	300	4
		Torquay	200	2
		Bradford	200	2
		Manchester	200	2
		Leicester	200	2
	Workshop 1	York	50	1
	Contracts	Birmingham	50	2
	Regional Commissioning	Runcorn	150	1
	Local Incentive Schemes	Bolton	200	2
January	Learning Exchange Events Part 2	Leeds	100	1
		Manchester	100	1
		Leicester	100	1
		Bristol	100	1
		London	100	1
		London	100	1
	Information Management	Cambridge	60	2
		Leeds	60	2
		Newcastle	60	2
		Heathrow	60	2
	National Event	London	200	1
	Local Incentive Schemes	London	200	2
February	Assessor Reviews	Birmingham	250	2
		Chester	250	2
		Newcastle	250	2
		Bradford	250	2
		Torquay	250	2
		London	250	2
		Cambridge	250	2
		Leicester	250	2
	Information Management	Bolton	60	2
		Bolton	300	3
		Leicester	300	3
		London	400	4
		Leicester	60	2
		Birmingham	60	2
		London	60	2
	Partners	Leeds	120	1
		London	120	1
March	Assessor Reviews	Heathrow	250	2
	Information Management	Torquay	60	2
		London	500	8
	Entrepreneurs	London	150	1
Totals: Nov–March	43 events, 12 event types	15 locations	7280 attendees	84 event days

FIGURE 6.5   Events team: staff groupings

does that matter? Surely, he knows where the item is displayed? As customers, we don't really care which team he's on. He may even work for an outsourced supplier company. And the colour of the uniform is irrelevant. When you're looking for a specific item, you expect the staff in the supermarket to be able to direct you.

Event attendees are just the same – only events are more likely to be made-up of people who work for a range of supplier organizations. And taking into account the pulsating nature of events organizations, it's all the more important that each individual involved in delivering the event knows that they need to be able to respond to any question or problem – to understand not only their own role within the scope of the event but also others' roles. The response might even be 'I'll take you to someone who does know', but this example highlights the importance of training and briefing staff who work on any event. Figure 6.5 above shows the split in responsibilities between different types of event staff, all of whom might be perceived as being in the same team by an attendee.

One solution, if you are going to run events on a regular basis, perhaps for a specific client, is to develop a wider team of people who will work for you regularly: a team that knows how the client prefers to operate, a team that understands each other, as well as understanding the event's purpose and delivery. With such a team it is not only easier and more effective to staff an event, the event attendees will gain a more consistent, quality experience. Having a larger potential 'temporary' on-site team than is necessary for just one event provides you with the flexibility to service more than one event at a time, and takes account of availability as well as skill sets and experience. Figure 6.6 shows a potential structure for developing such a team approach.

Useful team-building tools

Whether building a team from scratch or bringing together a group of people who have worked with each other in the past, induction and training programmes are vital to ensure the success of the event. When individuals work together there is a range of factors that can influence their interaction

FIGURE 6.6 Events team structure incorporating regular freelancers

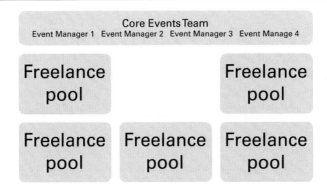

and ability to communicate. Personality and communication preferences add to the complexity of a team, and we have developed an interactive workshop for developing new teams, based on the characteristics of the Myers Briggs Type Indicator (MBTI®). Rather than complete the questionnaire (**www.opp.com**), each of the dimensions is explored using a narrative style related to real examples. Workshop participants take part in activities and discussions within the small teams in which they will develop and deliver an event, as part of a process in which they get to know each other, and learn about their own communication preferences and styles. A flavour of this process is given in the case study 6.2 below.

CASE STUDY 6.2 Developing teams with event-management students using the Myers Briggs Type Indicator (MBTI®)

Bernadette Theodore-Saltibus, Senior Lecturer, UK Centre for Events Management, UKCEM Graduate (BA (Hons) Events Management, 2006), and **Rev Ruth Dowson**, Senior Lecturer, UK Centre for Events Management

With approximately 1,000 students on our events management degree course, a core requirement includes preparing them to work in a range of events sectors; this includes developing their capability to work in teams that develop and deliver these events. Following their first year of academic study, most of our students spend a year working in the events industry, as part of the course. On their return to the academic environment for a further two years of academic instruction, one of their assessments requires them to work in a team alongside a real client, to develop and deliver an event from idea inception to conclusion. Most of these clients are from the charity sector and, as part of the students' preparation, we take them through a three-hour workshop to help them understand more about themselves and others, using a narrative approach and related activities.

The Myers Briggs Type Indicator (MBTI®) is often used by administering a questionnaire; however, we take a more experiential approach, which involves stories from our own experiences, and a series of activities that enable the students to identify their own preferences. In the UK, the MBTI is administered by Oxford Psychologists Press (You can read more about this at **www.opp.com** and **www.myersbriggs.org**). While there are many other psychometric instruments that could be used, we have chosen this one, in part because we ourselves (the writers) are opposites on each of the four dimensions, and we work closely together across a range of activities. Our aim is therefore not to promote MBTI above any other instrument but to add value to the professional and personal lives and skills of our students by sharing, in quite a personal way, our own preferences, and the stories we have developed from our experiences over the years. During the five years we have systematically used this process for the whole cohort of up to 350 students, on their return from placement (it was previously offered as an optional extra), we have found that the students have gained a language that enabled them to view others who were different from themselves in a positive light, as well as building relationships from the start of an important project and making friendships that last beyond graduation.

The four dimensions of MBTI are:

- Energy: identifying the individual's focus on the inner or outer world: EXTRAVERTS gain more energy from being with others, while INTROVERTS gain more energy from their inner life.

- Gathering information: identifying the individual's preference gathering information: SENSING people gather specific concrete data, while INTUITIVES make connections, interpreting and adding meaning.

- Making decisions: identifying the individual's preference when making decisions: THINKERS prefer rational logic, while FEELERS base decisions on an emotional level.

- Lifestyle: identifying the individual's focus within the outside world for structure or openness: JUDGING people prefer to live structured lives, using time to make decisions, while PERCEIVERS prefer to keep their options open to new information and emerging situations, putting off decision-making.

Once the students have heard the stories and experienced aspects of each dimension for themselves, they decide on their preference in each, which is expressed as a code with four letters. Bernadette is an ISTJ, which means she is an introverted, detailed, logical person with a preference for structure. Ruth is the opposite, an ENFP, which means she is an extraverted, big picture person, guided by the heart (rather than the head), with a preference for openness and not deciding. With this insight, students develop an understanding that working together and with others of differing personality types becomes a joy, as we can see the benefits of what the other brings, learn from each other and build a strong team that is able to communicate effectively.

Creatives and logics

While event teams are made up of a range of different people with different personalities, in our work with students at the UK Centre for Events Management, once the students have self-assessed for their Myers Briggs Type Indicator, we noticed that many students seemed to describe themselves as 'Creatives' or 'Logics'. Although these terms have not been officially researched, we found that events-management students often see themselves as in one group or the other. The success of a team may depend on its diversity – as well as in enabling people with different communication preferences to understand their own and others' communication preferences. Rather than seeing the other type in a negative light, we work with students to frame such difference as positive, and adding to the capability of the events team.

Companies working together – corporate personality style?

We have also worked in a range of corporate environments, some of which seem to have a strong bias in terms of personality, either as a whole organization, or a specific department. While not wanting to overstate the case, for example, actuaries might tend to be introverted, while marketing colleagues might be more extraverted. Whatever your preference, working in an environment that places more value on one preference than another, can be emotionally draining and demotivating; while some people will attempt to 'fit in' to the prevailing context (with different outcomes), others will fight against it. Overall, it is more effective for organizations to encourage and enable an environment that values difference and the range of contributions made possible by diversity, than to deny it and impose compromise or conformity.

Understanding communication preferences

Whatever tool you choose to use, it is always worthwhile first knowing more about yourself, identifying strengths and weaknesses, and then being able to apply that understanding to those you share similarities with, as well as to those different from yourself.

Another popular tool is the Belbin team roles, which can be identified using a short questionnaire, to identify different patterns of behaviour that individuals adhere to, and advises that the team should comprise of the range of roles available. Table 6.2 below shows the roles identified by Belbin, and the benefits and limitations of each type.

TABLE 6.2 Team roles, benefits and limitations

BELBIN team-role type	Contributions	Allowable weaknesses
PLANT	Creative, imaginative, unorthodox. Solves difficult problems.	Ignores incidentals. Too pre-occupied to communicate effectively.
CO-ORDINATOR	Mature, confident, a good chairperson. Clarifies goals, promotes decision-making, delegates well.	Can often be seen as manipulative. Off-loads personal work.
MONITOR EVALUATOR	Sober, strategic and discerning. Sees all options. Judges accurately.	Lacks drive and ability to inspire others.
IMPLEMENTER	Disciplined, reliable, conservative and efficient. Turns ideas into practical actions.	Somewhat inflexible. Slow to respond to new possibilities.
COMPLETER FINISHER	Painstaking, conscientious, anxious. Searches out errors and omissions. Delivers on time.	Inclined to worry unduly. Reluctant to delegate.
RESOURCE INVESTIGATOR	Extrovert, enthusiastic, communicative. Explores opportunities. Develops contacts.	Over-optimistic. Loses interest once initial enthusiasm has passed.
SHAPER	Challenging, dynamic, thrives on pressure. Has the drive and courage to overcome obstacles.	Prone to provocation. Offends people's feelings.
TEAMWORKER	Co-operative, mild, perceptive and diplomatic. Listens, builds, averts friction.	Indecisive in crunch situations.
SPECIALIST	Single-minded, self-starting, dedicated. Provides knowledge and skills in rare supply.	Contributes only on a narrow front. Dwells on technicalities.

Adapted from www.upwebsite.com

Collaborative working – potentially a new way forward for events

Traditional ways of working have included hierarchies and control methods, but in the current environment, some event organizations have developed new ways of working collaboratively with other organizations – including with their competitors – in order to survive and to thrive. Competition entails the need for a winner and for losers – while collaboration and building alliances can enable successful outcomes, whether for internal or external stakeholders. But such action depends on the structure of your own organization, as well as that of the client and suppliers. The development of such close partnership relationships involve high degrees of teamwork at all levels of the organizations involved, in which individuals are encouraged to contribute across teams, broadening their roles and responsibilities and encouraging contribution. Small businesses will find such flexibility easier than large corporations but the introduction of such approaches, while complex and challenging to manage, will facilitate the achievement of collaborative advantage for all involved. The case study below assesses the influence of building collaborative relationships for Silverstone, the UK home of Formula 1 racing.

CASE STUDY 6.3 Silverstone building collaborative relationships

Faye Briggs, Account handler and marketing coordinator, Oasis Events Ltd; UK Centre for Events Management Graduate
(BA (Hons) Events Management, 2014) & MPI Young Achievers Award Winner 2013

Silverstone, situated in Northamptonshire, is the UK's home of motor racing and has the impressive record of hosting the Formula 1 Grand Prix. A private sector organization with a range of sponsors and clients, Silverstone is solely owned by the British Racing Drivers' Club (BRDC), which is comprised of retired racing drivers who are the key decision-makers for any change.

Redefining partnerships

Not just a legal contract, a partnership can be redefined as a cross-organization group working together; managing such relationships effectively improves trust between the parties (Armistead and Pettigrew, 2004). The official partnerships held at Silverstone and their roles are identified in Table 6.3 below.

TABLE 6.3   Silverstone partnerships

Partner	Role
Pirelli	Pirelli provides tyres for the performance vehicles in the Silverstone fleet used during customer driver experiences.
Yamaha	Silverstone is supplied with Yamaha scooters which serve as an efficient mode of transport during race events around the circuit's 760 acres.
Laponie Ice Driving	Since the 2012 ice-driving season (January – March), Laponie recreates, in ice, a full-size version of the Silverstone Grand Prix Circuit, in Swedish Lapland.

Mohr and Spekman (1996: 34–43) define certain characteristics as inherent in successful partnerships including: commitment to the partnership and its progression, trust with all parties, openness when sharing information and strategic conflict resolution (persuasion and joint problem-solving). They argue that to measure success in partnerships, a combination of sales, volume and satisfaction must be considered. Huxham and Vangen (2005) suggest that although trust is recognized as a necessity in creating successful partnerships, it is extremely rare, noting that 'trust is frequently weak (if not lacking altogether), and suspicion is rife' in many existing partnerships. However, gaining trust is only half the battle and maintaining trust is the real challenge in collaborative relationships.

Since 2013, Silverstone has an additional partnership with commercial property company MEPC (**www.mepc.com/mepc/aboutmepc.aspx**), formed as part of a resolution to reduce the debt held by Silverstone. This financial deal allowed the BRDC to pay off long- and short-term loans from Lloyds Banking Group and Northamptonshire County Council, which had been used to make alterations to the track layout in 2010, and to enable the completion of 'The Wing' pit complex in 2011. MEPC is focused on developing the land around the Silverstone circuit to extend its business potential and paid £32 million for a 999-year lease of the Silverstone Industrial Estate and land that now has planning permission for development.

Our aim is to create a great Business Estate, with clusters of commercial activity and a sense of place and community, by building on the immense history of Silverstone and its current standing today as a venue for world class motor sport and a centre for high-end precision engineering.

(Dipple, 2014)

Here, the Chief Executive of MEPC identified a mutual goal for both MEPC and Silverstone, to improve the community built around the circuit and sharing the values for which Silverstone traditionally stands. The partnership is, therefore, potentially mutually beneficial as the investment opportunity for MEPC also allows Silverstone to pay off some of its outstanding debt and brighten the future for the Formula 1 sports ground.

However, there may be increasing pressure on Richard Phillips, Managing Director of Silverstone Circuits, as the business world is increasingly multi-faceted, and businesses are networking on a broader scale, resulting in further complexities. A large proportion of the client base at Silverstone is formed by the team providers for racing events (such as Red Bull, McLaren and Mercedes), by hospitality providers for corporate events, by organizations that hire the site as an event venue, and by the ticket providers for premium race days and other promotional events (Silverstone, 2014). Many of these organizations are repeat clients with whom Silverstone has contact throughout the year, and Silverstone needs to work collaboratively to maintain such relationships in an increasingly competitive international environment, and anticipate the imminent changes for Formula 1.

Read more:

www.oasisevents.co.uk

Armistead, C and Pettigrew, P (2004) Effective partnerships: Building a sub-regional network of reflective practitioners, *International Journal of Public Sector Management*, 17, Issue 7, 571–585, http://dx.doi.org/10.1108/09513550410562257

BRDC (nd) The British Racing Drivers' Club [Online]. Available from: www.brdc.co.uk/ [Accessed: 13 May 2014]

Dipple, J (2014) [Online] https://www.linkedin.com/company/silverstone-park [Accessed: 5 January 2015]

Huxham, C and Vangen, S (2005) *Managing to Collaborate*, Routledge, London

MEPC (2014) Silverstone Park [Online] Available from: www.mepc.com/silverstonepark/home.aspx [Accessed: 11 May 2014]

Mohr, J and Spekman, R (1996) *Marketing Management*, 4 (4), Spring/Winter 34–43. American Marketing Association, Chicago

Developing partnerships with clients, suppliers and others through ambassador programmes

Ambassador programmes are often based within universities (especially those with events-management courses), and consist of close working relationships with external event organizations. These partnership schemes are based around the provision of student and staff volunteers to work at the associated events. Leeds Beckett University has a number of such programmes that coordinate the relationship between the event organizers and their own students studying relevant degrees, from events management and photography, to journalism and PR.

The case study below describes an example of college students working at a large event, providing them with valuable work experience.

CASE STUDY 6.4   The engagement of college students with event volunteer programmes: The Skills Show 2013

Charlotte Jarman, Account Manager, Bluehat Group. UK Centre for Events Management Graduate; Winner, The Eventice 2014

In recent years, there has been a growing awareness of event volunteering amongst the public, mainly attributed to the successes of the Olympic Games Maker programme and the Tour de France volunteers. With this increased interest, the importance of harnessing a permanent volunteering legacy is created. Incorporating volunteering into the school curriculum is believed to be a fundamental way to achieve such a legacy.

'Find a Future' encourages young people to participate in volunteering through their college volunteer programme. The organization's flagship event, The Skills Show, is held at the NEC in Birmingham each year and is the nation's largest skills and careers event, attracting over 75,000 visitors during three days.

In 2013, The Skills Show engaged with 1,060 individuals who registered to volunteer at the event; some 794 of these were involved directly with the show, delivering 19,050 hours of service between them. The majority of participants were between the ages of 16–24, with some 391 (49 per cent) coming directly from nine local colleges.

Engaging with colleges not only provides a comprehensive method of recruiting large numbers of volunteers, it also provides a unique platform for training and development in line with participants' courses. For example, at the 2013 show, students enrolled on a Stewarding and Safeguarding course at a local college were positioned in car park stewarding roles allowing them to reinforce their theoretical classroom learning with practical experience.

An in-depth evaluation carried out by a third party after the event found that 93 per cent enjoyed being a volunteer at The Skills Show and would recommend the experience to others. The most popular benefits stated were the 'opportunities to meet new people' and 'work experience'. Najib Rahimi, a college volunteer, said the opportunity was 'invaluable due to the great on-site, real–life, work experience' and further commented on how his role at the show helped him develop valuable life skills.

As with any volunteering programme, as participants are providing their time and services free of charge, it is essential to carefully monitor participants to ensure they remain motivated and perceive value in the opportunity. Incentives such as reimbursed travel expenses, on-site food and branded uniforms were provided. However, it was noted, particularly within college groups, that there was a small minority not fully engaging with the programme. Ryan Johnson, Volunteer Team Leader, describes how: 'there was a clear differentiation between the motivated students and the students who didn't respond as well to the live-event situation at times'. It has been noted in the post-event evaluation that earlier engagement with colleges to manage expectations and ensure that placements are relevant to the courses could combat this in future years. Increased investment in Find a Future staff training and understanding of how to maximize the student volunteer experience may also help to maintain and build on the success of the college volunteer programme.

Miriam Farley, Volunteer Manager at Find a Future says:

At Find a Future our aim is to offer a unique work experience opportunity to any students with an interest in events management, customer support, health and safety or operations management. To do this we work in partnership with leading colleges to offer an invaluable work experience embedded within the events industry. Working with our partners and on-site suppliers we widen the students' experience, provide them with training, add to their CV and develop their skills in the workplace. In return we ask for their commitment to volunteer for three days at the show. The result is a really enthusiastic and energetic workforce who work together at one of the largest national shows in the country. It's great fun being part of the volunteer team at The Skills Show and I would encourage any student or college to get in touch if this interests them.

Read more: **www.theskillsshow/get-involved/volunteer**.

We have developed a range of sample job descriptions which you can download at **www.koganpage.com**. There are summaries of them in Chapter 8.

Chapter summary

- This chapter has explored the unusual nature of the events industry, which requires much larger numbers of staff to deliver an event than it does to develop it.

- It recognizes the reality that many events management teams face with multiple event delivery dates and ongoing development of new events in the planning stages. This all adds to the complexity of developing teams that are able to work together successfully, often at short notice, and with little time for introductions.

- The case studies outline some useful tools, such as Belbin and the Myers Briggs Type Indicator, that can be used to develop a team approach, and offer practical ways of communicating more effectively within a team, enhancing the team's ability to perform.

- It suggests partnership opportunities and provides a range of role descriptions that may be useful when planning your events team.

- Without a team, events don't happen. Developing a collaborative approach in which team members appreciate those who add value in different ways, is more likely to lead to a successful event.

Promotion and publicity

07

All events require some sort of promotional activity to get the word out to the target audience. This could be a simple reminder to previous event attendees to 'hold the date', or it could involve a more sophisticated, prolonged campaign to entice new attendees. A successful promotional campaign generally starts early and then continues to seize upon regular opportunities to generate publicity in the build-up to an event, which in turn generates a buzz and excitement ahead of the day. As a good event manager knows, when it comes to putting on an event, 'the anticipation is half the fun'.

There are many ways to communicate the message about an upcoming event, including television and radio campaigns, features in newspapers and magazines, leaflet drops and billboard displays and very few events today don't have some sort of online promotion and social media activity. A successful promotional campaign will often make use of multiple channels but with resource limitations (eg money, time and staff), deciding which tools are most effective requires careful consideration.

The most appropriate methods are largely determined by the target audience itself, where different target customers may be best reached using different channels. Before undertaking any promotional activities it is, therefore, important to find out as much as possible about the intended audience in order to understand the best way to make them aware of the event and attract them to it.

In the following chapter we will look at:

- Determining your audience and message
- Promotional tools used by event planners
- Ways to use social media to promote your event
- Developing a promotional plan for your event

If you have a natural flair for promotion and publicity, coupled with experience working within a Marketing and PR environment, then you can probably skim through this chapter. However, for those of you new to promotion and publicity, this chapter will be very useful since we cover the most important tools and techniques used to create interest and ultimately to attract the right audience to your event. Even more experienced Marketing and PR professionals may wish to read the chapter to ensure that they do not overlook anything important. Our case studies, in particular, will help you see how others have been successful in real-life situations.

Audience and message

There are many ways to promote an upcoming event (we will look at these in more detail later in the chapter) and there is always the temptation to 'leap right in' and start pushing out promotional messages – especially if the big day is fast approaching, the number of confirmed attendees is low, or there is another big event taking place on the same day. But before launching a promotional campaign for an event it is essential to determine the intended target audience and exactly what it is that you want to say to them. Of course, by now, you should already have a good idea of who you want to attend the event. As discussed in Chapter 2, developing the event concept (remember the Five Ws – Who, What, Why, Where and When), involves thinking carefully about who the event is being aimed at – the target audience. It can't be emphasized enough, however, that the more you know about your target audience the easier it is to develop an effective promotional campaign for an event.

Audience

Perhaps the most common mistake in determining your target audience for an event is to set your sights too broadly. For example – you have been tasked with organizing a business networking event for business start-ups, so ask yourself – who is your target audience? Easy, right? It's people who have recently started a new business. But what about people who are **thinking** about starting a business? It is important to be as clear as possible about your audience, because doing so will make it much easier to promote your event. Without a clearly formed definition of your target audience, you risk spending time and money on promotional activities that will not provide a worthwhile return on investment.

Thinking about the target audience as a homogeneous group (all of a similar nature) is much too simplistic, as there are likely to be many sub-groups (or segments) that make up the target audience for an event. Breaking down the target audience into smaller segments makes it much easier to determine how best to reach each group and the message can be tailored more precisely for each group, making the message more appealing to them. This process is known by marketing professionals and academics as the process of segmenting the target market (or audience).

Two commonly used approaches to divide a broad target market involve segmenting by demographic and psychographic variables.

Demographic segmentation

This involves dividing the target market into sub-groups, thinking about the profile of the attendees based on tangible characteristics such as their age, gender, occupation and so on. This helps an event planner to gain a better understanding of *who* typically attends an event. For many occasions, an event planner can often draw on historical attendance data to determine the audience profile.

When determining the profile of the target audience, it is important to consider the following factors:

- age
- gender
- occupation/profession
- marital status
- family life cycle
- location
- language
- education
- income

Some of the factors listed might not be particularly important for one type of event but could be extremely important for another. For instance, an event aimed towards celebrating the successes of high-flying young business women will be more concerned about the gender and age variables than any others. It would be wrong to think that an event can only have one target audience. Indeed, there are likely to be different sub-groups, each with different demographic profiles, as well as different motivations for attending. This brings us nicely to psychographic profiling.

Psychographic segmentation

This is the division of the target market according to variables such as their attitudes, interests and values. This helps to gain a better understanding of *why* the target audience chooses to attend a particular event. This involves detailed analysis and classification of target customers based on criteria such as their attitudes, interests and values to gain more insight into their motives for attending.

Possible motives for attending an event include:

- spend time with family and friends
- meet new friends
- experience something new
- visit somewhere new
- excitement and entertainment
- rest and relaxation
- meet key business contacts
- find potential customers

Combining psychographic with demographic data significantly improves our understanding of the target audience, giving us a much clearer picture of the typical event attendee – not only *who* they are but *why* they are attending – which improves our ability to target promotional efforts.

Top Tip

A helpful exercise to gain a better understanding of your target audience is to draw a picture profile of the typical event attendee. This is a great activity to undertake with other members of the event organizing team. Ask each other questions like: What does our typical attendee look like? What are they wearing? What are they holding? Who are they with? What are they thinking about? And even, what is their name? This exercise allows you to 'get under the skin' of your target audience, helping you and the team to learn more about the target audience – and it can be good fun too!

Who am I?

Message

Having thought carefully about the target audience for an event, the next step is to determine exactly what it is that we want to tell them about the event (the message). On the face of it the message we wish to communicate to the target audience seems straightforward – 'buy a ticket' or better yet 'buy a ticket today!' And, of course, there is a time and place for 'hard-hitting' messages such as these because it isn't much of an event without the attendees.

But care is needed with determining the right message – a message that is both appealing and deemed appropriate/relevant by the target audience. Sometimes a hard-hitting message (eg buy a ticket) might put off a potential customer, and a more subtle (or softer) message may be needed. In marketing terms, we talk about positioning messages which are designed to communicate something about the brand or image for a particular product (in our case the event itself). So rather than instructing the target audience to buy their ticket, the message might focus on compelling reasons for them to do so, such as, 'this event is the biggest of its kind', 'the best of its kind', or perhaps 'the first of its kind'.

It is helpful to think of two kinds of message that need to be communicated to the target audience:

1 The primary message is an overall message that expresses the main concept of the event and tends to focus on the benefits of attending an event.

2 Secondary messages are a series of more specific, targeted messages delivered to different sub-groups of the target audience.

Developing an effective message

The average person receives hundreds of messages (not all about events) and so each message has to work extremely hard to get noticed. No matter how the message is delivered, the target audience will select only those that they are interested in. It is, therefore, important to ensure that the message is deemed worth reading or listening to.

Speaking the language of the target audience (ie carefully choosing the words and phrases used) helps to ensure that the message is picked up on. A younger audience is likely to respond to different words and phrases than an older demographic. Similarly, target customers working in different professions are likely to have their own terminology and jargon. Be careful, however, not to use too much jargon, as this can be confusing. And focusing on the benefits of attending an event can help to simplify the message.

Creating an effective message isn't only done through the use of words; visual stimulation (images, shapes and colours) can also have a powerful impact on the recipient. Remember the old adage 'A picture paints a thousand words'? The right picture can say everything about an event without the target audience having to read any of the words.

Stop for a moment to glance at the tournament poster in Figure 7.1. You don't need to read the words to make an educated guess that the poster is promoting a tennis tournament where the participants are junior players and where both boys and girls will be taking part.

FIGURE 7.1   Tournament poster for Team Tennis Schools National Championships Finals 2014

Image courtesy of The Schools Tennis Team, www.schoolstennis.org

The AIDA model/acronym presented in Figure 7.2, can serve as a helpful checklist for coming up with an effective message structure:

FIGURE 7.2   The AIDA model

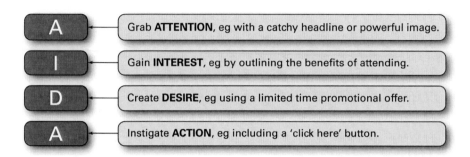

Promotional tools

There are many ways to get your message out to the target audience. Some methods reach a wider audience, some are more personal; some methods reach the audience immediately while others take a little longer; some are expensive and others reasonably cheap (there's no such thing as free promotion because all promotional activity requires at least an investment of time).

With a sound understanding of the profile of the target audience, it is now much easier to decide which methods are likely to be most effective.

Traditionally there are five main promotional methods or tools to choose from:

● advertising
● sales promotion
● personal selling
● publicity
● direct marketing

These traditional promotional tools still play an important part in promoting and publicizing an upcoming event.

Case study 7.1, The Zoe Challenge, is a good example of different promotional methods and techniques being used to target specific groups.

CASE STUDY 7.1   The Zoe Challenge

Ben and Phoebe Southall, Fundraising Team, Hope for Justice. UK Centre for Event Management Graduates (Ben graduated in 2013, Phoebe graduated in 2011)

In May 2013, Hope for Justice, an anti-human-trafficking organization launched a fundraising campaign called 'The Zoe Challenge'. Zoe was one of the first girls Hope for Justice rescued in the UK. Zoe's story was chosen to give an identifiable victim helping people relate to the cause.

The challenge had a core team of four cyclists follow Zoe's journey across 2,077 miles of Europe, starting in Latvia from where she was trafficked, and ending in Southampton where she was trafficked to. Having British television actor, Tom Lister (*Emmerdale*) as part of the core team, helped to generate publicity for the challenge event.

For the UK leg of the challenge, people were encouraged to take part in the cycle ride alongside the core team to help fundraise towards the £250,000 target.

The aim of the challenge was twofold:

1   To raise the money to pay for a second regional investigative hub in the West Midlands, where a team of specialist investigators work within the local community to investigate and rescue victims of human trafficking.

2   To promote awareness that human trafficking is happening in the UK, and each individual can play their part in ending it, by taking part in The Zoe Challenge.

To ensure that the challenge event was a success, Hope for Justice targeted four specific groups: general public, existing charitable supporters, business community, and influential figures.

To promote public awareness and to encourage donations from the public, the challenge used a number of PR opportunities, including: national TV coverage, features in local newspapers and local radio, and articles in more specialist cycling magazines. Hope for Justice estimates that the challenge generated around £475,000 worth of free publicity for the organization. A text donation number was created to make it easy for members of the public to make their donation.

Existing supporters of the organization received a mailshot in the post and via email to encourage them to take part in the UK leg of the cycle ride alongside the core team, or put on their own fundraiser that would count towards the £250,000 target. A six-month communication strategy in the lead-up to the cycle was put in place which used Hope News, a five-minute video bulletin, showcasing the training and preparation of the cyclists and encouraging supporters to take part. As a result, 90 cyclists signed up and 35 fundraising groups hosted a local Zoe Challenge which raised £48,000 towards the target.

To engage businesses in the campaign, a sponsorship package was put together with opportunities to support the challenge. This included both financial and non-financial support (eg providing energy drinks used by the cyclists). The 10 businesses sponsoring the challenge received premium placement of their logo on the cyclists' bikes and jerseys.

Influential figures from the local community, wealthy individuals and celebrities were invited to a series of high-profile fundraising dinners across the UK which were scheduled for the arrival week of the core cyclist team in the UK. The dinners included one in Leeds, where TV actor Tom Lister's support base attended, and an intimate prestigious dinner in London at the House of Commons.

Having such a targeted campaign helped Hope for Justice to achieve their fundraising target, increase their supporter base by 1,000 people and to set up their second regional investigative hub in early 2014, naming it Zoe's hub.

Read more: **http://hopeforjustice.org/stories/**

Advertising

Advertising is any paid form of communication designed to influence the target audience. Ultimately, the purpose of an advertising campaign is to generate a positive (or buying) response from the target audience (both existing and potential customers).

Advertising plays a particularly important role in new events, where no previous attendees or event community exists, and new customers must be enticed to make the event viable. In this situation, it is usual to set aside a large proportion of the budget (and time) on advertising activities as, essentially, you are starting from scratch.

Advertisements for events can be found in many different places, including:

- local newspapers
- national newspapers
- glossy magazines and brochures
- trade magazines and publications
- television commercial breaks
- local radio
- national radio
- cinema screens
- banners on websites
- pop-ups on search engines (eg Google ads)

- pop-ups on online videos (eg You Tube)
- social media advertising
- billboards, posters and leaflets
- buses, taxis and aeroplanes

Which advertising medium to use largely depends on the target audience (eg what TV channels they watch, what they read, listen to and so on) but also how much you have available to spend on advertising in the promotional budget. A national TV advertisement in the UK, for example, will cost in excess of £200,000 per 30 seconds during prime-time television. A 30-second advert slot during the last ever *Friends* episode in 2004 cost a staggering £1.2 million – still the most expensive ever in the UK (Connell, 2014).

While advertising can often be an expensive promotional method, there are different advertising rates to suit different budgets. Most magazines, for example, will offer full, half, quarter and eighth page advertising rates (see Figure 7.3 below) and some offer cheaper rates for black and white

FIGURE 7.3   Standard advertising sizes in magazines

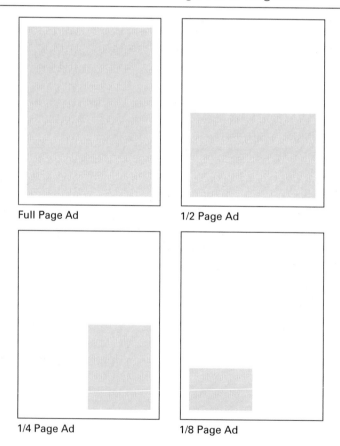

Full Page Ad   1/2 Page Ad

1/4 Page Ad   1/8 Page Ad

adverts. Cheaper rates are available depending on where the advert is positioned in the magazine, eg front page adverts are often the most expensive and then, closer to the print date, late offers can be available (but you are likely to be left with the worst position).

An effective advertisement must not only be seen and read, but acted upon. Thinking back to the AIDA model, it is essential, therefore, that a well-designed advertisement gives a potential attendee all the necessary information to respond to a call to action, eg where to go to buy or how to enquire. This means placing all of the essential information, such as telephone number, email address and website address, in a prominent position to make it easy for potential customers. More recently, QR codes, which can be easily scanned using a smart phone, have been used on advertisements (eg at the bottom of event flyers or posters). Try scanning this QR code and see where it takes you...

Example of a QR code

Sales promotion

Sales promotions and offers can be used in different ways, making them the most versatile form of publicity. Some promotions may be designed to tempt new customers to give an event a chance (eg a great deal), others to reward loyal customers (eg early bird ticket prices for existing customers) and some to give ticket sales a much-needed boost with the event only days away (eg last minute offers). Sales promotions work particularly well when combined with advertising with the offer (or deal) providing the central message for the advertisement.

Incentives and offers used to promote events come in all different shapes and sizes. But these are not very different to the promotions you find on the high street – half price sale, buy one get one free (BOGOF), free gifts or competition entry. Like the high street, the most effective promotions are usually those which are the most imaginative (ie offering the target audience something a little bit different).

In order to create the desired effect (ie a spike in sales or responses) it is also important that any promotion is time-limited. eBay and Groupon are two excellent examples of successful online businesses built on the concept of time-scarcity. It seems that our basic human instinct simply won't allow us to miss out on a great deal, thus creating the urge to act quickly so as to avoid disappointment.

Customers taking advantage of sales promotions and offers are generally required to give something in return (surely one good turn deserves another). Typically this will involve handing over their contact details (email, telephone or address) which, of course, means that next time around it is much easier for you to communicate about an upcoming event.

There are, of course, drawbacks to using offers and incentives as a means of promoting an event. Event planners need to be careful not to be seen to 'give away' too much too cheaply. A cheap deal on tickets is certainly not a suitable tactic for a 'luxury' event which offers attendees a touch of glamour, style and sophistication. In this case, a BOGOF offer will only serve to 'cheapen' the event and is more than likely a turn-off for potential event attendees. And, of course, with offers and incentives being time-limited the effectiveness of any promotion is only short lived. This short-term orientation may sometimes have a negative effect on the long-term future of the event.

Top Tip

Approach sponsors and other partner organizations to provide gifts and giveaways for competitions in the build up to an event. This will help you to generate excitement ahead of the event and is also a great promotional opportunity for sponsors and partner organizations. In return, you could give them some free tickets for their customers. A win-win!

Personal selling

The 'art' of personal selling is sometimes overlooked by those responsible for promoting an event. Personal selling involves person-to-person contact whether it is face to face or via a telephone conversation. There are no glossy brochures, no competitions and gimmicks, no publicity stories; just good old fashioned person-to-person selling (ie asking for the business). In a sense, person-to-person selling is what all other promotional activity leads up to, with selling positioned at the sharp end of any promotional activity (See Figure 7.4) – the act of moving a potential customer to an existing customer (often referred to as closing the sale).

FIGURE 7.4   Selling at the sharp end of promotional activity

Too often selling gets a raw deal with academics and theorists often looking upon selling as the poor relation in the promotional mix. Marketing guru Philip Kotler, for example, describing sales-led organizations as 'fearing' that customers will not buy unless a concerted sales effort is made (Kotler, 1991). The general public are often critical of selling, too, possibly because of one-too-many experiences with a pushy door-to-door salesman or tele-sales representative. Furthermore, culturally some people are more uncomfortable than others with explicitly commercial promotional activity. The British, for example, tend to shy away from what we may perceive to be an awkward encounter.

Not to put too fine a point on it – without selling, there are no customers, and without customers there is no business. Personal selling tends to be more prominent in the business-to-business (B2B) events sector where it remains the norm to call potential attendees during business hours to let them know about an event. Personal visits and calls are also commonly used to sign up exhibitors for large trade shows and exhibitions.

Hiring skilled sales people is the best way to ensure a 'full house' at your event. An experienced sales person knows the value of a pre-prepared call script to help them deliver a succinct sales message (ie why the event is relevant to the person answering the phone) and also that anticipating customer objections will help prevent them from becoming flustered. You know you are in the presence of a great sales person when they are able to register attendees there and then (eg filling out the registration form while still on the sales call).

Top Tip

Running contests between members of your sales team can act as a great incentive for them to deliver results. But an incentive programme only works if you offer a great prize. The perceived value of the incentive (or prize) will usually be closely tied to the extra effort put in by the sales team. And if you're trying to encourage a team approach, replacing individual sales bonuses with a team bonus is more appropriate.

Publicity

Getting someone else to promote your event is one of the most effective methods. Newspapers, magazines, radio stations and television channels all run features about upcoming events. Having a third party publicize the event gives it more credibility than say, for example, a commercially-explicit advertisement. Having a print or broadcast media publicize an event will also add perceived value to the event attendees and better still, it won't cost you any money!

It all seems too good to be true…

The downside of promotional messages delivered by a third party is that you lose control of the message content. Whoever said that there is 'no such thing as bad publicity' obviously didn't work in events. Bad publicity is hardly likely to encourage someone to purchase a ticket or register to attend an event.

To help ensure favourable media coverage for your event, you need to master the art of the press release. Most people working in PR, marketing and events have written a press release or two. And while writing press releases may be familiar territory for many, knowing how to prepare an effective press release can still be a little baffling. The following checklist gives 10 top tips to keep in mind when preparing your next press release.

When it comes to writing a press release, you're facing a tough crowd (journalists). Many journalists get a lot of press releases every day. You have to make their job as easy as possible for them. All of the important information (Five Ws – Who, What, Why, Where and When) must be included in the first couple of sentences to allow a journalist to scan quickly and decide if the story is of interest. Another good reason is that editors cut stories from the bottom, so the important information needs to be towards the top. Another thing to bear in mind is the editorial deadlines the media work towards. The best story in the world is of no use to them if it arrives too late. Don't be afraid to simply pick up the telephone and ask what deadlines they are working to, and whether your story is something that they might be interested in featuring.

CHECKLIST: Preparing a Press Release

1 All the important information is included in the first couple of sentences – think Five Ws!

2 A catchy headline is used to grab the reader's attention.

3 Relevant facts and figures are provided to back up the story.

4 Relevant and interesting quotes are used to flesh out the story.

5 A clear and prominent 'call to action' (eg do you want readers to buy a ticket?).

6 Use simple language, keep sentences short and avoid jargon.

7 Check the press release for typos and grammatical errors and then check again!

8 Photos bring a story to life so always include one or two high-resolution digital images with your press release.

9 Include all of your contact information (name, telephone, mobile, email and postal address).

10 Find out the newspaper or magazine's deadline and get the press release done and sent out.

Simply telling your media contacts that an event is happening isn't necessarily newsworthy. All good stories need a 'hook' and it is the particular hook (or angle) that makes the story newsworthy. Different media sources will have different ideas about what is newsworthy. The skill is matching a story (or more precisely the hook of a particular story) with an appropriate media source and subsequently their audience.

The following checklist includes 10 questions to help you determine if your event is newsworthy. If your event ticks one or more of the boxes then we would recommend contacting the media.

CHECKLIST: Is your event newsworthy?

1 Will there be a large number of people attending?

2 Will any high-profile individuals be at the event?

3 Are there a large number of people participating?

4 Is the event happening locally?

5 Will the event attract large numbers of tourists?

6 Is your event taking place on a memorable date or special occasion?

7 Does the event coincide with any other newsworthy events that are happening?

8 Is the event in any way considered controversial?

9 Does the event offer the opportunity for a human interest story?

10 Will there be an opportunity for good visuals (eg pyrotechnics display)?

Case study 7.2 is a good example of the use of celebrities to increase the amount of media attention given to an event.

CASE STUDY 7.2   Fire Walking at London Zoo

Rhiannon Bates, VIP Liaison and Press Officer, Zoological Society of London. UK Centre for Events Management Graduate, 2010

The Zoological Society of London (ZSL), the international conservation charity which runs ZSL London and Whipsnade Zoos, and operates conservation projects in more than 70 countries around the world, has introduced an ever-expanding suite of challenge events over recent years. Challenge events have become an increasingly important method of fundraising for charities and with competition high across the sector, encouraging participation is crucial.

Fundraising Director, James Wren, said, 'Challenge events are vital to ZSL as they help us inspire and engage with a wide range of people. We have developed a whole host of different challenges for people to take part in so there's something for everyone, from walking or running, to laughing, abseiling and even streaking!

'Money raised from challenge events supports our global conservation work, from funding anti-poaching patrols, to working with communities and providing equipment; the incredible support we receive at home is helping ensure a future for endangered animals around the world.'

One of the most daring challenges in ZSL's calendar of events is the annual Fire Walk. Held in November this event is a unique alternative to bonfire night, where participants walk across red hot coals to raise funds for ZSL's work. The event was introduced in 2012 at ZSL London Zoo and has since been held at ZSL Whipsnade Zoo as well.

In November 2012, the event focused on raising money for ZSL London Zoo's campaign, Tiger SOS for Sumatran tigers. Each participant was asked to pay a £30 deposit and pledge to raise a minimum £150. ZSL aimed to have 40–50 fire walkers sign up, therefore ensuring at least £4.5k in profit to support the organization's worldwide conservation work.

Work began months in advance to recruit participants and a multi-pronged approach is taken by the Fundraising and PR teams.

E-newsletters were distributed in advance, throughout the summer and autumn months, targeting people who had taken part in challenge events with ZSL before, and also those who had subscribed to ZSL newsletters through various channels, including attendance at other events, Zoo visits and members.

PR then focused on generating sign-ups from people not already on ZSL's mailing list, with a key target on local and London-based news outlets. A listings release was distributed to event listings press and resulted in pre-event coverage in *Time Out* magazine, and many online outlets including *Love Camden*, *All About London*, *All in London* and *Brit Events*; perfectly positioning the event in the areas ZSL was aiming for.

The event was supported by two cast members of television show *The Only Way Is Essex*. Lydia Rose Bright and Tom Kilbey were approached to take part with the aim of raising awareness of ZSL's Fire Walk challenge events to a wider audience.

Lydia promoted the event on her social media channels, with her tweets alone reaching 798k people. Further re-tweets and 'favouriting' of the mini-blog posts helped to spread the message to an even wider audience.

Quotes from Lydia helped to further endorse the event in media communications, with the reality TV star saying: 'I love animals so when I heard London Zoo was doing a Fire Walk to raise money for tigers I was really keen to take part. I was nervous about walking across hot coals but actually really enjoyed it, and it was for a great cause.'

Pictures of Lydia and Tom taking part were distributed to press with the aim of generating post-event coverage and using their position in the public eye and their popularity as a way of promoting ZSL's charity status and challenge events, as well as driving interest for future ZSL fundraising activities.

The event was covered by the *Sun* newspaper, helping reach a new audience for ZSL's challenge events. As a result of taking part, Lydia has also become a key celebrity contact of ZSL and ZSL London Zoo, and has supported other charity activity since.

The event surpassed its minimum targets for both numbers of participants and funds raised. The event was attended by 46 fire walkers, who between them raised £11,500, considerably more than the minimum pledge.

Read more: **www.zsl.org/challengeevents**

Direct mail

When planning a promotional campaign for an event it is easy to focus on attracting new attendees, but it is equally important to remind previous event-goers about the benefits of the event. This is where direct mail (including email) has an important part to play. Direct mail campaigns remain the cornerstone of many events' promotional campaigns, particularly within the corporate events sector. Many of the large corporate shows still rely on direct mail-outs to deliver 'save the date' teaser cards, personalized invitations, complimentary tickets and important updates to generate the largest number of registrations or tickets sales.

By definition, direct mail travels directly (point-to-point) from the event organizer to the target customer – doorstep-to-doorstep or email-to-email is perhaps a more accurate description nowadays with an ever increasing number of email campaigns. According to figures from the Direct Marketing Association (DMA), email marketing has now overtaken direct mail in terms of volume (Direct Marketing Association, 2012).

There are several factors that all email marketers should consider when creating an email campaign as part of their promotion strategy.

The following checklist will improve your email marketing success.

CHECKLIST: Creating a successful email campaign

☐ Your event (or company) name must be clearly stated in the domain name, which appears in the 'sender' line of the email.

☐ Don't use the CC or BCC fields. Personalized emails have a much better open and response rate. These emails often end up in the 'spam/junk' folder.

☐ Give your email a professional look by adding your event or company logo.

☐ Make good use of the top two to four inches of your email which is the prime reading space.

☐ Don't overload recipients with too many messages. Keep the body of your message short and scrolling to a minimum.

☐ Make both images and text clickable. Clickable links should send recipients through to a purpose-built landing page (eg registration page) to convert click-throughs.

☐ Don't send large attachments and images that may clog the recipient's inbox.

☐ Provide recipients with a clear way to contact you for more information.

☐ Provide recipients with clear instructions of how to unsubscribe from future mailings.

☐ Don't forget to test your email campaign before you send it out.

In spite of the popular image of junk mail and spam emails, direct mail remains an effective promotional tool and is, in fact, more than just a promotional tool enabling event planners to maintain regular contact with event attendees. There is, of course, a fine balance between keeping in regular contact with the target audience and 'pestering' them to the point of annoyance and irritation. By the time they receive their 99th event reminder they may decide that they no longer wish to come!

Direct mail is sometimes referred to as database marketing. For many events, a list of past attendees can be easily obtained. To a large degree, the success of a direct mail campaign is reliant on having an up-to-date list. If customer names, addresses and emails are out of date then direct mail is unlikely to prove to be an effective promotional activity. One of the best ways of maintaining an accurate, up-to-date customer contact list is by enticing customers to sign up for discounted tickets, free gifts and competition entries in exchange for their contact information.

Apart from targeting existing customers (ie those on your own database) you may want to attract new customers. It is sometimes possible to obtain mailing lists (including email) from publishing organizations and other event organizers although this is becoming more and more difficult with data protection laws. Customers in all walks of life (not just events) are becoming increasingly frustrated with the constant stream (some might say bombardment!) of junk mail and spam email. Devising a direct mail campaign in collaboration with partner organizations, such as sponsors, is a great way of gaining access to new mailing lists. A personal letter of invitation sent from the partner organization to their own customers is more likely to ensure customers pick up on the message.

Top Tip

Think carefully about the profile (demographic and psychographic) of the target audience of your partner organizations when it comes to doubling your efforts through a direct mail campaign as this offers the potential to double your reach.

Social media for event promotion

Today event promotion and social media go hand-in-hand with even the most traditional event audiences using social media. People attend events to connect and interact with one another (whether it is family and friends, work colleagues or even total strangers). Likewise, people join social media networks such as Facebook, Twitter, and LinkedIn to connect and interact with people. It makes perfect sense to use social media to get the word out about an event and generate a buzz and excitement.

A recent study of 1,335 event professionals found that nearly all respondents (93 per cent) were using social media to promote at least one of their events and almost one third (32 per cent) were using social media for all of their events (Event Manager Blog, 2014). Indeed, many event attendees will look sceptically at an event that isn't using social media to create a buzz and excitement, leading to questions about whether an event is outdated compared to other events that are making full use of social media.

The real benefit of social media, however, isn't simply about being perceived to be 'up-to-date', but is the value of connecting, interacting and engaging with event attendees before the event as well as during and after the event (often right up until the next event). Social media provides event organizers with an opportunity to create a community around their event; to converse with event attendees, to share ideas with them, to ask for feedback and even to ask for recommendations about how to improve the event (this process is known as co-creation and is discussed in more detail in the final chapter).

One of the most frequently asked questions about social media is 'should all events be using social media as a way of promoting and publicizing the event?' The short answer is that it depends on the target audience and the extent to which they engage (or not) with social media. If the target audience is using social media to connect and converse with others, then you probably should be also (if your competitors are already engaging with your target audience on social media, then you definitely should be!). When you consider the range of social media platforms currently available, most people are already engaged with at least one of the platforms. A statistic that is often used to demonstrate the influence and reach of social media is that if Facebook were a country then it would be the third largest in the world (Williams, 2012). Like we say, this statistic has been used often but nevertheless it is still quite remarkable.

There are quite literally hundreds of social media platforms. The following boxed feature offers a brief overview of the 'mainstream' platforms. Each social media platform appeals to different target audiences and so choosing the right platform (or platforms) for your event requires careful consideration (more about how to select the best social media platform shortly).

Before moving on, it's important to acknowledge that the social media landscape is continually evolving. The platforms that we've labelled 'mainstream' today will inevitably date; new platforms emerge and existing platforms create new ways of sharing content. But like we said earlier, one thing we're confident of is that event planners will continue to see social media as a vital promotional tool for connecting, interacting and engaging with event attendees.

Social media platforms

compiled by Jakki Sheridan-Ross

All statistics and figures sourced from those freely available on each platform, March 2015.

Jakki Sheridan-Ross's creative commons share alike licence applies throughout.

FIGURE 7.5   Different forms of social media

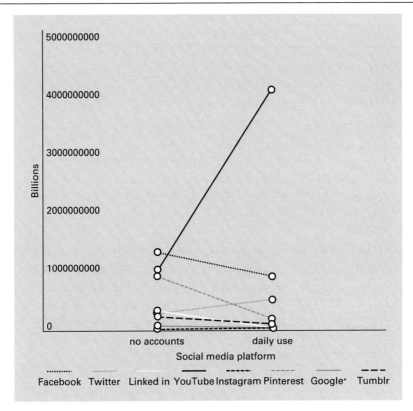

SOURCE: https://infogr.am/_/ZkRZ47n6WxaYIdypNoqQ

TABLE 7.1   Numbers of social media users

	Number of users	
	no. accounts	daily use
Facebook	1,300,000,000	890,000,000
Twitter	284,000,000	500,000,000
LinkedIn	322,000,000	38,000,000
YouTube	1,000,000,000	4,000,000,000
Instagram	30,000,000	70,000,000
Pinterest	70,000,000	40,000,000
Google+	900,000,000	189,000,000
Tumblr	224,000,000	113,600,000

FIGURE 7.6   Social media users

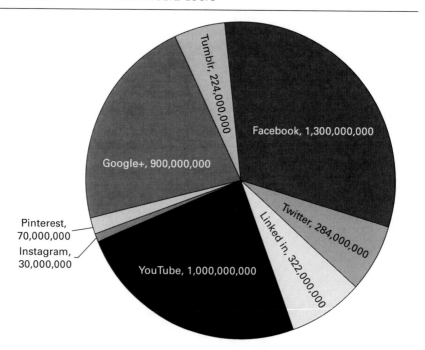

Facebook – often considered the domain of teenagers and 20-somethings but increasingly used by the over-50s and 'silversurfers'. Primarily used for leisure activities and personal interests – it's easy to upload and share photos, links and videos. It's also incredibly easy for people to share something they like with their networks – and with over 1.3 billion people logged in and active every single minute of every single day (with an average visit of 21 minutes per user each day) that gives you some pretty far-reaching and powerful opportunities.

Twitter – 5 billion tweets per day ... 25 thousand tweets per second. You'll find American users engaging in lots of social conversations while the British like to share links to internet content.

YouTube – over a billion accounts and a staggering 4 billion views every month, YouTube reaches 55 per cent of every demographic in the US: male; female; young; old; ethnic groups. It's quite simply the biggest video-sharing platform because they really do make it easy to share and tap into the viewing public.

Instagram – photo-sharing social media platform, primarily as a Smartphone App but can also be viewed on the web. Users take a photo with their phone camera, add a few filters or special effects and instantly upload it to the web to share with groups of friends or users across the world by adding a searchable hashtag. Over 110 billion photos uploaded daily and can easily be synced by the user to seamlessly share with their other social network platforms. Consider the numbers: you share one photo, your followers share it to their Instagram account and two other social media platforms and their friends share it on ... three for the price of one!

Pinterest – visual bookmarking tool for collecting web addresses for future use by saving pictures, most commonly for recipes, travel and arts and craft projects. Eighty per cent of Pinterest users are women and each user has an average of 67 people following the bookmarks that they are saving. With 70 million worldwide users that's a huge female audience to tap into.

Google+ – Google's competitor to Facebook though with only 900 million active users and an average visit by users of only seven minutes per day. Provides tools for engaging in communities, business pages, forums and general interests and is very powerful in allowing you to keep topics, user groups and interests separate.

tumblr – at least 224 million blogs with over a billion posts. tumblr started out as a simple blogging tool for people to tell their story and add a few images. Nowadays users can create a blog with a whole host of multi-media including photos, animations, links to web resources, videos, pretty much anything you like about anything you like, shared with whoever searches a keyword you're using.

LinkedIn – the largest networking platform for professional and business use. You will rarely find purely social interactions here but with 322 million worldwide professionals you'll open up a whole new world of connections.

Content is king!

The platforms may differ but one golden rule applies to them all when it comes to promoting your event using social media – content is king! No matter what platform you're using, the most important thing is to share valuable content that your target audience will find interesting. Essentially, all social networks revolve around content, whether it is pictures, videos, audio or words (refer to the earlier checklist for different forms of social media content that you can share) but only relevant, meaningful content will grab your audience's attention and gain interest in your event (think back to the AIDA model).

CHECKLIST: Different forms of social media content

☐ status update ☐ top tips

☐ blog post ☐ how-to guides

☐ webinar ☐ FAQs

☐ video ☐ client testimonials

☐ image gallery ☐ case studies

☐ presentation slides ☐ quotes

☐ ebook ☐ competitions

Before you start sharing content, think carefully about the type of information that is useful to your audience. Social media users want to receive information that is relevant and appealing, not just 'spam' that clutters up their social media feeds. To create a community around your event, you need to make it worthwhile for someone to follow you. For example, a live entertainment event could use social media to make announcements when a new artist/performer is confirmed or to give attendees a sneak preview of what's happening backstage. If your social media content doesn't provide any value to your audience then they're unlikely to remain part of your community long.

Top Tip

When it comes to grabbing your audience's attention, take full advantage of social media platforms that allow you to share pictures and images of your event. Increasingly, the best way to gain and keep your audience's interest is by using effective visual content. Visual social media platforms like Instagram and Pinterest are the fastest growing social media platforms.

This brings us to the question of 'How do you add value through social media content?' It's not our intention, in this book, to address this question in detail. You will, however, find a wealth of information on the internet about what social media marketers consider to be 'valuable' content. The Content Marketing Institute, for example, has an 'Essential Checklist for Creating Valuable Content' on their website **http://contentmarketinginstitute.com/2011/04/valuable-content-checklist/**

We offer the following set of questions as a checklist for you to consider when it comes to creating and sharing valuable social media content with your target audience. While this list is by no means exhaustive, if you're unable to tick at least some of the boxes, then you probably need to give more thought to the content you're sharing with your target audience.

CHECKLIST: Creating and sharing valuable social media content

- ☐ is it helpful?
- ☐ is it interesting?
- ☐ is it entertaining?
- ☐ is it exciting?
- ☐ is it funny?
- ☐ is it clever?
- ☐ is it educational?
- ☐ is it informative?
- ☐ is it inspiring?
- ☐ is it thought-provoking?
- ☐ is it innovative?
- ☐ is it unique?
- ☐ is it quirky?

Sharing valuable content creates what is often referred to as the 'ripple effect'. Your followers will see what you've shared, and if they like it they'll share it with their contacts, who in turn might share it with theirs, and so on, and so on. Anyone who is savvy with the internet has heard the phrase 'going viral' which refers to the fact that your content resonates so enormously that the ripple effect spreads across the web, and even across the world.

Part of the etiquette of using social media is not to be too 'pushy' or 'salesy'. If all that you do is sell, sell, sell continuously, then it won't be long before your followers are unfollowing you. The golden rule of content marketing is only 10 per cent of things you share should be self-promotional (eg promotions and offers). The good news is that you don't need to create the other 90 per cent of content yourself. As shown, the majority of the content that you share (60 per cent), can be 'cherry-picked' from trusted third party sources. So, for example, a conference and exhibition organizer could pick out the best content that is relevant to a particular industry sector as well as sharing interesting content created by the conference speakers or exhibitors. Sharing third party content is a very effective and also much quicker way of engaging with your community, without having to create original content yourself.

The Golden Ratio of Content Marketing 30:60:10

30 per cent of what you share should be first party content (ie original content you created);

60 per cent of what you share should be third party content (ie cherry-picked from trusted sources);

10 per cent of what you share should be Calls To Action (ie promotions and offers to incentive sales).

Top Tip

You can make it easier for your audience to find your content by creating a hashtag (#) for your event. Originally hashtags began on Twitter but now they have made their way onto all the most popular social media platforms. When creating your hashtag, make sure it's...

- Relevant – your hashtag should be related to your event (eg using the event name).

- Original – a quick search will let you know if your hashtag has already been used.

- Easy to remember – shorter hashtags are generally easier for people to remember.

Choosing your social media platform

Research carried out by The Event Manager Blog (2014) gives a helpful snapshot of the percentage of events professionals choosing each of the various social media platforms to share content and connect with their target audience (See Table 7.2). In 2014, Facebook was still top, followed by Twitter and LinkedIn; with more than half of the events professionals surveyed

TABLE 7.2 Event professionals using each social media platform

Platform	% of respondents using each platform for their events
Facebook	84%
Twitter	69%
LinkedIn	58%
YouTube	36%
Instagram	25%
Pinterest	18%
Google+	18%
Tumblr	3%

using the 'big three' for their events. What has been interesting over the last few years, however, is the rising popularity of image-based social media sites like Instagram, Pinterest and Tumblr. One of the reasons for this growth is the increasing number of smartphone users combined with the improvements on smartphone cameras. Image-based social media, therefore, is likely to become an even more important platform to engage event audiences.

As we have seen, each social media platform offers something a little different, so choosing the right social media platform for your event requires careful consideration. While there are no exact rules, here are three very important factors to consider, ensuring that you focus your promotional efforts in the right places when it comes to social media.

1. Audience

It may sound obvious but you need to find out where your target audience 'hang out' when it comes to social media. It's often a case of making some educated guesses. So, for example, if you're targeting an 'older crowd' then Facebook (sometimes described as the social media for mums and dads) is probably a good choice. A wealth of fascinating data about who is using social media is available (the majority is freely available on the internet) to help you choose the right social media platform for your target audience.

The following are among the key findings on social media usage from a new survey from the Pew Research Center's Internet Project (2013):

- Women are four times more likely to be Pinterest users than men.

- Facebook is ageing. At least 45 per cent of Internet users aged 65+ use Facebook.

- Pinterest attracts older people. Twitter and Instagram are still youth-dominated networks, but 23 per cent of Internet users aged 50+ use Pinterest.

- Facebook and Instagram users are the most engaged. Around 60 per cent of their users sign in every day (compared to 46 per cent of Twitter users).

- Almost all social networkers use Facebook. In fact, over 80 per cent of 'other' social network users also use Facebook.

- Instagrammers also use Twitter. There is a 50 per cent crossover between the networks.

- Pinterest and LinkedIn users are wealthier than the other networks with a high percentage earning over $75,000 per annum.

SOURCE: Our Social Times (2014) 10 Useful Social Networking Statistics for 2014. [online] available from: http://oursocialtimes.com/10-useful-social-networking-statistics-for-2014/ [Accessed: 3 December 2014]

2. Competition

Keeping an eye on your competitors' social media presence can provide valuable insight into where you should be focusing your own efforts. As well as seeing which social media platforms they are using, you can see exactly what content they're posting, how often they're posting and when they're posting. While it would be a mistake to simply copy your competitor's social media activity, if certain social media seem to be working for them (ie high levels of engagement with their audience), then we would recommend thinking seriously about doing the same – only better!

3. Content type

With social media the most important thing is to share content that will grab your audience's attention and generate interest in your event. A natural extension of this is selecting the best social media platform(s) to share that content. So, for example, if you want to introduce the guest speakers to your audience by sharing a professional bio, then select a platform suited to distributing written content. On the other hand, if you want to share humorous behind-the-scenes photographs of your event then choose a platform best suited to distributing visual content.

This case study encapsulates the importance of social media platforms to promote an event.

CASE STUDY 7.3   Twitter competition helps get the word out about the Conference and Hospitality Show

Emma Heslington, Event Service Co-ordinator, Leeds Beckett University and Dr Emma Wood, Reader at UK Centre for Events Management, Leeds Beckett University

The Conference and Hospitality Show (CHS) takes place each year in Yorkshire, England. The one-day show, which began in 2010, gives attendees the opportunity to network with one another, discuss topics with influential speakers, increase their industry knowledge and talk to potential suppliers face to face.

In 2012, the show expanded by moving to a new venue, the Pavilion at Leeds United Football Club, welcoming more than 100 exhibitors, speakers, celebrity chefs and hundreds of meeting and event professionals. Event organizer, Emma Cartmell, from the CHS Group, embraced social media to get the word out about the new event venue and expanded programme for the show.

'We had used social media in an ad hoc way before; but this was the first year we used it fully to get people talking and create a buzz ahead of the show,' Cartmell said.

As part of its social media strategy for the event, CHS ran a Twitter competition. The prize was a two-night stay at the Radisson Blu Hotel in Milan with flights from Leeds Bradford International Airport.

'We were aware that many of our past visitors and exhibitors were tweeting great things about the show, and we wanted to express our thanks,' Cartmell said.

Cartmell and the CHS team worked with a company called Ideonic, which ran the contest using tweet analysing software. The Ideonic software tracked the CHS12 hashtag and a series of 40 keywords, including 'show,' 'Leeds' and 'career'. When a tweeter used one of the keywords, they received a message congratulating them on unlocking a badge. Ideonic set up a leader board that automatically updated each time someone won a badge.

There were also badges for certain numbers of individual tweets (10, 50 and 75) containing #CHS12. At the beginning of the competition no one knew what the keywords were; delegates had to discover them in the build-up to and during the event. All of the keywords linked strongly to the show and could be found on the website. This encouraged participants to research the event in more detail.

More importantly, it helped the show align its brand identity through direct and tweeted messages.

As a result of the Twitter competition, more than 3,000 tweets were sent about the event, with Cartmell describing the competition as a 'great way to get attendees, exhibitors and the press talking about the show'.

Show attendees agreed that the competition was a great success. Lindsay Taylor, Director at Your Excellency Ltd, said, 'It was a huge incentive for people tweeting about the event, the fact that there was a prize at the end. That was a huge plus and a really, really good marketing tool.'

The Twitter competition gained CHS press coverage in e-zines such as *Conference News* and *My Venues* and in *M&IT* magazine.

Read more:

www.conferenceandhospitalityshow.co.uk

www.ideonic.com

www.mpiweb.org/FOM

Social media advertising

Having warned against being overly 'pushy' or 'salesy' when it comes to using social media to engage with your audience, there are, however, certain situations when directly advertising on social media can go a long way to growing your audience and engagement. You should consider using social media advertising when...

- Your event is new with no established social media community.
- There isn't enough time to create and share 'valuable' content before the event.
- There aren't enough people to create and share 'valuable' content.
- Your promotional budget won't stretch to other forms of advertising (social media advertising is relatively inexpensive).

You can advertise on nearly every platform but we'll focus on the top three: Facebook, Twitter and LinkedIn.

Facebook

Advertising your event on Facebook is fairly straightforward. The four steps to advertising your event on the site are:

1 Create a Facebook Event on your page – Facebook will ask for your event name, event details, location, a link to get tickets, time, etc.

2 Choose your campaign objective – Facebook offers a specific advertising campaign objective for promoting events called 'Event Responses'.

3 Choose your campaign budget – You have an option to set a total budget which will automatically stop the campaign once the budget is reached. You can also set the start and end dates for your campaign.

4 Choose your audience – You can segment your target audience on Facebook in lots of ways, including: Location, Age, Gender and Interests.

Twitter

There are two types of Twitter Adverts:

Promoted Accounts are used to get your account in front of more people with the aim of increasing your follower base.

Promoted Tweets are used when you have important information to share (eg important announcement) and want to reach a larger audience than usual.

For both Promoted Accounts and Promoted Tweets, there are two basic steps:

1 Choose your target audience – Twitter gives lots of targeting options, including: Location, Gender, Interests and more.

2 Set a budget – You have to set a daily maximum which you are willing to spend. You also have an option to add a total budget.

Top Tip

Two great features on the Twitter advertising platform to help you target the right users are:

- look-alike-only targeting – this allows you to target users who are most like your existing followers;

- keyword targeting in timelines – this enables you to target users based on the keywords in their recent tweets and the tweets with which users recently engaged.

LinkedIn

LinkedIn has a smaller audience than both Facebook and Twitter but creating a LinkedIn sponsored update is a very effective way of spreading the word about an upcoming event to a professional audience.

The three basic steps to follow are:

1 Design your post. Be sure to create a headline and short description that will attract attention. Adding an image or a video to your post will make it more eye-catching.

2 Target your update. LinkedIn profiles contain more detailed 'professional' information compared with what people list on their personal profiles on other social media, eg job title, roles and responsibilities, level of seniority, company size, etc.

3 Set campaign options. You have the option of setting a total budget and duration for the campaign.

Developing a promotional plan

As we've seen, there are many choices regarding how and where to promote your event. While there is no one right way to create a successful promotional campaign, there are practical steps you should take to give focus and direction to your efforts.

Here are five simple steps to follow:

1 Set objectives
2 Establish the budget
3 Select promotional tools
4 Create a promotional calendar
5 Measure the results

Like any good plan, there needs to be an element of flexibility but careful planning helps to ensure that resources (namely money, time and staff) are used effectively.

Set objectives

Before beginning any promotional activity, you need to set yourself some objectives to provide you with focus and direction. At this point, it may be helpful to refer back to the section 'Establishing the objectives' in Chapter 2. Setting objectives will also enable you to measure the effectiveness of your promotional efforts (more about this shortly).

Every event is different and each promotional campaign should have its own set of objectives.

Possible objectives may include the following:

- raise awareness
- create interest
- stimulate demand
- stimulate sales

- provide information
- reinforce the image
- differentiate the event

Establish the budget

Bowdin *et al* (2011) suggest four approaches to establishing the budget:

1 **What the event can afford**

Here a figure that is deemed to be 'affordable' is set and then a promotional plan is developed using the financial resources allocated. This approach is common at many smaller events (eg community festivals and amateur sports tournaments) where limited resources are available to put on the event.

2 **Percentage of sales method**

Here the promotion budget is set at a percentage of the forecasted sales revenue. Clearly this method is only suitable for an event that will generate revenue. It is often the case that the promotion budget will be set as a percentage of forecasted ticket sales.

3 **Competitive parity method**

Here the budget set is deemed to be in line with the budget for other similar events. So, for example, an organizer of a product launch for a motor car will seek to determine the budget for a product launch of a competitor motor car (ie the norm for the sector).

4 **Objective and task method**

Here the focus is on what needs to be achieved – the objectives of the promotional campaign – before setting a budget. This method consists of three steps:

- Establish the objectives
- Determine specific tasks to meet these objectives
- Calculate approximate costs of tasks

Select promotional tools

Each promotional tool (or element) has its strengths and weaknesses. Part of developing a promotional plan is deciding which tools will be most effective within the allocated budget and timescales.

The Four Cs is a useful way of assessing the suitability of each element of a proposed promotional campaign (Figure 7.7).

While each promotional tool can be used in isolation, they are more effective when used together for greater impact. Integrated marketing communications is a strategy aimed at unifying different tools by presenting them with a similar *'look and feel'*. Helping to ensure that the recipient immediately recognizes that the promotional message is about the same event and not a competing promotion.

FIGURE 7.7 Four Cs of promotional planning

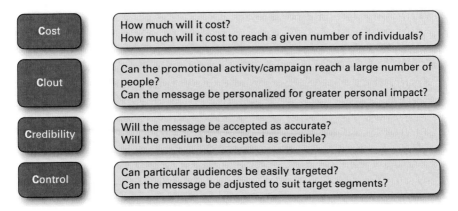

Adapted from Chartered Institute of Marketing (2009)

Here are some simple questions to help you deliver an integrated promotional campaign:

- Are the promotional tools working together?
- Does the choice of tools help to give you widespread exposure?
- Is a clear and consistent message being delivered?
- Do you maintain consistent branding and 'house style'?
- Have promotional efforts been scheduled and coordinated?

Create a promotion calendar

Once you know the tools (elements) you'll be using, the next step is to create a promotion calendar (timeline). Your promotional calendar will show when the campaign is scheduled to begin, for how long and the specific promotional activities taking place.

Timing is one of the most important factors in a successful promotional campaign. Start too soon and people won't be ready to consider attending, start too late and their diary is full. Furthermore, the various promotional elements need to be carefully coordinated and launched at very specific times to ensure the successful delivery of an integrated promotions campaign.

Creating a promotion calendar is an effective tool to help you plan ahead and stay on top of your promotional activities. There are different ways to set out the layout of your promotion calendar. Keep it simple. Figure 7.8 provides a simple template to get you started. This can be easily amended to suit your specific needs.

FIGURE 7.8 Promotion campaign calendar template

Promotion Campaign Calendar	Jan	Feb	Mar	Apr	May	Jun	Jul	Aug	Sep	Oct	Nov	Dec
Printed Media												
Local												
National												
Radio												
Local												
National												
Social Media												
Facebook												
Twitter												
LinkedIn												
Blog Posts												
Post 1												
Post 2												
Post 3												
Video Posts												
You Tube												
Email Campaigns												
1. Topic/Objective												
2. Topic/Objective												
3. Topic/Objective												

Measure the results

Tracking the results of your activities will enable you to measure what return on investment you are getting for your promotional spend. What you measure could vary for each promotional objective, but as long as you are clear on objectives and then measure them specifically you can ascertain success or failure.

Chapter summary

- All events require some sort of promotional activity to generate a buzz and excitement ahead of the event.
- Before launching a promotional campaign it is essential to determine the intended target audience and exactly what it is you want to say to them.
- Combining psychographic with demographic data will significantly improve your understanding of the target audience giving you a much clearer picture of the typical attendee and their motives for attending.

- The AIDA model can serve as a helpful checklist for creating an effective promotional message that will grab ATTENTION, gain INTEREST, create DESIRE and instigate ACTION.
- Social media is increasingly used to promote events but the more traditional methods (eg direct mail and personal selling) still have an important role to play.
- The level of promotional activity for an event will vary but drawing up a promotional plan in the lead up to your event is advisable.

Reference list

Bowdin, G, Allen, J, Harris, R, McDonnell, I and O'Toole, W (2011) *Events Management: Third Edition*, Butterworth Heinemann, Oxford

Chartered Institute of Marketing (2009) *How to plan marketing communications*. Chartered Institute of Marketing. Available from: www.cim.co.uk/files/marcomms.pdf [Accessed: 3 December 2014]

Connell, C (2014) *Not just a show, a record of all our lives: As Friends reaches a milestone anniversary*, Daily Mail online, available from: www.dailymail.co.uk/femail/article-2752307/Not-just-record-lives-As-Friends-reaches-milestone-anniversary-Claudia-Connell-s-addicted-20-years-on.html [Accessed: 3 December 2014]

Direct Marketing Association (2012) *National Client Email Report 2012*, Direct Marketing Association (DMA), available from: http://dma.org.uk/uploads/National per cent20Client per cent20Email per cent20Report per cent202012_53cfc69ad269d.pdf [Accessed: 3 December 2014]

Event Manager Blog (2014) *Social Media for Events* [online] available from: www.eventmanagerblog.com/social-media-events-free-ebook [Accessed: 29 November 2014]

Kotler, P (1991) *Marketing Management: Analysis, Planning, Implementation, and Control*, Financial Times/Prentice-Hall, London

Pew Research Center (2013) *Social Media Update 2013* [online] Available from: www.pewinternet.org/files/2013/12/PIP_Social-Networking-2013.pdf [Accessed: 3 December 2014]

Williams, R (2012) *Revealed: The third largest 'country' in the world – Facebook hits one billion users* [online] available from: www.independent.co.uk/life-style/gadgets-and-tech/news/revealed-the-third-largest-country-in-the-world–face-book-hits-one-billion-users-8197597.html [Accessed: 3 December 2014]

Finances and procurement

08

If the first task of an event organizer is to identify the objectives for a specific event, it is clear that without a good understanding of the extent and sources of income and expenditure, an event is destined to fail. Whether through sponsorship, ticket sales or advertising, financial resources may be obtained from outside the client organization, as well as from within. Resource requirements must be identified at an early stage in the event-management process. In this chapter, we explain how this can be achieved, and provide and explain examples using relevant and useful tools, techniques and templates.

This chapter includes:

- in-house or outsourced events management
- outsourcing, commissioning, purchasing and procurement of suppliers
- budgeting and forecasting
- cash flow and break even

A key aspect of event evaluation (see Chapter 9) will include an analysis of the costs of the event. The more detailed and specific your objectives are in developing the event – including its intended purpose and expected outcomes – the more likely your organization is to know whether an event has been worthwhile – and perhaps whether it might be repeated. The financial aspects form part of these important measures. All too often, an event takes root in the mind of an executive, without a realistic assessment of the potential costs and benefits of the activity. And this not only includes costs paid out by the company, for example, hiring a venue, but it should also include an accurate valuation of less visible internal costs, such as staff time and measuring the negative impact on the organization's brand or reputation if the event fails. Chapter 9 covers evaluation more fully, and other sources such as 'Return on Investment in Meetings and Events' by Jack J Phillips, M Theresa Breining and Patricia Pulliam Phillips, provide valuable models and in-depth discussion of the evaluation issues identified here.

Outsource or in-house?

With any event, one of the decisions you will need to make is whether you can or should use the resources you have within your own organization, or whether there are some resources you need to obtain externally. This could include sourcing a venue for the event, to a range of service suppliers (such as audio visual equipment and technical support), or help with creating and managing the event itself, from advance planning to on-the-day delivery.

Outsourcing

- Definition: Outsourcing is the transfer of an organizational function to a third party.

- Why outsource?

  Cost – outsourcing can be more cost-effective than outright purchasing; this is discussed in more detail in the following sections.

  Time – in the tight timescales of events management, combined with the peak of the pulsating nature of events that requires a bigger workforce on-site, there isn't always the luxury of time to deliver all the different aspects within the resources of one company.

  Expertise and specialist equipment – supplier companies may provide a range of skills, knowledge, experience and/or specialist equipment and facilities that are not needed within the company on a full-time basis, so buying in these resources as needed makes more efficient use of financial resources.

  Risks – bringing in expertise spreads the burden of responsibility and reduces the overall risk to the event. Each supplier is responsible for undertaking risk analysis for their specialist area.

  Quality – using specialist resources – whether people or equipment – enables the event management team to deliver a higher quality event experience.

  (With thanks to Simon Bell for inspiration.)

If you are participating in or sponsoring someone else's event (such as the Wimbledon Lawn Tennis Championships, for example), you will need to consider how best to use the opportunity to meet your objectives as well as retaining a level of control. It may be easier to purchase corporate hospitality tickets for a well-known event than manage an event of your own, but controlling quality, information and communication is then out of your hands, and the resulting experience is no longer unique. So, in considering the benefits of outsourcing versus delivering an in-house event, it is important to identify the potential costs involved. However, outsourcing activity does not make the cost problem go away, as considerable time is spent in managing the relationship with the outsourcing provider. Many events organizations will choose to outsource some of the services required for an event, and this leads to what can become a complicated web of in-house/outsourced communication and relationships. One option is to retain the majority of the event management process in-house, which may be done by recruiting new staff with relevant events skills and experience.

Scoping a budget for an in-house core events team

This example shows the process followed by a large UK-based organization in scoping and costing the fixed and variable aspects of setting up an in-house core events team to develop and deliver an ongoing series of residential training events.

Resource requirements

Resource requirements can be split between internal and external aspects, as shown below in Table 8.1:

TABLE 8.1 Internal and external resource requirements

Internal	External
• Staffing – events team, in-house events facilitators • Events delivery processes (see Chapter 2 for an example used by a public sector organization, Case Study 2.4)	• Venues • Audio visual services • Event design, development and facilitation support • Event-management system • Facilitator pool • Consultancy support (eg external presenters and facilitators)

Staffing – events team

Table 8.2 maps the functions required within the team against relevant team roles.

TABLE 8.2   Team roles and functions

Functions required	Roles required
● Venue sourcing, selection and management;	● Events Manager/Events Coordinator role
● Speaker/facilitator selection and management;	● Events Coordinator role
● Outsourcing and management of AV requirements;	● Events Coordinator role
● Preparation/coordination of communication materials, handouts and exhibition materials;	● Events Coordinator role
● On-the-day event management;	● Staff with appropriate experience/training
● Delegate bookings and communication;	● Events Administrator role
● Team admin including travel, badges, event resources, team email inbox management.	● Events Administrator role

The levels of resource required to staff such a core team would include the following:

- Events Manager role: one fte (fte = full-time equivalent)
- Events Coordinator role: two fte
- Events Administrator role: two fte

Events team support to deliver additional events – say as a separate project – would require an additional Events Coordinator and Events Administrator, to sit within the team and be managed by the Events Manager, rather than recruiting a whole new team.

Role summaries

The Events Manager role includes the following responsibilities:

- Lead strategic planning, management and delivery of national and local events.

- Manage external resource sourcing, selection and procurement processes, eg venues, AV, personnel.
- Manage events team.
- Lead coordination of event facilitation, administration and technical support requirements.
- Manage event evaluation and initiate improvements.

The Events Coordinator role includes the following responsibilities:

- Coordinate and deliver event management, including venue liaison.
- Coordinate speakers and facilitators.
- Use online events management tool to deliver high-quality event administration.
- Organize exhibitions, communications, eg delegate packs, email.
- Provide on-site event management, including managing relationships with external suppliers.
- Maintain requisition and ordering processes.

The Events Administrator role includes the following responsibilities:

- Deliver all aspects of event administration, including delegate bookings, production of delegate packs and delegate resources where required and providing post-event online access to materials.
- Use online events management tool to deliver high-quality event administration.
- Respond to queries; manage team email inbox.
- Organize team travel and accommodation.

Facilitators

For events that require facilitators, it is possible to use in-house staff who are trained and experienced facilitators, thereby reducing the need for a large team of permanent staff and developing internal levels of expertise while retaining funding within the organization.

Level of resource required:

- Event facilitation and content team lead role: one fte
- Facilitator role (permanent): one fte
- Facilitator pool: minimum of 10, covering 20–30 events per year (two facilitators per event)
- Event Content Manager: one fte

Hosts

Event hosts can be drawn from relevant in-house staff and key local personnel, from a team of freelance staff, or hired in.

Developing in-house event-planning processes

Table 8.3 shows the event management processes required to deliver the team's events. See Chapter 2 for more details about developing the event-planning process.

TABLE 8.3 Event management processes

Inputs	Action	Outcomes
• In-house guide to running events • Event management experience	• Share existing processes with staff from other teams who run events • Develop agreed organizational processes	• Shared understanding of requirements for running events • Shared processes • Professional delivery of events • Consistency across organization in event delivery • Expectations of service and stakeholders met/exceeded
• Online events management tool	• Training	• Organization-enabled local delivery of events

It is important to scope the costs of this activity. Staffing costs have been addressed in the previous section, and the next section will consider the outsourcing of key suppliers.

Outsourcing key suppliers

Venues

Each event requires a venue with meeting space, catering and overnight accommodation. The requirements will vary with each event. The sourcing process will include:

- Obtaining three or more quotes from different venues that meet the event brief *specifications*, using a specific venue search company.
- Selecting a venue from the list.
- Direct liaison with the venue including signed contracts.

Potential issues that need to be resolved:

- Understanding the organizational procurement and finance processes and policies, (including deposits and advance payments, where required), and agreeing processes for confirming variations between the purchase order amount and the final invoice.
- Timescales for processing of purchase orders and payment of invoices.
- Authority to sign off budgets.

Audio visual services

Each event will require audio visual support. The Project A events will require a standard list of equipment and technical personnel, to include the following:

- For PowerPoint presentations – laptop and LCD projector, screen, set/backdrop.
- Sound is not required for presenters, but would be needed if DVDs/videos are shown, or if presentations are to be recorded.
- DVD player.
- Technician.
- Memory sticks, loaded with all the presentations and additional resources, and handed out to delegates at the end of each event.
- Equipment for small exhibition/roadshow which may include: laptop, portable branded exhibition stand, large (42-inch) plasma screen and possibly on-site internet access.
- Portable printer for on-site use.
- Flipchart stands and paper.

A key consideration is whether some of the equipment should be purchased and owned by the organization (and possibly held, maintained and transported by the AV supplier), or hired from the AV supplier. If equipment was to be purchased outright, two sets would be needed, to provide backup and logistical cover for multiple events. **Estimated** costs of the two options (purchase or hire, excluding VAT) are given below in Table 8.4.

However, organizations may still choose to hire, despite the higher costs, if they lack the appropriate technical support to maintain equipment and deliver a quality service. The likelihood of equipment becoming obsolete should also be considered, as the pace of technological change is inevitable. This shifts the risk to the AV supplier instead.

Events management system

Table 8.5 outlines the benefits of purchasing a specific online events management and booking tool for use for all events delivered by the in-house events team and any other in-house staff.

TABLE 8.4   Estimated costs of purchasing equipment v hire

Equipment	Purchase cost	Hire cost
Laptop	2 x £650 = 1300	£55/day 2 x 40 days = £4400
Projector (2000 Lumen desktop)	2 x £1000 = £2000	£65/day 2 x 40 days = £5200
Screen (8' x 6' Fastfold front or rear projection)	2 x £1350 = £2700	£35/day 2 x 40 days = £2800
Totals	£6000	£12400

TABLE 8.5   Events management system

Actions Required	Benefits of Brand X online events management tool
Online events management tool to be procured	• Has been tested and proven, running over 260 events with over 30,000 bookings in 18 months • Has also been replicated across the wider organization • Uses the existing capabilities of the Events Team and frees up administrative time through online booking and automated processes • Provides a professional look to the organization's event management capability • Can be used by trained staff across the organization • Will provide visibility and evidence of delivery for the events team and will register actual levels of engagement with stakeholders

Event design & development and facilitation support

This service includes developing the event format and content, facilitator training, and attendance and facilitation at events.

Consultancy support

Consultancy support would include the use of external presenters to deliver sessions as required, including support for event design and development, and delivering specific session(s) at events.

Annual cost estimates for events delivery

Table 8.6 shows a breakdown of estimated costs per year, based on an in-house events team, and outsourced key suppliers. In this example, the anticipated numbers of delegates is 30 per event.

TABLE 8.6   Breakdown of estimated costs per year

Resource	Number	Estimated cost for 1 year/40 events	Estimated total cost for 1 year/40 events
Events Team			
Events Manager	1	£48,000.00	£48,000.00
Events Coordinator	2	£35,000.00	£70,000.00
Events Administrator	2	£26,000.00	£52,000.00
Event facilitation and content team			
Team Lead	1	£48,000.00	£48,000.00
Facilitator	1	£48,000.00	£48,000.00
Content Manager	1	£48,000.00	£48,000.00
Facilitator pool (10 p-t)	180	£500.00	£90,000.00
Event design & development/facilitation support	1	£16,000.00	£16,000.00
Online events management tool			
Hosting	1	£2,000.00	£2,000.00
Implementation	1	£3,000.00	£3,000.00
Support & development	1	£5,000.00	£5,000.00
Venues	40	£10,000.00	£400,000.00
AV Service			
AV support and additional equipment	40	£1,750.00	£70,000.00
Equipment	2	£15,000.00	£30,000.00
Materials	40	£250.00	£10,000.00
Total cost – 1 year			£940,000.00
Average cost/event			£23,500.00
Average cost/delegate			£783.33

While many organizations will not require such a large team, it is important to note that the actual cost of in-house delivery can be substantial, but is often invisible, as resources (such as staff) can be spread across a range of activities. However, once a team is in place, it can provide support to numerous events. If additional projects emerge, an in-house team can be increased in size to meet the extra capacity, as needed. The cost of outsourcing such a capability is likely to be much higher (our own experience is that the cost could be in the region of six times higher to outsource), but outsourcing has the flexibility of enabling costs to be monitored more effectively on an event-by-event basis, as well as providing events expertise that may not be available in-house. Some organizations – particularly in the public sector – have restrictions on allowable headcount, so outsourcing is often used to get round this 'problem'.

Budgeting

It is unlikely that the event manager will know exactly how many people are due to attend until the day itself, so managing numbers accurately and keeping historical data on booking trends and no-show rates is vital. Even if the event is cancelled, there are still costs involved that need to be recorded and justified. This section addresses the possible options that might be encountered in different circumstances:

- single event
- series of events
- complex event
- cancelled event

Budgeting for a single event

Figure 8.1 illustrates a budget for a conference for 400 people, and provides three views: projected spend, any revisions during the planning process, and the final actual amount spent delivering the event.

In this example, there was an overspend on audio visual requirements, which included the making of a video on the day, filming 'vox pops' of attendees, to be shown in the final conference session, while there was an underspend on the development of conference content. The final numbers for the event may have been less than 400, but most venues will charge for the final number given, as stated on the venue terms and conditions, and signed for in the contract (unless of course the final number is larger than that contracted).

Budgeting for an event series

If the event is part of a series, it is important not only to review the cost of each event, but also to be aware of the overall costs of the event series as a whole.

FIGURE 8.1 Example budget, for a conference of 400 people

Conference – Venue C

Date

Total Budget: £170,000.00

	PROJECTED			REVISED			ACTUAL		
	Unit Cost	Qty	Total	Unit Cost	Qty	Total	Unit Cost	Qty	Total
Set up costs (Great Hall & Atrium)	£3,400.00	1	£3,400.00					1	£3,400.00
DDR (Day Delegate Rate)	£63.00	400	£25,200.00					400	£25,200.00
Bedrooms	£134.00	40	£5,360.00					40	£5,360.00
AV (equipment, technicians)	£16,000.00	1	£16,000.00					1	£20,000.00
AV (Vox Pops film)	£11,000.00	1	£11,000.00					1	£15,000.00
Content development	£50,000.00	1	£50,000.00					1	£43,000.00
Drama	£10,000.00	1	£10,000.00					1	£10,000.00
Promotional Material	£12.50	400	£5,000.00					400	£5,000.00
Travel Expenses (Delegates)	£1,000.00	1	£1,000.00					1	£1,000.00
Travel Expenses (Facilitators)	£1,000.00	1	£1,000.00					1	£1,000.00
Contingency			£10,000.00						
Running Total (excluding VAT)			**£137,960.00**			£0.00			£128,960.00
VAT @ 17.5%			£24,143.00			£			£22,568.000
Running Total (including VAT)			**£162,103.00**						**£151,528.00**

Budget
Underspend −£10,575.00

This is because it is very easy for incidentals and new costs to creep in on one event and then continue without challenge, which means that small amounts can add up to become much larger ones (especially incidentals), so accurate records are vital.

> **Top Tip**
>
> It's best practice to include a 'comments' column in the budget spreadsheet, which helps to explain the rationale behind any decisions or changes, such as small incidental costs added to each event.

FIGURE 8.2 Budget for an event series

Total Budget:	£125,000.00	Based on anticipated numbers of 100 (lunchtime/ afternoon session) + 50 (evening session) × 11 dates		
	PROJECTED	**REVISED**	**ACTUAL**	
Room Hire	£15,664.34	£14,660.82	£14,736.13	
Lunch	£16,435.50	£8,689.94	£8,429.89	Changed finger buffet to brown bag lunch
Broadband	£0.00	£943.24	£68.09	
Staff meal	£0.00	£2,031.25	£1,721.31	
AV	£31,978.70	£32,035.20	£30,675.70	
Teas & coffees	£4,318.50	£3,377.80	£4,340.69	
Staging	£0.00	£555.45	£555.44	
Bed & breakfast	£5,871.80	£4,240.30	£4,163.85	
Speakers expenses	£0.00	£0.00	£1,014.20	
Courier	£0.00	£0.00	£1,275.79	
Incidentals	£0.00	£1,337.40	£1,596.90	
Contingency	£0.00	£0.00	£6124.70	Venue cancellation charges – venues not used
Running total (Net)	**£74,268.84**	**£67,871.40**	**£74,702.69**	
VAT @ £17.5%	£12,997.05	£11,877.50	£13,072.97	
Running total (Gross)	**£87,265.89**	**£79,748.90**	£87,775.66	
Underspend	£37,734.11	£45,251.11	£37,224.34	

Once you have run an event or a series of events, it is worthwhile reviewing all the different types of expenditure and the amounts, so you can amend your spreadsheets for the next time. Make sure you consider whether an item is really a one-off, or whether it is possibly going to recur.

Budgeting for a complex event

A key challenge in compiling an accurate budget is that for a longer event, which includes an overnight stay, for example, there will be some people who dip in and out of the event at different times. As a result you don't want to pay for all the elements of the event for those who aren't attending the whole event.

This next example shows a complex two-day conference, which has 130 participants (including the events team and speakers) staying overnight at the venue. However, we already know in advance that 50 attendees don't stay overnight, because they live locally, but they do join the group for dinner, so you are charged for the day delegate rate (DDR) plus the cost of dinner for this group.

FIGURE 8.3   A complex two-day conference

Event name: Venue			
Dates:			
Total budget:	**£70,000.00**		
	Unit cost	Qty	Total
Room hire (Suite A)	£2,978.72	1	£2,978.72
Room hire (Suite B)	£4,680.81	1	£4,680.81
Room hire (Suite C)	£1,276.59	1	£1,276.59
24hr rate	£221.27	130	£28,765.10
Day delegate rate	£59.57	50	£2,978.50
Evening dinner	£34.04	50	£1,702.00
Tea & coffee	£3.20	200	£640.00
Tea & coffee	£3.20	40	£128.00
AV	£10,376.00	1	£10,376.00
Contingency			
Running total (Net)			**£53,525.72**
VAT @ £17.5%			£9,367.00
Running total (Gross)			**£ 62,892.72**
Over / Under Budget			£7,107.28

One way of minimizing costs for an event like this is to reduce the number of 24-hour and DDRs booked, and add in extras such as room hire and refreshments.

It is well worth the money they receive from the venue to use the expertise and contacts of a venue search agency. So rather than just accepting the DDR or 24-hour rate quoted, if you have some attendees at your event for part of the time, or as non-residents, consider whether it is worthwhile splitting up the costs into different headings, thereby paying for what you have used, rather than assuming that everyone is there all the way through an event. For example, many people leave events early – say, if they have a long journey back home – and it is possible to calculate the proportion of teas and coffees you won't need at the end of the day.

Top Tip

A good venue search agency will negotiate on your behalf to obtain the best financial agreement for your event. Not everyone finds negotiation easy, so using an external company can help you to minimize unnecessary costs. What you save here could be used for another event!

Budgeting considerations for event cancellation decisions

Many events are cancelled prematurely in an effort to save money, due to low take-up of event places. However, before making any final decision about cancelling an event, it is advisable to consider the full cost implications of such a decision. Whatever the reason for cancelling an event, it is often worthwhile continuing with an event booking, as once a contract is signed, 100 per cent of the invoice will have to be paid out to companies such as the venue and caterers, on the basis of these signed contracts. It is also important to consider the possible negative PR aspects of making cancellations, including the views of potential attendees and media coverage about wasted money, especially in the public sector. Here is a worked example of costings for a cancelled event. This demonstrates that the actual cost savings are minimal, and restricted to certain areas. It should be noted that the AV cost-saving is more due to the kindly nature of the AV supplier, who would have been within rights to adhere to the contract, or at least charge a cancellation fee.

In reality, once the contract is agreed (not necessarily signed, as verbal agreements can be binding), you are liable for up to the full amount, whether the event goes ahead or not.

FIGURE 8.4 Cancelled event – budget

	PROJECTED			ACTUAL		
	Unit Cost	Qty	Total	Unit Cost	Qty	Total
Room Hire	£3,084.38	1	£3,084.38	£3,084.38	1	£3,084.38
Lunch	£8.25	300	£2,475.00	£8.25	300	£2,475.00
AV	£2,839.00	1	£2,839.00	£2,839.00	0	£0.00
T&C	£2.25	300	£675.00	£2.25	150	£337.50
Bed & Breakfast	£118.00	5	£590.00	£118.00	0	£0.00
			£9,663.38			**£5,896.88**

Responsible finances

Planning an event can be a complex process, not just in terms of logistics, but in managing the event finances, such as deciding who will pay for what – and in some cases, who is **able** to pay for specific elements. For smaller events, the bill can be handed over to the one client, a simple task. When several organizations collaborate to host an event, their internal politics and circumstances add layers of complexity to the decision-making process, such as policy restrictions, funding limits and corporate governance.

The following case study examines the restrictions on charitable organizations when using events as a source of fundraising.

CASE STUDY 8.1   Events for Variety Club of Great Britain: the Children's Charity

Ruth Dowson, Senior Lecturer, UK Centre for Events Management

Variety, the Children's Charity (formally known as The Variety Club of Great Britain) was one of the first UK charities to work with disadvantaged children. Founded in the UK in 1949, Variety has its roots in the film and entertainment industry, and provides resources and support for children with disabilities and those living in poverty or other difficult circumstances, far beyond the well-recognized Sunshine Coaches.

Variety has always been an events-driven organization when it comes to fundraising – in 1960, it hosted its first event in Yorkshire at York Racecourse. In the Yorkshire Region, Variety regularly hosts successful fundraising events:

- The Yorkshire Business Awards are attended by 500 people every year and hosted by the prestigious Queen's Hotel (**www.qhotels.co.uk/our-locations/the-queens/?gclid=CM-G3qbm7cACFZTLtAod1gQAAw**) in the centre of Leeds. This event is held in the run-up to Christmas and grosses £160,000–£170,000 each year, with a net contribution towards Variety projects of £135,000.

- The Yorkshire Property Awards have been held at Rudding Park (**www.ruddingpark.co.uk/**) since 1997 and have grown from an audience of 200 to over 800, with a waiting list in 2014, having reached the venue's capacity, grossing £120,000–£130,000 a year and netting £58,000 for the charity's causes.

In Yorkshire, Charlotte Farrington heads up the team that delivers this impressive financial contribution. Supported by a volunteer group of professionals their approach to ticket sales and sponsorship is to make contact within their own professional and business networks to identify potential attendees and interest. Gaining informal commitments to purchase tickets/source sponsorship well in advance, this process ensures that events are guaranteed to minimize the potential financial risk to the charity and maximize the profit that can be donated to Variety's projects in the region. Charlotte was previously a volunteer committee member for three years prior to joining Variety's professional fundraising team. Previously experienced in events in a corporate marketing role, Charlotte's involvement with Variety came through her boss, and her enthusiasm for the task is evident in the stories she tells about the children whose lives she personally has helped to influence.

Working with a committee of volunteers has its challenges, juggling multiple priorities. It's a very different environment from that experienced by the older generation – there are no longer the 'ladies who lunch' to take on organizational tasks. Instead, Charlotte works within a small team alongside the many volunteers from different sectors to raise funds for this worthy cause, through a range of mass participation events such as marathons, bike rides and treks, to those related to special interests, including golf and bridge.

As a charity, Variety have to abide by the legal and financial constraints imposed by the UK's Charities Commission (**https://www.gov.uk/government/organisations/ charity-commission**), which also provides guidance and regulations to fundraisers on responsible activities, as well as pointing to other avenues of advice, for example, from the Institute of Fundraising (**www.institute-of-fundraising.org.uk/home/**).

The financial environment within the charity sector means that all overheads and costings for events have to be approved well in advance by the charity's Head Office and Financial teams. Minimizing the financial risk to the charity is key and so control over all event expenditure is required, along with timely planning and detailed preparation. Professionalizing the events function has meant that instead of always taking the lead from the committee of volunteers (of which she was once a member), the events team is able to initiate activities and develop new ideas, with the potential to increase income for the projects funded by this much-appreciated children's charity.

Read more: **www.variety.org.uk**

The 'AIG effect' was born in 2008, when the American International Group, then sponsors of Manchester United, the world's most recognizable football team, succumbed to the global economic crisis and received $85bn from the US Federal Reserve. Days later, one of its subsidiaries hosted insurance agents at a luxury California hotel, at a cost of $443,000, and the company was lambasted across the board. The next event it was due to hold was summarily cancelled, beginning a retreat by large corporations from anything remotely luxurious, and sending economic shivers down the spine of the hotel industry around the world, as company after company cancelled their bookings, for fear of a press backlash. Years later, questions are still asked of corporations if shareholders – or even onlookers – deem expenditure unwarranted. And it doesn't necessarily mean that a room costs what the rack rate states – many events result in upgraded bedrooms at a fraction of the advertised charge. So – when you run an event – any event – make sure you know why you're running it and how much everything costs. And consider what it would look like if it made it into the press...

The following example focuses on the issues experienced in running an important international conference that aimed to enable collaboration between a government body and two international commercial organizations.

International conference with three major sponsors

The following example describes some of the complex financial issues faced by the professional event management team attempting to coordinate the delivery of an international conference for three major organizations collaborating on a joint project. The combination of public sector and commercial involvement indicates a requirement to abide by not only strict government procurement rules but also be sensitive to commercial interests and potential embarrassment in the press. The key organizations were:

- An international industry association, which had its own requirements, expectations, internal procurement policies and funding limitations.
- A UK public sector body, which meant that there were significant procurement restrictions on any contributions, and that any activity could be subject to requests under the UK's Freedom of Information Act 2000 (FOI) (**www.legislation.gov.uk/ukpga/2000/36/contents**).
- The third partner provided one of the four venues used for the prestigious event.

In addition, there were smaller corporate sponsors of specific activities, such as drinks receptions and conference dinners, that might pose problems for governance in public sector or charitable organizations.

Factors to consider

For this particular event there were two UK public sector bodies, collaborating with international commercial organizations. The rule of thumb many public sector organizations operate is: 'would it pass the test of appearing in a national newspaper?' ie would it pass the scrutiny of the harshest critic looking for scandal? Government departments are often subject to negative press articles about events deemed unsuitable by whoever is throwing the first stone, and regularly receive FOI requests from journalists on events-related expenditure.

The Taxpayers Alliance (**www.taxpayersalliance.com/**), which claims to be 'an independent grassroots campaign for lower taxes', is often the named source of information received from FOI requests, which can, of course, be interpreted as 'needless expenditure' by local and national government, easily taken out of context.

The 2010 Bribery Act (**www.legislation.gov.uk/ukpga/2010/23/contents**) recognizes bona fide corporate hospitality or other promotional expenditure as an important part of doing business. However, care (and advice) should be taken when planning such events, whether for public or private sector clients.

Finances: for international conference with three major sponsors

A key financial challenge for this event was caused by a lower than anticipated level of registration income, alongside a higher level of registrations, which was partly due to a much higher number of invited guests than predicted: invitations given to special guests and VIPs who were not expected to pay for their attendance.

This situation resulted in higher variable costs that were not covered by registration income, but which needed to be paid for by someone; in this

FIGURE 8.5 Promoter expenditure

	Forecast Budget	Actual	Variance
Sponsor A	£69,311.00	£89,132.16	£19,821.16
Sponsor B	£40,000.00	£46,150.67	£6,150.67
Sponsor C	£9,005.00	£11,005.00	£2,000.00
	£118,316.00	£146,287.83	£27,971.83
	Anticipated	**Actual**	**Variance**
Sponsorship Income	£68,744.00	£32,901.00	−£35,843.00
Registration Income	£30,800.00	£10,560.00	−£20,240.00
Promoter Income			
Sponsor A	£30,000.00	£46,150.67	£16,150.67
Sponsor B	£20,000.00	£45,671.16	£25,671.16
Sponsor C	£9,005.00	£11,005.00	£2,000.00
Total Expenses	£118,316.00	£146,287.83	
Total Income	£158,549.00	£146,287.83	

case, it resulted in a tense negotiation between the three key collaborators, to the detriment of their ongoing relationships.

However, this problem is not uncommon and occurs at many events – whether festivals, music gigs, corporate hospitality or even conferences, all can be subject to the idea that 'we have to invite X – but we can't make a charge'. Although music events and festivals often have guest lists, they are not the only ones to face the challenges of long guest or VIP lists, and controlling the availability of free tickets can make or break any event. Saying 'no' on the day is not only embarrassing for the guest and the box office crew or registration desk, it can ruin customer or client relationships built up over time, in an instant.

Finances: itemized expenditure

It is always useful to be able to provide a logical rationale for each line of expenditure, not only for internal purposes but also for justifying costs to clients. As the previous example showed, when there are multiple sponsors and a range of stakeholders involved in an event, clear lines of responsibility are even more important for maintaining (or breaking) relationships before, during and after the event.

TABLE 8.7   Example of itemized expenditure – multiple sponsors

Item	Budget	Actual	Variance	To be paid by	Comment
Reception & dinner (invitation only) – private venue A	£15,000.00	£15,000.00	£0.00	Sponsor A	Sponsored by corporate Sponsor D
Sponsor venue conference costs	£9,005.00	£11,005.00	£2,000.00	Sponsor C	All Sponsor venue costs paid for by Sponsor C; final number 250; initial estimate based on 150 delegates
Additional Av tech hire (at sponsor venue)	£6,000.00	£3,185.43	–£2,814.57	Sponsor B	In-house procurement regulations followed; paid for by Sponsor B
Reception – private venue B	£6,311.00	£6,311.00	£0.00	Sponsor A	Sponsored by Sponsor E £3,000; final numbers 180
Event Management	£25,000.00	£25,000.00	£0.00	Sponsor B	Agreed contribution by Sponsor B (in kind)
Event Management	£15,000.00	£15,000.00	£0.00	Sponsor A	
Coaches	£0.00	£2,673.16	£2,673.16	Sponsor B	New item; procured and paid for by Sponsor B

TABLE 8.7 *continued*

Item	Budget	Actual	Variance	To be paid by	Comment
Photographer	£0.00	£800.00	£800.00	Sponsor B	New item; procured and paid for by Sponsor B
Speaker expenses & costs	£0.00	£2,000.00	£2,000.00	Sponsor B	New item; procured and paid for by Sponsor B
Financial management fee	£0.00	£1,500.00	£1,500.00	Sponsor A	Cost of financial event management including billing and receipt of delegate fees
Conference programme	£3,000.00	£520.00	–£2,480.00	Sponsor B	Sponsored by Sponsor F; procured and paid for by Sponsor B
Hotel conference costs	£33,000.00	£51,321.16	£18,321.16	Sponsor A	Additional costs due to increased numbers; final number 140; estimate based on 110 delegates. Also increase in scope due to inclusion of conference dinner Thursday evening
Conference hotel AV costs	£6,000.00	£11,972.08	£5,972.08	Sponsor B	In-house procurement regulations followed; paid for by Sponsor B
Totals	£118,316.00	£146,287.83	£27,971.83		

If one organization has different financial policies or procurement procedures from another, always make sure that you strictly abide by them. It is worthwhile treating all expenditure according to the criteria of the 'strictest' financial guidelines for that project.

Top Tip

When negotiating a contract with potential sponsors, make sure you know about any financial restrictions or practices that could impact on the financial aspects of the event.

Finances: income sources

The sources of income for any event are limited; funding for expenditure comes from three sources: the client, from sponsorship other than the client, or from ticket sales. Costs can be minimized in various ways before the event but generated income is what pays the bills afterwards.

This table is related to the previous event example and shows the range of sources of income provided by sponsors, ticket sales and exhibitors at the end of the event. Other sources might include advertising and, for larger events, media rights.

The lesson to be learned here emerges from a series of questions about whether the positive impacts of what, in other terms, was an amazingly successful event were overshadowed by disagreements over finances. (This takes the individual calculation of who pays what for the restaurant dinner tab, to another level!) So, who felt the pain afterwards? Did the positive

TABLE 8.8 Sources of income

Item	Anticipated	Actual	Variance	Funds Held By
Exhibition	£38,194.00	£5,876.00	−£32,318.00	Association – with two paying corporate exhibitors
Delegate sales	£30,800.00	£10,560.00	−£20,240.00	Financial event manager
Sponsorship – private venue A	£17,625.00	£17,625.00	£0.00	Association – with corporate sponsor
Sponsorship – private venue B	£7,050.00	£3,525.00	−£3,525.00	Association – with corporate sponsor
Sponsorship – public sector venue (coffee break)	£2,350.00	£2,350.00	£0.00	Association – with corporate sponsor
Sponsorship – programme	£3,525.00	£3,525.00	£0.00	Association – with corporate sponsor
Sponsor A	£20,000.00	£46,150.67	£16,150.67	Sponsor A
Sponsor B	£30,000.00	£45,671.16	£25,671.16	Sponsor B
Sponsor C	£9,005.00	£11,005.00	£2,000.00	Sponsor C

impacts of a successful event fade once the final financials were known? Did the three original event partners regret their initial ambitions? Each of these three sponsoring organizations may have had many long internal debates as they sought to pay for the event. But it is often the case that partners who end up paying more than they originally bargained for, may choose not to do business with each other again.

Other events may provide different lessons but the complexity of relationships between different stakeholders should be recognized up front in any event-planning process, from the financial perspective. In addition, there are elements of real life that may intervene, requiring a total rethink of the plan. The following case study outlines the need for contingency planning for income streams, and the dangers of relying too heavily on one sponsor.

CASE STUDY 8.2   The death of a sponsor is contagious...

Ivan K Cohen, PhD, Associate Professor in Finance and Economics, Richmond University, the American International University in London

Brian Damage has been the chairman of his local semi-professional football club for three years. A self-made multi-millionaire, Brian came from humble beginnings but made a name for himself as the inventor of a number of Apps for smartphones. When he sold his App company to one of the big software providers he decided he wished to 'put something back' into his local community and took a controlling stake in Buggswood and District Football Club.

As with many smaller football clubs, match attendance is often measured in the hundreds rather than thousands, so that match-day revenue is not enough to cover the salaries of the players, all of whom are part-time. It is barely enough to cover the club's fixed costs: maintenance of the stadium, electricity and other utilities, and the salaries of a full-time administrator and a small team of coaches and physiotherapists, who all work part-time for the club.

As something of a local personality, Brian has been able to persuade many local businesses to sponsor elements of the Buggswood team. Each week a local high street shop sponsors the match ball, for example. However, his biggest coup as manager was to persuade national insurance broker, LifeCharm, to sponsor the club *in toto*. This meant a significant revenue stream – more than 35 per cent of Buggswood's entire revenues – which has enabled Buggswood to employ players of better quality than previously, including some who had played earlier in their careers in the Championship. This has also enabled Buggswood to improve their League position and even increase attendance as a result.

Recently, however, LifeCharm have not led a charmed life, having encountered increasingly serious financial difficulties. This began in 2013 when rumours of 'accounting irregularities' started circulating. These rumours led to a call from shareholders for an investigation, which prompted the financial regulators to get involved. The costs of investigation by the financial regulator are not cheap and, even when a company is cleared, the impact can remain deleterious for some time. However, as the regulatory investigation dragged on – these things take a considerable time! – LifeCharm's policyholders began to cash in and move their insurance elsewhere; many shareholders opted to sell and invest elsewhere, pushing Life-Charm's stock price down, making it difficult for the company to raise additional funds even by borrowing from the bank with which they had been involved for decades.

It was a cold winter's day, with a blanket of snow on the ground when Brian received the fateful phone call he had been dreading from LifeCharm's head of PR, Sima Chakravarti. She regretfully informed Brian that LifeCharm was no longer in a position to honour its sponsorship agreement with Buggswood and would immediately cease its monthly transfer of sponsorship funds. The loss of 35 per cent of revenues would make it difficult for Buggswood to continue to pay its bills on time, and before long would likely see the club go out of business as a result. The possibility of finding another sponsor or two to bridge the gap was virtually impossible, as this had been a one-off deal, unlikely ever to be repeated.

The death of a sponsor is a contagion... a costly contagion.

Cash flow and break-even

A primary reason for the failure of many businesses is lack of cash flowing into the business when it is needed. It is important to ensure that you have enough income to pay the bills as they come in for each event that you manage. To work out the cash flow for an event, first develop an event budget, listing all income and expenditure. In this instance, we have started with an estimated income of £60,000, and included some details for clarity.

> ### Top Tip
>
> As a supplier you can check that your client is capable of paying you, using Companies House records (**www.companieshouse.gov.uk/toolsToHelp/findCompanyInfo.shtml**) before entering into a contractual agreement (or doing any work!). As a client for event services, you can also check the financial background of suppliers.

A month-by-month cash flow statement can be developed and updated monthly to reflect accurate transaction details.

FIGURE 8.6   Cash flow and break-even statement

Event								
Event title								
Event date								
Client name								
Event budget as at .... Date								
Description	**Unit**	**Unit cost**	**Volume**	**Cash budget**	**Actual cash spent**	**+/− Cash variance**	**Budget notes**	**Actuals notes**
Income analysis:								
Income sponsorship								
Income – tickets								
Income: budget = £60,000: Client company want to pay £10,000 a month, starting October				60000				
Total Income	0	0	0	60000				
Expenditure Analysis:								
Venue hire non-returnable deposit at time of booking				1000				
Venue final payment one month before				9000				
Guest entertainer paid one month before				6500				
Prizes bought two months before the event				3000				
Food initial deposit five months before event	people	10.00	200	2000				
Food final payment one month before	people	25.00	200	5000				
Drinks paid one month after event	bottles	20	72	1440				
Sound system paid one month after event		1500	1	1500				
Music fee paid to agent three months before event	band	1900	1	1900				
Events Team staff costs	hour	15	400	6000				
Event Management fees	month	2000	8	16000				
Additional staff for the night paid one week after the event	hour	15	250	3750				
Contingency				2000				
Total Expenditure				59090				
Client Profit/Loss				910				
Budget Notes								
1 food is £35 per head, 10% on booking, balance 1 month before.								
2								
3								
4								
Actuals notes								

FIGURE 8.7   Month-by-month cash flow statement

Event								
Event title								
Event date				**Date**				
Client name								
Cash flow as at ..... date								
	October Booking Date	November (−5)	December (−4)	January (−3)	February (−2)	March (−1)	April: Event Date	May (+1)
Opening balance	0	6200	11400	18800	15300	19700	14850	6700
Cash received analysis:								
Cash – sponsorship								
Cash – tickets								
Income: budget = £60,000, Client company want to pay £10000 a month starting October	10000	10000	10000	10000	10000	10000		
Total Cash Received in Month	10000	10000	10000	10000	10000	10000	0	0
Cash Spent Analysis:								
Venue hire non-returnable deposit at time of booking	1000							
Venue final payment one month before				9000				
Guest entertainer paid one month before						6500		
Prizes bought two months before the event					3000			
Food initial deposit five months before event		2000						
Food final payment one month before						5000		
Drinks paid one month after event								1440
Sound system paid one month after event								1500
Music fee paid to agent three months before event				1900				
Events Team staff costs	800	800	600	600	600	850	1400	350
Event Management fees	2000	2000	2000	2000	2000	2000	2000	2000
Additional staff for the night paid one week after the event							3750	
Contingency						500	1000	500
Total cash spent in month	3800	4800	2600	13500	5600	14850	8150	5790
Net cash in month	6200	5200	7400	−3500	4400	−4850	−8150	−5790
Cumulative closing cash balance	6200	11400	18800	15300	19700	14850	6700	910

The examples above can provide useful templates that can be adapted for your own use, as well as forming a basis on which to begin a discussion with the client to enable an accurate assessment of the services required and develop a cost.

Purchasing and procurement

Within events management, organizations rarely have the internal resources to deliver all aspects of the event. As has been said earlier, they often need to outsource (buy in) specialist services, equipment and support from a range of other companies.

Purchasing and procurement terms:

- Definitions: Larger organizations will have specialist functions (even separate departments) to manage the process for outsourcing resources. These may be known as 'Purchasing' or 'Procurement' teams.
- Purchasing involves the outright acquisition of services, equipment or other goods for monetary payment.
- Procurement includes the acquisition of goods or services in any way, which could include leasing, temporary hire, borrowing or contra-deals (swap).

The following case study assesses the financial implications of corporate and public sector collaboration. Some organizations find it acceptable to provide in-kind services (or contra-deals) to contribute towards a project but this can complicate the process of drawing up event budgets when a range of different parties are involved, or if they withdraw their support even at an early stage. Global Coaches House found themselves in challenging circumstances and required a creative approach to sourcing the goods, equipment and services needed to host their Olympic event, as shown in the following case study.

CASE STUDY 8.3 International Council for Coaching Excellence, Global Coaches House

---

Karen Livingstone, Technical Project Officer, ICCE Global Coaching Office and UK Centre for Events Management Graduate (MSc International Events Management, 2005)

The Global Coaches House (GCH) is the brainchild of the International Council for Coaching Excellence (ICCE), an organization dedicated to improving the quality of coaching at all levels of sport. The ICCE works with International Federations, national coaching associations, education institutions and international partners to achieve its vision of leading and supporting the global development of coaching as a profession.

GCH is, first and foremost, a global community of sports coaches who connect virtually, on a daily basis. Secondly, it is a programme of events taking place in the setting of a top multi-sport competition – to date the GCH has taken place during the London 2012 Olympic and Paralympic Games; Sochi 2014 Winter Olympics; and the XXth Commonwealth Games in Glasgow 2014. The event can last anything from four days to three weeks, depending on the length of the associated Games. Typically, an event will attract 400–500 coaches throughout the programme.

The model for GCH is such that the ICCE works with two partners: one which is usually the venue, for example, for the Commonwealth Games, the University of Strathclyde and another agency responsible for sport and coaching in the host location/country, such as **sport**scotland. The GCH offers an in-depth programme, providing coaches with a great opportunity to accelerate their development by learning from some of the best coaches in the world, within the special atmosphere of a top multi-sport competition.

Through sharing and learning from each other, coaches are able to improve coaching practice and enhance the athletic experience for millions of sport participants across the globe. Whether they are a coach shaping the next Commonwealth champion, aspire to coach at this level in the future, or just want to get better at coaching young athletes on their quest to improve their fitness levels and lead a healthier life, the Global Coaches House challenges and stimulates self-improvement for coaches.

The ICCE is a private company limited by guarantee, an alternative type of corporation used primarily for non-profit organizations that require legal status. GCH is a non-profit making activity and any income generated from the event covers running costs. Although speakers recruited for the programme are of a high calibre and would ordinarily charge a large fee, they waive this, understanding the nature of GCH and budget constraints. On-site staffing consists of the core Local Organizing Committee and a pool of unpaid volunteers. As a partner of the event, the venue is encouraged to provide a location for the event free of charge as their contribution. Other operational costs include marketing, accommodation, event materials and travel expenses. This expenditure is met through a small registration fee paid by each delegate and sponsorship arrangements with other organizations.

A budget is drawn up at the beginning of each GCH and is agreed by all the primary partners. The budget holder is the ICCE and all transactions are managed by the ICCE Global Coaching Office (GCO). All budgetary decisions are agreed by the Local Organizing Committee. Any purchasing and procurement is managed by the GCO and all event bookings are managed through an online event management system.

By the middle of 2014, planning was in place for a GCH in Rio during the Olympic and Paralympic Games 2016. The ICCE has tasked a GCH Leadership Team with continually improving the event model and financial processes.

Read more: **www.globalcoacheshouse.net**

The procurement process will depend on the cost of the service being procured, the client and the type of supplier. If there is already a relationship with a potential supplier organization, it may be possible to justify the use of a 'preferred supplier' to the client, perhaps on the basis of previous experience and skills, favourable rates, good working relationships or availability. Alternatively, you may need to obtain several quotes from different companies. For public sector clients – and increasingly, with private sector clients, as we have said before, transparency is an important factor in procurement, so it may be appropriate to put the business out to tender. For public sector organizations in the UK (and European Union) there are financial restrictions against which this should be measured (**www.ojec.com/Threshholds.aspx**). As a rule, it is appropriate to go to tender for projects on which expenditure is approximately £100,000. The pressures of financial transparency for corporate governance mean that for a service costing about that amount, it would be good practice to issue a tender document.

If sustainability is a consideration for the client or for your organization, it might be appropriate to advertise the opportunity locally, to reduce the carbon footprint of the eventual supplier as well as encouraging local businesses. The ITT (invitation to tender) is a formal communication to potential tenderers and can be used to emphasize your own or the client's commitments to current issues such as sustainability and quality, while enabling an equal opportunity to potential suppliers.

Procurement of goods or services for events may be achieved through a range of options:

- Three quotes: the event manager issues a request for quotes for services, equipment or other goods, to three companies, who will respond with a price and possibly other relevant information, eg delivery date, availability, previous experience. In the public sector, three quotes would be limited to expenditure of up to and around £10,000. Increasingly, private sector companies will use more formal tendering processes for larger purchases due to the constraints of corporate governance.

- Tendering process: this is a formal process where the ITT (or invitation to provide a quote) is advertised more formally. In the case of public sector organizations, expenditure above set limits (just over £100,000 for event-related purchases) must go through a complex and lengthy European-wide process. There are specific websites, eg **www.tendersdirect.co.uk**, which list the range of tenders currently available. The tender process is outlined in detail below.

- Preferred supplier: once a tender process has been undertaken, an organization may decide to appoint one or more preferred suppliers, with whom they develop an ongoing relationship for supplying specific goods, equipment and services. In smaller companies the process for appointing a preferred supplier may lack the rigour required by public sector and larger organizations, such as using a supplier because your bother-in-law owns it.

The following case study examines the uses of the three-quotes method.

CASE STUDY 8.4   Balancing the budget

Becky Hughes, UK Centre for Events Management Graduate

The immediate reaction of most staff when tasked with researching equipment, consumables or staffing for events is usually to seek out the cheapest product available within the desired category, but it is important to balance budget against objectives and expectations. Equally, if a client or company has a large budget, it's not necessarily prudent to maximize spending if resources aren't worth the cost of the service provided. This is where the concept of value for money becomes important.

Whether sourcing products for an agency who must watch their margins, a not-for-profit accountable to its benefactors, or a company whose reputation is at stake, value is potentially more important than raw cost, though isn't always regarded as such. To take the example of sourcing temporary event staff, three agencies were approached for quotes, returning the following results:

Brief: supply five staff for one evening event at a city centre venue, staff to wear standard industry uniform and arrive half an hour prior to the start of the event for briefing;

Company A quote: staff to be supplied at a rate of £9.50 per hour plus VAT with 50 per cent of payment required up front;

Company B quote: staff to be supplied at a rate of £12 per hour plus VAT with payment upon receipt of invoice post-event;

Company C quote: staff to be supplied at a rate of £11.50 per hour plus VAT, payment expected within 30 days post-event and additional staff available at short notice if required.

Based on price, Company A would seem to be presenting the best deal, but how would their payment terms impact on cash flow? What would happen if they failed to deliver, with the client having already paid 50 per cent of the booking fee? Company B are the most expensive – are we to assume that they are therefore the best? Company C are neither most expensive nor cheapest, and offer the additional bonus of flexibility – something which is of huge benefit to event managers. Although this would appear to be a simple situation, when considering pros, cons and objectives more carefully, it is clear that the procurement process isn't as straightforward as analysing quotes based upon cost price alone, but it is, instead, about ensuring that there are clear expectations of what will be gained from any expenditure.

When making any purchase, be it of consumable equipment, hire of a venue or contracting of a service, it is vital that event managers decide beforehand what it is that they really need, what must be included, the quality expected and the price they are willing to pay for the right result. The cost of making the wrong decision during the procurement process may be far greater than the saving made on the balance of an invoice.

Read more: **www.kickingon.wordpress.com**

Within the tender process, there are four distinct phases:

Phase 1: Pre-tender

- Set up core team; agree the roles required (eg events team, finance, legal); agree the levels of responsibility and areas of expertise required by team members; establish specific objectives for the procurement project.
- Formulate plan: agree actions, dates, complexity of the tender, the value of the tender.
- Develop a specification for the required goods, services or equipment and criteria for evaluation; outlining the purpose of the purchase and the shared values required of any potential supplier company.
- Develop tender documentation: develop and use templates for a common structure; include roles, objectives, instructions to tenderers (examples follow in sections below).

Phase 2: The tender

- Invitation to tender: examples of documentation are given in the section below.
- PQQ – for larger procurement processes, there may be an initial stage that involves a Pre-Qualification Questionnaire (PQQ) which enables finance/legal departments to filter out any unsuitable potential suppliers.

- Initial visit and briefing: this depends on what is being procured. For a venue selection, a site visit is always recommended (see Chapter 3 on Location). Particularly for locally-based supplier companies, the beginning of managing the ongoing relationship might begin with an initial meeting prior to the selection decision. For larger purchases, there may be the opportunity for potential suppliers to meet and ask questions for clarification about the purchase.

- Submission of tenders: for legal reasons, in the public sector (and for best practice elsewhere), responses to tenders are kept securely in a locked (or if electronic, password-protected) place, to ensure equal treatment for all submissions.

Phase 3: Evaluating the responses

- Evaluation of the tender: decide which roles and individuals are required to undertake evaluation (eg permanent staff as opposed to contractors). During this process ensure that professional relationships are maintained and any bias or prior relationship is acknowledged.

- Shortlisting: Set up a shortlisting meeting, decide which roles are required to attend.

- Meeting/interview: if the decision is made to interview potential suppliers, ensure that there are no undue influences on the process.

- References: feel free to request formal or informal references from organizations with prior experience of working with the supplier. This can range from a set tickbox proforma to a telephone call.

- Visit existing sites/customers: if needed you may choose to arrange visits to the supplier's existing customers but be sure to have a clear purpose for the visit, and a means of gathering and giving feedback.

Phase 4: Appoint the successful supplier/s

- Appoint the preferred supplier: having marked each supplier against specific criteria, add up the scores to compare the ratings. The company that is appointed must be the highest scorer.

- Negotiate and sign contracts: again, agree the relevant roles with authority to appoint, negotiate and sign contracts.

- Commence service: this may be the first project of many, or a one-off arrangement, but either way, there needs to be a formal recognition of the start of the relationship.

- Monitor and evaluate: this may be undertaken by the use of Key Performance Indicators (KPIs), measurable targets, two-way feedback, regular meetings and identified process improvements.

- Debrief unsuccessful tenderers: this task may be given to the procurement team, to ensure a robust process.

Ultimately the event management company still maintains overall responsibility for the quality and success of the event and so needs to carefully manage the selection of suppliers and partner organizations. Key to this is having appropriate financial and procurement processes and supporting documentation.

Documentation templates

This documentation for financial management of an event can be built on a solid foundation of openness and transparency, whether internally, or between client and supplier. The templates below (some with worked examples), can also provide a useful basis on which to begin a discussion with the client to enable an accurate assessment of the services required and develop a cost.

Budget holder details

This template provides the basic information about the client and estimated initial budgets.

TABLE 8.9 Budget holder details template

Title of event(s):	Event owner (Client):		
Budget holder, team and contact details:			
Total budget:	Venue budget:	B&B budget:	AV budget:
Cost code:			

Financial Information: developing a Service Level Agreement to support financial planning

This template is useful for gathering the important financial and other relevant information you will need from your client to help you plan the event, and can form the basis of a Service Level Agreement between your organization and the supplier (or even with the client). The detailed approach helps to identify where responsibility sits, in a clear fashion, so as to avoid assumptions about who is doing what (and the ensuing mistakes). You could adapt it to use with your own suppliers or clients.

FIGURE 8.8   Template for developing a Service Level Agreement

Baselined budget:		Preferred spend:	
Staffing budget:		Contract/ permanent:	
Venue budget:		B&B budget:	
AV budget:		Other budgets:	
Cost Centre code:		Subjective code:	

Budget holder, team and contact details:
Name:
Team:
Contact details:
Location:
Accountant: Name
Statement of intent: both parties will work in partnership and service delivery will be monitored on an ongoing basis to ensure that services are provided in line with the service schedules and that the appropriate quality standards are being met. Any changes/refinements to service provision will be subject to formal variation.

	Responsibility			
Project initiation meeting (event planning brief and Service Level Agreement)	**Event Manager**	**Client**	**Due by date**	**Date completed**
Project initiation meeting (event planning brief & SLA)				
Event planning brief drafted				
Event planning brief approved				
SLA drafted				
SLA signed & agreed				
Event planning schedule drafted				
Event planning schedule approved				
Programme and content				
Identify – three to five potential suppliers				
Draft tender				
Approve tender				
Issue tender				
Reply by date				
Evaluate tenders				
Discuss with event owner				
Agree supplier				
Inform tenderers				
Venue				
Venue search brief completed				
Venue search brief approved				
Venue search brief issued				
Venue search results collated				
Venue search results approved				
Venue visits				
Venue booked				
Venue contract signed				

FIGURE 8.8 *continued*

Catering				
Catering options discussed				
Menus agreed				
Clarify payment of catering in terms of minimum numbers				
Final numbers and dietary requirements required				
Accommodation				
Outline number of non-delegate bedrooms required				
Outline allocation for dinner, etc				
Outline where charges are to be allocated				
Check if VIP/private dinner required				
Book VIP/private dinner (if applicable)				
Date when booking can be changed without charge				
Clarify cancellation charges				
Final B&B numbers required by hotel/venue				
Audio Visual and Technical Requirements				
Spec and agree AV requirements				
Issue mini-tender for AV spec				
Evaluate AV replies				
Appoint AV team				
Decline other AV tender bidders				
Supplier Requirements				
Spec and agree supplier requirements				
Issue mini-tender for supplier spec				
Evaluate supplier replies				
Appoint supplier team				
Decline other supplier tender bidders				
Finance				
Event budget agreed and signed off				
Event budget updated				
Raise requisition for venue				
Raise requisition for AV				
Raise requisition for other suppliers				
Receipt venue spend				
Receipt facilitator spend				
Receipt AV spend				
Final event costs reported				

The procurement process – invitation to tender

The following is an example of a template for issuing an ITT for supplying a vox-pop video for use at a conference. It is by no means a perfect example but the purpose of each section is explained. The potential suppliers should be provided with a written description of the service required – this may be called an 'invitation to tender' (ITT), a 'brief' or a 'specification'. The more detailed this document is, the more insight the potential supplier will have as to what is required – and the more accurate a costing will be provided in return. However, as events are generally one of a kind, rather than a standard off the shelf, it is possible that these costings will only act as a guide.

There should be a letter with instructions to tenderers with terms and conditions, contractual details and relevant policies, with a response proforma and timetable for progressing the procurement process.

The event background profile in Figure 8.9 provides a context for the event and should outline the event's aims and objectives, the target market for the event and the full contact details of the event manager. This section enables potential suppliers to gain an understanding of the level of service required and sets standards that must be achieved to ensure event-quality by setting down effective management systems and procedures. The more detail provided about the event, the more accurate a financial quotation will be in response.

Figure 8.10 outlines the details of the event and the service required.

FIGURE 8.9   Template for the event background

AUDIO VISUAL SERVICES (VOXPOP PRODUCTION)	
Event: title, audience	
Venue: venue name & location **Website:** venue website **Please visit the link below for all venue technical specifications should that be necessary:** Venue website link to floorplans	**Event date: date**
Session timings – Date: 09:00 – 15:30	**Estimated numbers: 450**
Set-up date & time: **Date: 18:00 – 22:00**	**Return to: Contact details** **Name:** **Email:** **Tel. No.:**

Event background:
This conference will be an opportunity to hear how [audience] across England are using [purpose of event] within their roles and how it has benefited them and [other stakeholders].
It will build on the success of the first event which was held in [date]. It will provide delegates with an opportunity to learn more about [organization] and how it will deliver better and safer [purpose], from a [stakeholder] perspective. There will also be an update on the progress which has been achieved over the last 12 months, and an opportunity to see live demonstrations of some [technology] packages. A Q&A panel will provide people with an opportunity to ask questions and provide feedback about their own experiences of using [technology]. An interactive session will demonstrate key areas of the [product]. Speakers at the conference will include [List name/s, role/s and organization/s], who will share their experiences and explain how [product] could have improved their [experience].

FIGURE 8.10 Template for the event details and services required

Event details				
Date	**Start time**	**End time**	**Function**	**Room**
01/05/07	09:00	10:00	Registration	Ground floor reception
01/05/07	10:00	11:10	Plenary session	Room A
01/05/07	11:10	11:30	Refreshment break	Lounge B
01/05/07	11:30	12:50	Plenary session	Room A
01/05/07	12:50	13:30	Lunch and exhibition	Lounge B
01/05/07	13:30	15:30	Plenary session	Room A
01/05/07	15:30		Conference close	

Objective of the vox pops

The vox pops will be used to open a [organization] conference which is taking place on [date]; they will be 10 minutes in length. The aim is to capture a range of views from [vox pop subjects] who are now using [products] in their everyday roles. For example [example of product use]; their experiences, and the benefits.

Vox pops	**Additional points**
The views of [stakeholders] will be gathered using the following sources: ● [list sources]	*Numbers of days work anticipated for this piece of work: four *Please note that in order to obtain the information required for the vox pops, extensive travel around the country will be necessary *The vox pops will also need to be produced in the following formats: – DVD – MPEG 1 in 352x288 resolution

Please specify the cost and number of crew, equipment and additional resources needed for this piece of work. This must include editing, both pre- and post-event. Evidence of similar past video work should be included in your bid for the tender (on DVD or similar).

Please also specify the day rates for crew, equipment and additional resources. Should you require further information in regards to this tender, please feel free to contact us on xxx xxxx xxxx.

Eligible companies must meet the following criteria:

● Have adequate personal, public and employers' liability insurance
● Ensure work is carried out in a safe manner in compliance with the Health & Safety at Work Act 1974
● Adopt best-practice procedures and work safely to reduce risk as far as is reasonably practicable
● Be prepared to work and liaise with venue Health & Safety officials to ensure adherence to any specific venue requirements
● Provide up-to-date risk assessments and method statements to show safe working practice
● Ensure staff/technicians are fully trained
● All electrical appliances must be PAT tested and certified for safe use

Other requirements:

● It is expected that the AV team will be prepared to work unsociable hours in accordance with AV industry habits and the event requirements
● The AV director is responsible for members of their team at all times. An assigned technician will be fully responsible while on-site recording the vox pops

Please quote for all above, with all items including options, costed separately

There are three aspects of a specification that will assist potential suppliers reach a better understanding of the service required. These are:

- Specification by function: created within the event-planning process, this tells the supplier the purpose of the service – what the service is supposed to do – including resources the supplier should provide for the client, to appoint the right person for the right role and complete the project.

- Technical specification: a detailed breakdown of resources, including staff and technical equipment by type, quantity and days needed. It may request additional documentation from the supplier, such as risk assessments, method statements, legal requirements, site maps/floor plans to assist the tenderer in making the decision.

- Specification by performance: it should include relevant health and safety, ethical, quality and sustainability issues, and address delivery of service, with attention to detail to meet the event's quality standards. Could be stated in terms of performance results and criteria for verifying compliance, such as KPIs. Could identify shared corporate values.

For a fuller description, any specification should include details of the required support service/equipment based on the above three headings. The Purple Guide (see Chapter 5 for details) lists all relevant legislation and regulations that can be included in these sections.

Costing additional items separately will aid consistency in comparing responses. It is important to agree costing and pricing strategy in advance to ensure value for money and an ability to measure return on investment. Providing a pro forma for responses will aid this clarity.

A process for agreeing changes to the contract should be included to minimize disagreement during and after the event.

Evaluating tender responses

Evaluation criteria can be weighted for relative importance and will enable consistency across different evaluators in selecting potential supplier/s for final negotiations. Sample criteria are listed in Figure 8.11.

FIGURE 8.11   Sample evaluation criteria

Please note that this tender will be evaluated on the following criteria:
1 quality
2 meeting the specifications
3 cost vs budget
4 availability
5 past experience

Below is an example of responses to a tender for AV and vox pop video that demonstrates the usefulness of a consistent response format. The suppliers are being judged against specific criteria, and providing prices against details in an ITT. The different responses from the four companies are compiled within the template to enable a comparison and, ultimately, a decision on the choice of supplier. The responses are split into different sections, listing the equipment (human) resources, miscellaneous additional costs, discounts and a cost summary.

FIGURE 8.12   Tender responses example

Event title – date – AV TENDER RESPONSES
Tender ref:

Item	Supplier A	Supplier B	Supplier C	Supplier D
Laptop	DECLINED	£750.00	DECLINED	£385.00
Wireless remote control		£10.00		Not quoted
LCD projector (main)		£600.00		Only quoted for one – dual screen projection requested £180.00
Projection screen (main)		£92.00		£63.00
Large plasma monitor/screen		£2400.00		£2016.00
Stage set		£1450.00		£1800.00
LCD TFT Floor screen		£100.00		£50.00
VGADA – Signal splitters		Not quoted		Not quoted
Lectern		£80.00		£31.50
PA system		£550.00		£486.50
Radio microphones (lapel)		£250.00		£157.50
Radio microphones (hand held)		£250.00		£157.50
Portable printer for on-site use		£82.00		£45.00
Flipchart stands and paper		£125.00		£52.50
Spare power extension cables		FOC		FOC
Poster display boards		£240.00		£88.00
TOTAL		**£6979.00**		**£5512.50**

3. RESOURCE COSTS

Company	Total Price
Supplier A	**DECLINED**
Supplier B	**£2130.00**
Supplier C	**DECLINED**
Supplier D	**£2650.00**

*Double resource costs as only quoted for one day not two

FIGURE 8.12   *continued*

4. ADDITIONAL COSTS

Company	Description	Total Price
Supplier A		**DECLINED**
Supplier B	£11,330.00 included in this cost for vox pops. Additional equipment and transport	**£11,852.00**
Supplier C		**DECLINED**
Supplier D	£7715.50 included in this cost for vox pops Additional equipment and transport	**£10425.10**

5. DISCOUNTS

Company	Discount	Discount %	Total discount
Supplier A			DECLINED
Supplier B		40% equipment 10% set & stage/display boards	£2289.40
Supplier C			DECLINED
Supplier D		30%	£5576.28

6. SUMMARY OF TOTAL COSTS

DESCRIPTION	Supplier A	Supplier B	Supplier C	Supplier D
EQUIPMENT COSTS	DECLINED	£6979.00	DECLINED	£5512.50
RESOURCE COSTS		£2130.00		£2650.00
ADDITIONAL COSTS		£11852.00		£10425.10
LESS DISCOUNTS		£2289.40		£5576.28
INTERACTIVE SERVICES				
TOTAL COSTS		£18671.60		£18587.60

Evaluated by:

Name	Position	Date
Name	Position	Date

Once the financial evaluation has taken place, the responses should be rated against the evaluation criteria. These could include a demonstration of an understanding of the requirements, the ability and capacity to meet the event requirements, quality, sustainability and other policies, financial reliability and liquidity of the supplier company, and references.

Responding to suppliers with the decision

Once the decision has been made, confirmation emails should be sent to the successful and unsuccessful suppliers. Templates are shown below.

Dear

Thank you for your AV quote in regards to .
Having considered the various quotes that we received in regards to this event we have decided on this occasion to use another supplier.
If you would like to discuss things further with us please feel free to contact us either by email or telephone.
Thank you once again for taking the time to submit a quote.
Yours sincerely

Events Team
Organization name
Web: **www.webaddress.com**
Please address event emails to events@organisation.uk
Events on-line: **http://eventsonlinesystem.co.uk**

Dear   [supplier contact]

Thank you for your quote for the above event to be held in   [location] this month.
We have reviewed all the quotes and I am pleased to tell you that we would like to appoint [company name] to cover all AV requirements for this event. We hope that you and your team are still available on less [date]. We will contact you by [date] to go through the finer details. In the meantime if you have any queries please do get in touch with us.
Thank you once again and we look forward to working with you.
Yours sincerely

Events Team

Organization name

Web: **www.webaddress.com**

Please address event emails to events@organisation.uk

Events on-line: **http://eventsonlinebookingsystem.co.uk**

Following this process and using these templates will save time and effort when sourcing suppliers, and enable you to keep financial control more effectively. Further templates are available online.

A final word on effective procurement and good financial management for events

As we have shown in this chapter, managing finances and procurement processes are not easy tasks for event managers. However, we have included a range of templates to make this task easier, and end this chapter with some key points that should be considered:

- Control supplier expenditure by agreed per diem expenses – or cover them yourself (eg booking overnight accommodation for on-site staff).
- Availability and responsibility of staff to sign off against the budget – including from the client side. Make sure you have sign-off from the client for any expenditure you incur, as it may not be possible to claim back unauthorized expenses. Make sure that the staff who are signing off expenditure are authorized to do so.
- Make sure you have the relevant insurances to cover your event, guests and staff, both on- and off-site.
- Put in place a variation to services agreement as part of the procurement process – to agree changes to the original commission, and costs.
- Agree an advance payments and deposits schedule, and check all terms and conditions thoroughly before you sign the contract.
- Agree feedback processes as part of the contract, from your organization to the supplier, and from the supplier to you. Feed back relevant improvements to the client.
- Beware of hidden charges made on the day for last-minute items such as photocopying or internet access.
- The Purple Guide is one of a number of extremely useful event-related publications by the Health & Safety Executive and can be downloaded free at **www.thepurpleguide.co.uk/**

Chapter summary

- Without a full appreciation of the potential costs of an event, organizers risk, not only the failure of the event, but also of the company, whether in terms of finances or reputation.
- Decide whether you have that capacity and capability to deliver the event using in-house resources, or whether you need to outsource.

- Ensure you have a signed-off budget from the client, and that any expenditure is accurately estimated in advance. The complexity of the event will have a direct bearing on the finances of the event.

- Ensure that you abide by financial regulations and company guidelines, as well as planning what you might do in the case of an emergency – always have a plan B and contingency funds in case things don't go to plan.

- Make sure you keep a record of financial aspects, from cash flow to ensuring you are allowed to spend budgets. If you don't manage the cash flow, you could be out of business, no matter how popular the event!

- There are detailed processes to enable you to identify and procure suppliers. We have provided a range of templates and examples that can be adapted and implemented, as well as online resources.

Evaluating your event

09

Events cost money and they take time to organize, using valuable resources. Evaluation is essential to learn what works and doesn't work, from the inception and planning stages, throughout the event itself and beyond, while the information gathered can be used to plan future events. Evaluation is also necessary to understand the impacts of your event – whether positive or negative. Evaluation can also be a useful way of showing others (eg clients, sponsors, internal event funders and partners) that your event was a success, which can ultimately help to justify future events. The days when events just happened with no justification or clear objectives are long gone, and for those of us who have responsibilities for developing and delivering events, there is a requirement to understand how to measure effectiveness and outcomes for those event activities.

As well as evaluating the purpose of the event and the effectiveness of the teams involved, what is more commonly undertaken is a scant assessment of the success of the event itself. This chapter aims to raise some ideas and provide examples of a range of tools and techniques for traditional evaluation, as well as encouraging a review of the way teams work, and relationships between event organizers, suppliers and clients, as well as participants.

In this chapter we will consider:

- the purpose of evaluation
- how to identify what works and what doesn't work within your event and planning process
- impacts and legacies of events
- developing an evaluation plan
- evaluation models
- what to evaluate
- emerging evaluation tools
- using the findings of your evaluations

For an in-depth strategic study of tools and techniques that can be used to measure events, Jack J Phillips' specialist work, 'Return on Investment in Meetings and Events' (Phillips, Breining and Pulliam Phillips, 2008) is unsurpassed. One of the key characteristics of an event is that it is an activity 'with a purpose' (Bowdin *et al*, 2011, 14–15). Some events have the potential to have a lasting impact, or legacy, and indeed this is why many larger events take place. Events may provide a catalyst for change; have an educational purpose; strengthen relationships, whether with staff, customers or other stakeholders; build a sense of community; promote goods and services: the list is seemingly endless – but it is different for each individual event. The key is to identify the purpose for your particular event – which may be simple or complex – and this will help you to plan and implement your evaluation process and content.

The purpose of evaluation

Because events use so many resources, whether financial, people, or other physical resources, being able to measure their effective use and make improvements is important. As previously discussed, in Chapter 6, having clear roles and identifying the scope of the contribution of the different parties involved will support your evaluation of the event planning process.

It may be helpful to distinguish between the teams delivering the event logistics and the development of the event content, particularly in a large or complex event. While many event agencies can shape suggested structures, advise on content and engagement styles, as well as inform on processes and locations for events, the initial content for an event may best come from those with an understanding of the client's objectives and the specific purpose of the event, and any sensitivities around delivery. However, it is vital that where such separate teams exist, there is frequent and effective two-way communication between them to ensure that the differences in their roles are clear, that the allocation of all activities is agreed, and that both teams understand the purpose and context of the event.

In order to be able to justify future events it is important to be able to demonstrate the success of past events. A major problem for many events is that there are either no event objectives agreed, or that objectives are unclear or not measurable. Feedback from experienced event managers indicates that this continues to be the case, despite global economic pressures. The reasons for this lack of focus may not come from the event managers themselves, but may be due to pressures of time within the client organization, for example, if senior managers do not make the time to consider the event objectives, as they do not see the event as an immediate priority.

Good event managers will work proactively with the client (and potentially within the client's organization), to facilitate the development of objectives that are clear and measurable. Such measures take time and effort, but the client will thank you for it, and will be more likely to commission future events. Developing a process that is applied rigorously (even if that process changes), will assist the client, and templates for taking a brief can be developed. This is where the role of the lead event manager working with the client is important – as event expert, do you act as a consultant, leading the process to develop the event objectives? Are you an integral part of the client-supplier team where your opinion is valued? Or are you simply included in meetings with little input, if any? It has even been known for event managers to be excluded from initial planning meetings, or side-lined by those who perceive themselves to be more senior, yet who are not events experts, and who will attempt to take a brief but lack the experience or expertise to ask the right questions, or who might interpret incorrectly what has been said or agreed. There's no substitute for being 'in the room' and part of such discussions when they happen, keeping an accurate record of what is said and agreed, and by whom. Audience research is not carried out as a matter of course, but it should be, in order to test their perceptions of the proposed event and feed back their views into the content develop-ment process. There have been many occasions when an organization decides that a specific audience needs to know certain information, but when the potential audience doesn't recognize the need, such efforts are wasted.

So, events need clear objectives with links to an agreed purpose that connects with the client organization's aims, that can be applied across a variety and range of events. And events also need measurable outcomes, that demonstrate links to the client organization.

Throughout this book, there is a range of activities involved in planning and managing an event. As such, it is vital to evaluate what has worked and what hasn't worked so well. The following checklist provides the most important aspects when it comes to evaluating your team's success in delivering an event.

CHECKLIST: Evaluating your team's activities

☐ Event programme and content development, advice and support

☐ Event programme coordination and delivery

☐ Venue search, site inspections and selection

☐ Venue liaison, including overnight accommodation and catering requirements

☐ Procurement and management of event suppliers

☐ Managing event bookings, attendee communication and registration

☐ Managing logistics of associated facilities and activities, such as exhibitions

☐ Guest liaison, especially VIPs and speakers – ensuring that everyone at the event is registered

☐ Event communications – sign-off by relevant parties, including client corporate communications, events logistics team

☐ First point of contact for all event participants via email/telephone/ social media and ensuring all queries and issues are resolved promptly

☐ Confirmation of event bookings, issuing venue and event details, and event evaluation questionnaires

☐ Development and production of document templates and maintaining controlled documentation and communication records

☐ Production of event materials and collateral including signage, name badges

☐ On-site event-support on the day

☐ Developing, issuing, collating and analysing event evaluations, and presenting the results to appropriate stakeholders, including suppliers

☐ Completing budget and payment processes

☐ Collecting, uploading and maintaining event resources (online) for future access by different stakeholders

Scope of roles

In addition to identifying the activities allocated to each team, the scope of their remit is also key to enabling a full evaluation of the resources available and in use. The following example adds insight into the importance of setting such objectives prior to the start of any new event project, by listing the scope and objectives of a new events team for future evaluation:

Scope of events team support

The events team activity includes the management and coordination of key events that provide engagement with (Client X) and their (specified) prioritized external stakeholders.

Out of scope

Staff training events, internal communication events – these are in the remit of Corporate Services and Communications departments

Benefits of events team support – the event will:

- Achieve or support achievement of organizational objectives as agreed in business plans.

- Build new or strengthen existing identified high-priority stakeholder relationships. It will build on stakeholders' levels of awareness, understanding and support of the client organization and its products/services. It will prioritize issues identified as high priority for those stakeholders.

- Strengthen the client organization's image and build trust in achievement with a key stakeholder group.

- Include two-way communication with the target group and provide intelligence to support the improved effectiveness of the client's engagement activities.

- Ensure risk management whereby insufficient support would or could damage the client organizations or our reputation or relationship.

Assumptions that support the achievement of the benefits listed above:

- That the events team has the capacity or potential to expand capacity to deliver the level of events planned; that the client has the financial resources to meet the costs incurred.

- That the event objectives have been clearly expressed and approved by the client with appropriate signatory level assigned to the event manager.

- A clear view of the size, locations and complexity of the event/s.

- A realistic budget is available, and the budget holder identified.

- Adequate notice to attract the appropriate audience and deliver a successful event.

- Should there be a cancellation or postponement of an event, the potential cost of such an action is recognized and agreed with the event manager.

Agreement on the scope of the event team's work and responsibilities feeds in to the overall evaluation of the event, in terms of whether or not they have been achieved.

How to identify what works and what doesn't work within your event and planning processes

There are many different methods for identifying success, failure, or improvements. One that was developed in the 1970s by the Xerox Corporation has been used in many different contexts and for many different purposes, but it is a simple approach that works well, consistently.

The 'Three Qs' approach can be introduced at any point in the process, for example in a 'hot debrief' (immediately at the end of the event, on-site), or in a 'cold debrief' (at the end of the event process, given time for reflection and input from event attendees). This approach can be used to build in continuous improvement and review into your event management processes, or content development.

The 'Three Qs' approach consists, not surprisingly, of three questions that are posed for anyone involved to respond to, informally – as ideas and thoughts and reflections arise.

The questions are:

1 what has worked well? (and how can we improve it?)

2 what hasn't worked well? (and how can we learn from it?)

3 what issues, ideas or concerns does this raise? (and how can they be progressed?)

The key part is not really this first part of the question (eg 'what has worked well?'), which is captured as bullet points, perhaps on a flipchart for all to see, but what happens next. For once each question has been asked, a second action comes into play, that attempts to identify potential solutions or options, without casting blame, but looking for improvement at every turn. This process can be as detailed as you like (or have time for), and can be applied at any stage of the event process. The questions can be asked of different stakeholders, about any aspect of the event development or delivery, including the usual participant evaluations. And it works. But do feel free to develop your own method of asking questions, and reflecting on the event. It's more important that you apply *something* for evaluation, than nothing at all, but you may wish to adapt or develop your own evaluation process that becomes part of the way you 'do events'. Evaluation may include reviewing agreed implementation and event-planning processes, but it's more important to map and agree processes and ensure that they are adhered to, than not to have any processes at all, and re-create the wheel every time you run an event. And processes are not written in stone

– they can be improved too, and should be reviewed regularly to make improvements. But they do need to be communicated to those who need to work to them.

The event evaluation process can begin at any time – the earlier the better, and finish as late in the process as you wish. The stages of evaluation and research can include the following:

- the planning stages of the event;
- immediately pre-event;
- during the event – on-site;
- at the end of the event;
- post-event after a gap of some months.

Examples of questionnaires and questions

Evaluation questions might often cover the following:

- event participants' experience;
- what they have learned or how much;
- how they will change what they do as a result, what specific action will they take?
- relating to the specific event objectives, whether directly or indirectly;
- whether the event was memorable or worthwhile (you would have to word this question carefully to get a useful result).

Different sections of the questionnaire might cover a range of aspects, such as: the event objectives, different sessions within the event, specific issues facing the organization or its clients/customers, and the overall experience of the event. Different types of questions will provide different types of information. Quantitative questions might be Yes/No, a scale of 1–5 or 1–10 (known as a Likert scale), and these give results that can be counted and measured. Qualitative responses might be sought by having an open comment box, the results of which can be analysed to identify themes, and positivity or negativity, in terms of tone.

The questions below have been used on a consistent basis by one organization, but the software provides the facility to add or delete specific questions, although there may be a core set of questions that are asked every time an event is run.

FIGURE 9.1   Sample initial evaluation form

Please rate the following:

	Comfort of meeting rooms	Audio visual	Venue location	Car parking	Venue staff
Excellent					
Good					
Satisfactory					
Poor					
N/A					

- Do you have any other comments regarding the venue?
- Knowledge & skills: Please use the sliders below to record where you felt you were before the event and where you feel you are now. Rate between 1 and 10 as follows:

   0= I had/have no knowledge of the subjects discussed at the event and how I could use them in the future

   10= I fully understand the subjects discussed at the event and how I can use them in the future

   Before the event: 0–10

   After the event: 0–10
- What did you like best about this event?
- How could this event be improved?
- How did you find out about the event?
- How would you improve publicity and encourage participation?
- Please identify up to three actions that can be taken away today and implemented in your work/organization
- What further support would be useful to help you implement these actions?
- Where would you or your organization have accessed the information presented at this event if it had not been held?
- What further support can we offer you or your organization?
- Your evaluation entry is anonymous. If you would like to be contacted by us to discuss the event or your feedback, please leave your email details here.
- Please rate the event overall in terms of the headings below:

	Administration and event organization	Content	Venue	Event overall
Excellent				
Good				
Satisfactory				
Poor				
N/A				

- Any other comments?

For specific sessions, from keynote speakers to breakout sessions, the following rating structure could be used:

FIGURE 9.2   Alternative rating system

Please rate each session on a scale of 1 to 5, where 1 is poor and 5 is excellent:			
	Content	Presentation	Usefulness
Title of session			

CASE STUDY 9.1   Online event evaluation using the Kent House EventManager™ software

Kevin Holdridge, Managing Director, Kent House Consulting

Recognizing the time and effort required to plan and organize events, Kent House developed an automated online event-management process, working collaboratively with a team of experienced event managers. EventManager™ is a web-based application that can be used to create, organize and manage a range of events, including seminars, conferences and meetings.

The software is aimed specifically at teams organizing large and complex programmes of events whether for themselves or as an agency. As such, it allows for convenient centralized management of events in distinct streams, each of which can have their own branding and identities, and different administrator access levels.

Using the Kent House event management system is easy and it can be accessed from anywhere in the world, on any device with an internet connection. Over a period of nine years, the award-winning EventManager™ software has handled millions of online bookings and tens of thousands of events for hundreds of satisfied event managers. EventManager™ is used for event planning, issuing online invitations, and managing online bookings, event evaluations and reports. Self-service online registration provides a consistent, quality approach and improves attendees' experience, significantly reducing organizational administrative costs and workload. The reporting functionality of the software enables data tracking that provides detailed statistics per event and per client, providing useful information for accurately measuring return on investment.

For evaluation purposes, the system includes:

- A quick and simple issue of template-driven evaluation questionnaires using a set of core questions but with the option to add as many supplementary questions as required. You can evaluate speakers, workshops, sessions, per-day options, all via an email sent direct to event attendees.

- A chase option that can be sent only to those participants who have not already completed the online evaluation questionnaire.

- A manual completion option for those users who wish to return their evaluation by email or post.

- The option to communicate separately with different types of attendees, from delegates, to speakers and exhibitors, suppliers and clients.

- Immediate anonymized aggregated statistics and comments that save time and enable fast assessment of your event's success.

- The ability to issue a follow-up evaluation so you can measure knowledge change and the longer-term effectiveness of your event on attendees.

- Standard and advanced reporting functionality enables you to interrogate data for powerful management and board reporting. There is a built-in report generator which has access to all data items so that powerful custom reports can be built once and then run whenever needed.

Formats for reports can be changed but a summary and detailed report is the norm which can be analysed by copying the raw data from the EventManager™ and interrogating it using Excel.

Example summary report:

Event X Evaluation Headlines:

Jan–Feb (Year)

Four events took place, attended by a total of 274 attendees – an average of 69 per event.

The 11 speakers were rated for content, presentation and usefulness.

With an average 24.1 per cent response rate, some 184 qualitative comments, grouped as follows: Programme Structure: 2.7 per cent, Venue: 7.6 per cent, Support: 15.2 per cent, Good event: 10.9 per cent, Content: 31.0 per cent, Networking: 9.8 per cent, Speaker: 10.9 per cent, Admin: 12.0 per cent.

Some 42.4 per cent of these comments were positive, 52.2 per cent were negative and 5.4 per cent were neutral.

Satisfaction ratings (Good/Excellent) were as follows: Overall event: 66.15 per cent, Administration: 85.55 per cent, Venues: 88.08 per cent.

Training

Varying levels of training can be undertaken for the EventManager™ and access is granted once sufficient training for the system has been undertaken with a recognized EventManager™ trainer. The reason for this training is to ensure that a level of competence has been achieved prior to using the system, as the vast majority of the work that the EventManager™ is used for will be public-facing.

Kent House offers client support every step of the way, starting with providing in-house support and training by experienced event managers, on-site. Update training sessions can also be requested should new functionality be developed or users' skills need to be refreshed. There are five different levels of access:

- Event owner

- Event administrator

- System administrator

- Power user

- Head of events

System users have access to ongoing web-based support from the Kent House portal, with live chat and email communication. Our track record speaks for itself with issues resolved quickly and clients kept informed of progress at regular intervals. The system is constantly updated and improved to offer more efficient solutions for clients. New system developments are rolled out to all clients free of charge as part of the ongoing development path for the system. If a client has a bespoke development that they wish to have implemented, this is costed for them as a fixed cost project and once deployed, is offered to all other clients free of charge. Costs for installing EventManager™ are divided into a one-off set-up licence fee and then annual hosting, maintenance and support costs, with no limitations on the number of users, events or bookings.

TABLE 9.1 Comparison of Kent House EventManager™ against generic event booking tools

Area	EventManager™	Generic online booking
General	Excellent product tailored to meet specific needs of the client.	Excellent product with no flexibility beyond standard configuration.
Core features	Provides all the core features needed to host, promote, and manage events online, including delegate self-booking.	Provides all the core features needed to host, promote, and manage events online, including delegate self-booking.
Branding and programme management	Designed for professional event managers to support the whole event marketing and management service as transparently as possible. With EventManager™, events are run using your own website, email domain name and branding, and operate from your own branded website (with microsites for individual events if required). EventManager™ is focused on your audience and your events programme rather than on one event or a series of events in isolation. So, once a delegate has registered for one event, they have easy access to future events and you have powerful reporting and communication options across the full community of delegates.	Built as a third party service to facilitate easy set-up of ticketing for events, which it does well.

TABLE 9.1   *continued*

Area	EventManager™	Generic online booking
Flexible payment	EventManager™ charges a flat fee for the system with no additional charges per booking or for higher activity levels. The only other charges are those levied by your payment processor (eg PayPal, WorldPay, SecureTrading). This provides for easy budgeting and planning, and works out at better value for larger events and multiple event programmes. He does not take a percentage of sales revenue. Any mainstream payment-processing service can be integrated, so you can use whichever one you prefer.	Charges 2.5% of the ticket value plus £0.65 per ticket; this is on top of the payment processing fee (typically 3.5% to 5% of the ticket price). Gives the option only of using PayPal or themselves as payment processor.
Post-event evaluation	EventManager™ was built with evaluation at its heart and provides built-in evaluation tools to enable easy generation of feedback and measurement of effectiveness for individual events and for series of events.	Allows you to send delegates to third party feedback tools such as SurveyMonkey.

Read more: **www.kenthouse.com**

Evaluation issues

Having looked at an example, there are a number of evaluation issues to consider:

- Anonymous or named responses: anonymity often inspires respondees to be more open and honest in their responses – but they need to be able to trust that their thoughts are *really* anonymous. Some online systems will anonymize the data collected, but will keep a record of who has or has not responded. It may be that you want to know who has submitted a specific response, so it can be followed up afterwards (it may also be the case that you can guess who said it). In this case it is better to include a specific question that invites respondees to add their email address if they would like a follow-up from the event organizers on a specific matter.

- Online or paper? Some organizations continue to use paper forms handed out at the event, often 'encouraging' completion by responding with a free gift when the form is handed in. However, paper format requires typing up the content, an onerous and time-consuming task. While online formats are immediate, they may get lost in the attendee's email inbox, or be discarded as spam mail, and response rates are never as high as those 'coerced' by free gifts. However, there are advantages, in that some people prefer to reflect on their experience and may make a more considered submission after the event. Online systems can accumulate responses automatically, providing initial analysis of anonymized data, relieving the event team of the task of manually inputting data. Some online response systems can also identify who has not responded, and chase them up at a later date, as well as sending subsequent questionnaires on different topics.

- The importance of developing an ongoing picture of event delivery through consistent evaluation cannot be overestimated. Online systems provide the ability to compare and contrast evaluation and other reporting measures – such as attendance rates, no-shows, booking lead times – that can be used to improve and enhance delivery of any event as well as specific events in a series through the analysis of trends. Feedback should not only remain with the client or events team, but event participants should be informed of changes that have been made as a result of their input.

- The types of questions used in evaluation questionnaires are important, and there needs to be a balance between a quick yes/no or rating response and a considered answer with comments that add depth of understanding, and which can provide matter for qualitative analysis.

Question type:
- yes/no
- yes/no with don't know
- scale 1–5
- scale 1–10
- rank options according to preference
- multiple choice – single answer
- multiple choice – multiple answers
- free text (comment box)

Is the question mandatory?

- If a question is mandatory, this could lead to non-completion of the questionnaire

Consider the wording of the question itself:

- Open/closed questions
- Single question not multiple
- Specific
- Measurable
- Does it relate to the event objectives (explicitly or implicitly)?

Demographics

- Consider how you want to be able to analyse your event participants

Piloting a questionnaire is always useful – and the more feedback received, the better able you will be to make improvements.

Impacts and legacies of events

For larger events (known as 'mega events') such as the Olympics, or the Football World Cup, thinking about the environmental, economic and social impacts of the event are key to success in the bidding process. These three aspects are known as the 'triple bottom line', (Elkington 1997) and they include planning for a post-event legacy. A well-known example in bidding for mega events, such as the Olympics, would be the use of build-ings after the event has taken place. While for the London 2012 Olympics and Paralympics, much was made of the potential for use of new buildings constructed for that purpose, there are far too many photographs of unused and dilapidated buildings in Greece (from the 2004 Athens Olympics) and even in Australia (Sydney 2000).

An essential part of the bid process is outlining the intended legacy after the event has moved on, and this often makes the difference between successful and unsuccessful bids. So how does that translate into a successful event? Most of us will not be responsible for developing a bid for such a mammoth undertaking, but it is still worthwhile considering the impacts and legacy of our smaller events as part of the evaluation process. It is clear that understanding the impacts of the events we run is more important today than ever before – and that applies to planners of events of all sizes, not simply global mega-events.

The following case study describes what is involved in impact analysis for mega events and how this feature is developing.

CASE STUDY 9.2 The 2008 Beijing Olympic Games – economic impacts and legacies

Xi Wang, China Meteorological Administration, China Foreign Affairs University, China

Governments are seeking consistently to bid for international sports events, like the Olympic Games, mainly because of their economic role which leaves lasting marks upon the countries that are chosen to host it. But what is the true impact of the Games? Does it have a positive effect on the host city/country's economy?

China was the third developing country to host the Olympic Games – in Beijing in 2008 – and is notable in the world in terms of its population as well as being the host city with the longest history. Over the 16 days of competition, a total of 11,028 athletes from 204 countries and regions around the world competed in 28 sports in more than six host cities other than Beijing.

Economic legacies of the 2008 Beijing Olympic Games

Almost six years after hosting the 2008 Olympic Games, Beijing's Olympic legacy appears to be a lasting one. China has avoided a post-Olympic slump, largely because of the impetus of its powerful economy; the Olympic Games is a catalyst of change which brings a positive economic legacy for the host country.

The legacy left behind by the Olympics is multifarious. 'It's been generally positive,' said Zhang Wenjia, a 36-year-old taxi driver. 'The infrastructure is much better, more tourists are coming and business remains good' (CNN).

Li and McCabe (2012) created a framework for the definition, dimensions and measurement of the legacies of mega-events. For the purpose of this case study, the economic legacies are in three areas: the influence on tourism, the event stadiums and other economic activities. The following is the reflection of these three elements following the 2008 Beijing Olympic Games.

Venue and infrastructure legacies

The Olympics has speeded up the modernization of the city's infrastructure and the expanding city's capacity for development, from roads to telecoms, to subway lines. A new airport terminal and high-speed rail connections as well as new metro lines or extensions to existing lines are having a significant effect. In 2008, the subway network of Beijing was only 200km long. By the end of February 2014, it had grown to 465km. Also, the city's expansion is gradually moving into its northern suburban areas where the Olympic Games complex is situated.

The Olympic venues are used extensively for sports events, cultural activities, exhibitions, business, tourism and recreation, demonstrating the post-Games social benefits. The main Olympic venues such as The Bird's Nest and the Water Cube have seen their special significance integrated into the commercial development. The figures below graphically display the wide use being made of the Beijing Olympic venues in the post-Games period: shopping, body-building, catering, training, exhibitions, performances, competitions, conferences and entertainment.

Tourism legacies

The tourism infrastructure improved significantly because of the 2008 Beijing Olympic Games and many new scenic spots were created which added momentum to the development of the local tourist industry. To make the most of the post-Games period, some of the Olympic venues have been converted into tourist destinations to supplement the UNESCO World Heritage Sites such as the Forbidden City, the Great Wall and the Summer Palace. This has helped to create new tourist itineraries combining traditional places of interest and contemporary scenic spots.

The following two charts indicate that both the visitor and tourism revenue of Beijing increased steadily for the five years following the Olympic Games in spite of the fluctuation of the exchange rate because of the world financial crisis and the various emergencies and incidents in some years.

FIGURE 9.3 Beijing visitors and YOY% (2008–2013)

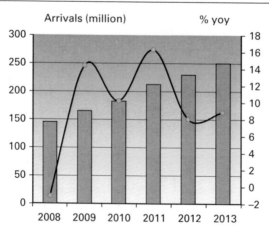

SOURCE: Beijing Municipal Commission of Tourism Development, Beijing Municipal Bureau of Statistics

FIGURE 9.4 Tourism revenue & YOY% (2008–2013)

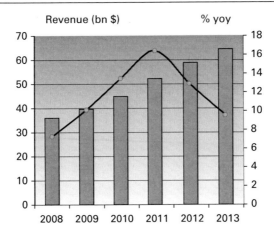

SOURCE: Beijing Municipal Commission of Tourism Development, Beijing Municipal Bureau of Statistics

Business and export legacies

Li and McCabe (2012) argue that a successfully held event demonstrates the capabilities of a host country to organize large events, manage venues, create a friendly and safe environment and formulate supportive and effective policies. Such a demonstration brings a growing confidence in investment from foreign companies which will help to stimulate the economy and local businesses.

Through the success of the 2008 Beijing Olympic Games, China's international prestige and its national strength have been confirmed. According to AT Kearney's Global Cities Index for the world's best cities in 2010, Beijing ranked 15th, while for 'commercial activities', the area in which Beijing performed best, it ranked sixth. 'Commercial activity' is defined as including the value of a city's capital markets, the number of Fortune 500 company headquarters and its attraction for the talents of different groups and ethnicities. In a list of the world's richest and most influential cities carried out by HSBC and Knight Frank's real estate consultancy, Beijing ranked ninth, with New York, Paris and London being the top three. To compile this list, the analysts took into account each city's economic vitality, political influence, science and technology expertise and living standards.

Read more:

Li, S and McCabe, S (2012) *Measuring the Socio-economic Legacies of Mega-events: Concepts, propositions and indicators*, International Journal of Tourism Research, **15** (4)

The triple bottom-line: environmental, social and economic sustainability

The concept of 'green' events is linked to environmental sustainability (see the case study below for a more detailed view on measuring and improving event sustainability). A useful, detailed handbook and practical guide to running 'green' events is by Meegan Jones: *Sustainable Event Management* (2014). Most events involve travel of some kind, for participants as well as organizers and suppliers, perhaps only a few miles, but sometimes across the globe. Event organizers aiming to encourage participants out of their cars might follow the example of some festivals where the only way to attend is to purchase a coach ticket (one of the more sustainable forms of transport) that includes the cost of the festival ticket as well. An event might be delivered in multiple venues located in different geographical regions, with online streaming linking up the sites, and hybrid events (linking face-to-face and virtual audiences) are increasingly popular. While in the past, exhibitions were the most wasteful events, discarding carpets after one use, it is now festivals that suffer from the plague of 'throwaway everything', from tents and sleeping bags to clothing and cutlery. Registration no longer needs to be paper-based or postal, and technology today enables a variety of online registration options from the simplicity of EventBrite to more complex bespoke solutions with much broader functionality.

From a social perspective, event sustainability may be related to an organization's Corporate Social Responsibility (CSR) that includes fair pay, using Fairtrade or organic products – but also might incorporate sessions for event participants getting out and doing some good, say, working in a local school. It can been seen as an opportunity to educate attendees about making healthy lifestyle choices for healthy eating. However, this too should be viewed through the lens of whether such actions represent lived-values versus a tick-box approach. For example, former UK events agency, Universal World Events, regularly sent members of its staff team to work with African charities on projects supporting underprivileged children. PR companies and their clients might ask themselves how this appears to outside observers, as well as considering the extent to which actions and decisions are congruent with an organization's stated values.

Economic sustainability is a broad topic that encompasses the economic viability of an event, for the present and future, as well as considerations of state support and sponsorship. Australian regional government backing is vital to the success of the events sector in Sydney (**www.businesseventssydney. com.au**), where Business Events Sydney promotes the region and co-ordinates bids for new business, developing collaborative relationships between suppliers, influencers and potential clients. In a similar vein, the 'Keep Britain Meeting' campaign was developed by the British Business Visits & Events Partnership (BVEP) (**www.businesstourismpartnership.com**) to encourage new events business into the British economy. Such organizations have huge resources that might be harnessed towards a specific geographic region. From another angle, economic sustainability also relates to the idea of using local suppliers for an event, generating (and keeping) cash within the local economy. Questions relating to what should be included in evaluating the economic impact of an event to a specific locale are addressed by different methodologies developed by academics and practitioners, but it is acknowledged to be notoriously challenging to calculate an accurate gauge of the economic contribution of a specific event. The potential sources of event expenditure include: travel, including airfares, event or conference attendance fees, accommodation, catering and entertainment, as well as on-site and off-site spending by event participants, but should be measured against the cost of developing facilities for use by participants. (Remember the Brazilian demonstrations against the impact on public services and corrupt officials around the time of the 2014 Football World Cup?) (**www. telegraph.co.uk/news/picturegalleries/worldnews/10133833/Brazil-World-Cup-protests-teenager-dies-as-a-million-people-take-to-the-streets.html**)

Sustainability in events have been measured, initially using the British Standard BS8901 (**www.eco.co.uk/content/uploads/files/BS8901per cent 20Caseper cent20Study.pdf**), and the more recent ISO 20121 (**www. iso20121.org/**), developed as part of the London 2012 Olympic legacy. By 2014 many event-related businesses are accredited or working towards accreditation, so if this is important to your client, be sure to pick your venues and suppliers carefully. The following case study describes the key features of implementing ISO 20121.

CASE STUDY 9.3   Developing a sustainability monitoring and evaluation plan using ISO 20121

Dominique Wallace, Events Manager & UK Centre for Events Management graduate

In 2012 an International Standard for Sustainable Events Management was launched: ISO 20121. The standard is based on (and replaced) the British Standard BS 8901, first developed in 2007 and the only British Standard created specifically for the events industry. ISO 20101 aims to support organizations with making their business operations and events more sustainable. This requires a commitment from the business in wanting to achieve sustainable development, which involves considering the three 'P's': People, Profit and Plant. Put simply, sustainable development means identifying ways to run your business in the most positive way for your stakeholders and bottom line, while reducing the negative impacts on the planet.

Monitoring and evaluation of your business aims and objectives are essential when working towards ISO 20101 and the standard is based around a simple 'Plan, Do, Check, Act' management cycle, which aims to support continual improvement.

FIGURE 9.5   The plan, do, check, act management cycle

Adapted from www.aleanjourney.com

In order to ensure successful monitoring and evaluation, you firstly need to identify what it is you will be evaluating. One of the first steps is to recognize and assess your issues. Roger Simons, MCI Group Sustainability Manager, says:

> *When trying to identify our issues, we find the best method is to brainstorm the biggest sustainability issues affecting us and prioritize these, both in terms of their impact and the control we have over changing them.*

At this stage, remember to consider the three 'P's'; some areas you may wish to consider are:

Planet:

- waste
- travel
- utilities

People

- staff welfare
- staff volunteering

Profit:

- revenue
- economic impact on event location

The next step is to set objectives, targets, and plans to achieve the targets; for example, these could be:

TABLE 9.2 Example objectives

Issue	Objective	Target	Plan to achieve target
Waste	Identify and measure all waste sent to landfill.	Identify all waste streams. Measure waste per stream on a weekly basis and record.	Ensure all staff responsible for waste disposal are advised on what is required from them. Ensure methods of measuring and recording data are available.
	Reduce the amount of waste sent to landfill.	Reduce waste to landfill by 30 per cent in 2015.	Identify waste which can be reduced, reused or recycled. Identify largest streams of waste and see how these can be managed to reduce the amount sent to landfill.

It is essential to remember to work out what you are actually going to evaluate and measure and develop key performance indicators (KPIs) which will let everyone know what data you need to collect.

TABLE 9.3 Example Key Performance Indicators

Issue	Objective	Target	Plan to achieve target	Key Performance Indicator
Waste	Identify and measure all waste sent to landfill.	Identify all waste streams. Measure waste per stream on a weekly basis and record.	Ensure all staff responsible for waste disposal are advised on what is required from them. Ensure methods of measuring and recording data are available.	Measure 100% of waste streams. Measure waste per stream in tonnes on a monthly basis.

Sustainable food is especially important to Sarah Watson from Bournemouth and Poole Sustainable Food City Partnership:

> *Our aim is to ensure none of the food at our events is wasted. To do this, we cater for as near to the exact attendee numbers as possible and any leftover food is taken away by the attendees or caterers. Should any food waste occur, we ensure we weigh and record this and take steps to see what we can do to avoid this in the future.*

Once you have set your targets in place, you need to ensure you communicate these to all staff and suppliers, so that they can support you in meeting your objectives.

One of the key things to remember is that ISO 20121 is a management system approach and not a checklist, which means all of the policies and procedures are specific to each business. In order to successfully evaluate the sustainability of your event, you need to consider the issues that are relevant to your business, how you can best work towards improving these and set clear, achievable aims and objectives. Once you know what it is you want to evaluate, it is easier to find the tools to support you in capturing and recording the relevant data.

It is important to remember that once you have evaluated your event, you re-asses your aims and objectives to identify if you achieved everything you set out to. If so, then you start from the beginning with re-evaluating your issues and setting targets. If you didn't achieve everything you set out to, then you continue working towards it and put plans in place to support your aim.

Read more: **www.iso20121.org**

Evaluation models

While there are thousands of evaluation models, Jack J Phillips' ROI model (Phillips, Breining and Pulliam Phillips, 2008) is one endorsed by Meeting Professionals International (MPI) (**www.eventroi.org/roi-week/faculty/**) and establishes five levels of assessment for any event:

- Level One considers what most end-of-event questionnaires address – were the participants 'happy' with their experience?
- Level Two focuses on measuring the learning achieved by participants within the event
- Level Three addresses the extent to which learning gained at an event has been implemented in the workplace
- Level Four measures benefits to the organization from individuals attending an event
- Level Five compares the financial costs against monetized benefits of a meeting

Ideally, according to the Phillips model, evaluation should demonstrate progression through each level as knowledge gained and skills learned at an event are applied to day-to-day work practices to benefit the organization as a whole.

The systematic Kirkpatrick model (**www.kirkpatrickpartners.com/ OurPhilosophy/TheKirkpatrickModel/tabid/302/Default.aspx**) forms the underlying basis of the Phillips model and is derived from a training environment, developed in the 1950s by Dr Don Kirkpatrick to measure individual and organizational learning from training interventions. It again covers the experience, the learning (often through tests on course or event content) and the extent to which that learning is embedded on the individual's return to the workplace through changed behaviour, and the results – or that it brings in benefits to the wider organization.

CASE STUDY 9.4   implementing Strategic Meetings Management (SMM) to enhance ROI: the case of Cisco Systems

---

Dr Eliza Hixson, Senior Lecturer, UK Centre for Events Management and **Emma Heslington**, Events Support Services, UK Centre for Events Management, Events Management Graduate 2011

Cisco Systems is a multi-national organization with close to 70,000 employees worldwide. With employees working in a range of departments in over 165 countries around the world, difficulties can arise when managing the meetings and events that are held in this organization. Cisco realized that SMM can help them to gain value from meetings and contribute towards their Return on Investment (ROI) and Return on Objectives (ROO) by ensuring that meetings and events are aligned with business objectives. Carolyn Pund, a Senior Manager and leader of the Global Strategic Meetings Management team, explains that, 'for the effort that we put in we want to bring value back to the company... the metrics of success are the return on the objectives'. Creating value and reducing costs through partnerships with suppliers is a key element of SMM and many large, global organizations use their purchase power to negotiate deals that enable them to gain the best ROI from their meetings and events.

It was up to Carolyn Pund and her team to implement strategies to manage meetings and events within Cisco. In order to govern the management of all operational meeting processes, Carolyn Pund and her team established an SMM programme in 2008. Like many SMM programmes, the Cisco SMM version was developed in order to streamline meeting processes, such as sourcing, budgeting, planning, approval, accounting and reporting.

At the start of the SMM process, Carolyn Pund and her team analysed the meeting spend throughout Cisco and worked closely with numerous departments to understand their needs in terms of meetings and events. A key decision was to develop one global team to manage meeting operations, therefore reducing the duplication of resources across the organization.

Another key outcome for Cisco was the use of SMM to collect and report on meetings data. Reporting and measurement are crucial for Cisco because the evaluation of meetings and events helps with making future decisions. To capture meetings data, Cisco developed a robust customized portal in which all departments must log event details and get their events approved before planning can commence. The approval process allows the Global Strategic Meetings Management team to evaluate the 'what and why' of a meeting or event in order to determine whether it is likely to produce business results which will outweigh the cost of the event.

'At the core of what we do is technology that tracks all of the data around a meeting,' says Carolyn Pund. Cisco also uses this technology platform to access and analyse data in order to monitor the value of their business partnerships so they can review and assess whether they are achieving their maximum ROI. As part of their analysis, Cisco has found that their SMM programme has led to 18–23 per cent savings on strategically managed programmes. However, cost is not the only metric for success and Cisco considers a range of data when analysing their SMM programme. Carolyn Pund considers that a key measure of success of an SMM programme is the ROO. As such, an SMM programme should demonstrate value through meetings that achieve business objectives. Through their high levels of customer satisfaction, Cisco has demonstrated that they are capable of creating valuable meetings and events through the implementation of their SMM programme.

Leeds Beckett University has recently developed research materials for the MPI Foundation. Read more: **www.mpiweb.org/SMM**

Some event planning models consider evaluation to be key to the first stage. This is particularly true when thinking about repeat (often annualized) events, for example, an annual conference or AGM, building in learning from the successes and failures of the previous event to plan and prepare fully for the following year in a cycle of continuous improvement. So where does evaluation begin – potentially with pre-event input? And where does it end? Evaluation is an iterative process that informs future events, related or not. We advocate a stakeholder approach that evaluates success from the different perspectives – of the client, delegates/participants, planners, suppliers, staff, any local community affected by the event, and any health and safety partners. We also recommend piloting the content of certain types of events, such as conferences, by involving and engaging potential partici-pants in the information-gathering exercise that will inform the type of event that is appropriate for your audience. Meeting participants' needs may be more challenging than might be imagined, as such needs may not be explicit – and at times, unrecognized by the participants themselves. It is always important to demonstrate to event participants that their needs are being met, as well as those of the client. Online questionnaires are not the only form of gaining feedback for evaluation purposes – you could also include focus groups and interviews, video diaries, collecting data from Twitter hashtags and other social media. But there is no point in collecting data if you're not going to use it.

Evaluating procurement is a key aspect of ensuring that you have ap-pointed the most appropriate suppliers for your event. Chapter 8 covers this procurement function but the process begins with developing clarity about the purpose and role of each type of supplier and agreeing the criteria against which these aspects will be measured. Regular meetings with suppliers to obtain and give feedback on delivery and planning processes should in-clude two-way feedback – to and from the supplier. Chapter 3 explains how to evaluate venue requirements using simple tools and templates.

Developing an evaluation plan

In order to develop an evaluation plan, the following structure might be used:

- Event purpose.
- Background to the client and the event.
- Description of the context of the event.
- The overall (strategic) aims of the client organization and of the specific part of the organization procuring the event.
- Identified and named roles and responsibilities.
- Objectives of the event and how they relate to the overall strategy of the client organization.
- Event branding, visual identity (including online) and fit with the client's brand values.
- Key audiences for the event, segmented and described (eg in terms of attitude).
- Key messages for the event, applied to audience segments.
- Communication channels, applied to specific audience segments.

- Internal (client organization) communications, including how information will be cascaded.
- Activities required and their relationship to organizational objectives.
- Communication dissemination plan.
- Key tasks and allocated responsibilities (on the client side and for event management).
- Resources required and dependencies against a timeline.
- Event timing.

Once these aspects are agreed, they form the core of the event plan and evaluation against progress is possible. Any evaluation strategy or plan sits within an organizational context, so make sure that all aspects of the evaluation are appropriately developed within such a framework.

Evaluation timeline

Using the structure of your event plan, you should develop an ongoing evaluation plan that runs alongside the plan to evaluate actions, decisions and processes that affect the development and delivery of your event.

FIGURE 9.6   Develop an ongoing evaluation plan

Phase 1	Phase 2	Phase 3
Pre-Planning Event concept Determine budget Establish objectives Stakeholder mapping Prepare bid proposal Feasibility study	**Detailed Planning** Location selection Programme plan Site plan Logistics & Operations plan Recruit event team Contract suppliers Promotional plan Financial planning	**Post event** Evaluation Debrief Follow-up

Event Planning Process

Evaluation Pathway:

| Phase 1: Evaluate: Event concept with stakeholders; Value for money in budget; Feasibility study | Phase 2: Evaluate: Location & Venue; Event content, style & structure; Logistics & Operations processes; Promotion; Team & roles; Budgets & procurement processes | Phase 3: Evaluate: Event delivery with stakeholders, Hot & Cold debriefs; Next steps; Review processes |

Emerging evaluation tools

Online social media tools such as Twitter and Facebook can be a useful source of feedback about your event. You can encourage such feedback by communicating a hashtag with your event name (abbreviated) #event that is included in tweets. Encouraging more followers is also useful – and this will only happen if you engage in 'tweety' online activity. During the event it is useful to respond to feedback, and following the event the hashtag quotes can be analysed as part of data evaluation.

Companies such as The Live Group (**www.livegroup.co.uk/**) have developed interactive software that gathers data during discussions, which is also useful for later analysis, such as seen at a conference on sexual health, where pre-prepared questions were asked, discussed at each table and responses generated by each table agreed and input on a tablet. Some questions may be held in reserve, while new questions may arise from the table discussions. This can be illustrated as follows:

FIGURE 9.7   Example of evaluations rating questions

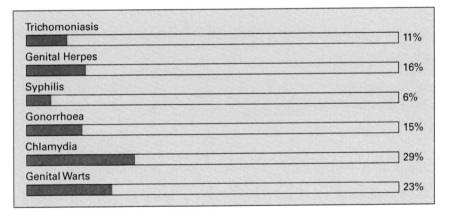

Question: Please rank these sexual health diseases in order of annual incidence

Trichomoniasis	11%
Genital Herpes	16%
Syphilis	6%
Gonorrhoea	15%
Chlamydia	29%
Genital Warts	23%

Responses to the question: 'Is there an issue not on the agenda that you would like us to cover today?' can be measured easily:

TABLE 9.4   Example of response count

Response	From which Delegates' Table
Reporting.	2
If you could cover any sites which are already live.	2
Is money and resources to be available to support deployments?	2
Can we differentiate policy for chronic conditions like HIV from sexual health?	3
Chlamydia screening and what level of sharing is acceptable between GU services and the screening programme if any.	4
Rights of under age.	5
Children's issues/parental access.	6
Need to cover partner notification issues and circumstances where sharing is done without consent.	8
What protection does use of GUM Numbers give over and above use of NHS Number?	8
How are you informing children about consent/dissent?	9

These topics can then be added to the agenda and included in any discussions planned for the event.

Responses to the question: 'Should it be possible to share identifiable clinical information, for patient care and with the patient's consent, with other same-service clinics, ie GUM/GUM or Reproductive Health/Reproductive Health?' give a clear picture of the opinion in the room:

FIGURE 9.8 Examples of question responses using software

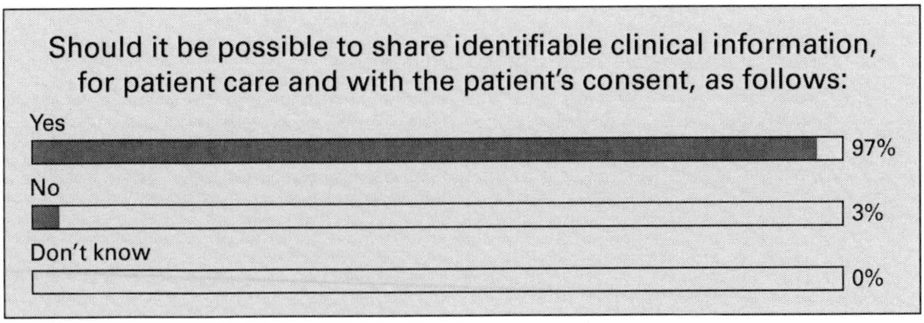

> Should it be possible to share identifiable clinical information, for patient care and with the patient's consent, as follows:
>
> Yes
> 97%
> No
> 3%
> Don't know
> 0%

Such software can provide valuable insights into opinions of event participants, but is best managed by experienced facilitators.

Analysing and using the findings of your evaluations

The following example provides a range of data analysis that contributes to the overall evaluation-reporting process. Using the evaluation findings is vital!

FIGURE 9.9 Example evaluation report

> **Selected data from online Event Management System: Diocesan Day Conference**
> **Attendee data:** This section provides a summary of the booking statistics:
> 511 delegates (as registered on EMS) attended plus children, KidzKlub and Team
> **Total 556**
> **Did Not Attend**
> 22 delegates DNA; No Show Rate: 3.95% (Industry best average 10%)
> **Cancellations**
> 18 delegates cancelled
> (3 delegates self-cancelled; 15 cancelled by Team)
> 6 cancelled during the week up to the conference
> 6 cancelled on the day
> **Booking Sources**
> 21.65% of bookings made direct to website
> 67.8% of bookings made by Liz (NB within two years, these figures had reversed)
> 10.55% of bookings made by Matt & Ruth
> **Email and Postal Bookings**
> 181 participants with no email address supplied
> 32.55% of participants with no email address supplied
> Evidence suggests that a significant proportion (possibly 50%) of these may either have an email address of their own or share an email address with their spouse. However, even with one-third of participants having postal confirmation, significant savings in stationery and postal costs achieved overall through use of internet-based bookings.

In Figure 9.10, these workshops were evaluated under three criteria: for usefulness, presentation and content, on a score of 1 to 5.

FIGURE 9.10 Workshop evaluation: Example of analysis

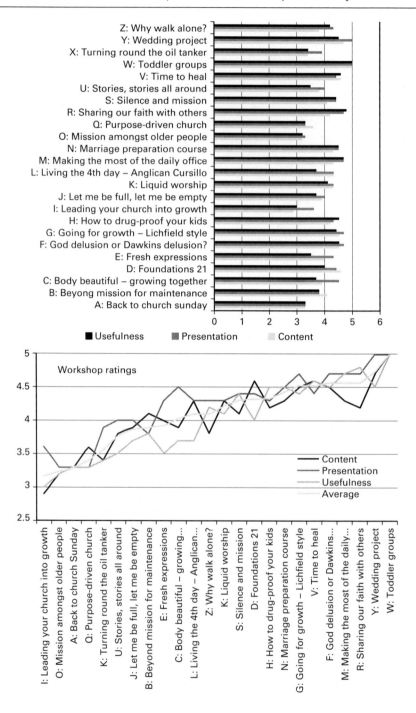

Using the same data, the above graphs show how it is possible to rank the workshop ratings based on a calculated average (mean).

Using a scale of 1 to 10, participants are asked to rate their skills and knowledge before and after the event.

FIGURE 9.11   Example of knowledge and experience ratings, before and after event

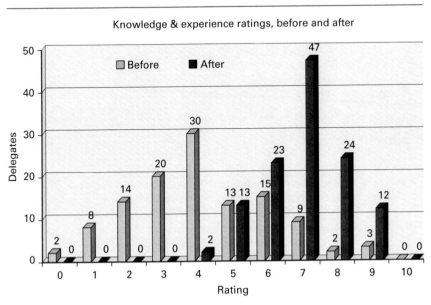

The averages for the before and after scores are accumulated, providing a measure for the level of change as recognized by the attendees.

TABLE 9.5   Example of knowledge and skills averages

Knowledge and skills: averages			
Before	After	Change (number)	Change (per cent)
3.97	6.42	2.45	61.71%

Individual elements of the event can also be measured. The example below shows the scores for satisfaction with car parking, shown in number and graph forms.

FIGURE 9.12   Example of evaluation: question

Please rate the car parking:

Option	Number	Percentage
Excellent	68	51.13%
Good	53	39.85%
Satisfactory	11	8.27%
Poor	1	0.75%
Total:	133	

Figure 9.13 shows the accumulated responses for prioritized personal actions post-event, some of which emerge from the workshop titles.

FIGURE 9.13   Analysis of responses to 'What are the three priorities for you from this event?'

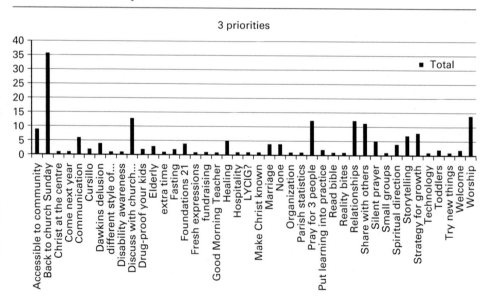

In Table 9.6, questionnaire respondees were asked to provide a comment on the venue. These have been filtered according to themes, and then allocated a response rating for the tone of the comment, from 'negative' to 'neutral' to 'positive'.

TABLE 9.6   Analysis of comments on venue theme

Theme – Venues	Negative	Neutral	Positive
Access	1		
AV	1		
Car parking		1	2
Catering	1		
Children	1		
Exhibition	2		2
Location		2	8
Overall event			5
Signage	10	3	4
Space	5	1	2
Structure		1	
Toilets		1	
Travel	1	1	1
Venue	1		26
Worship	2		
Total	25	10	50

Questionnaire respondees were then asked to provide a comment on the venue. These have been filtered according to themes, and then allocated a response rating for the tone of the comment, from 'negative' to 'neutral' to 'positive'.

FIGURE 9.14   Analysis of comments on venue theme

Theme – Venues	Negative	Neutral	Positive
Access	1		
AV	1		
Car parking		1	2
Catering	1		
Children	1		
Exhibition	2		2
Location		2	8
Overall event			5
Signage	10	3	4
Space	5	1	2
Structure		1	
Toilets		1	
Travel	1	1	1
Venue	1		26
Worship	2		
Total	25	10	50

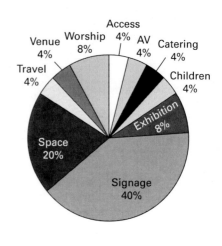

The graph in Figure 9.14 provides a picture of the results (easier for some to analyse than numbers).

The figures and graph below show a similar analysis for the question 'what did you like best?'

FIGURE 9.15   Analysis of 'what did you like best?'

Theme	Negative	Neutral	Positive	Grand Total
Childcare			3	3
Discussion			1	1
Fellowship			58	58
Learning from others			9	9
Organization			11	11
Overall			9	9
Speakers			58	58
Worship	1	1	47	49
Grand Total	1	1	196	198

These examples of analysis of the evaluation responses provide a powerful set of data for the future event planning and measuring success against objectives.

Chapter summary

- Events use a huge amount of resources – financial and otherwise – and it is increasingly important for those of us involved in developing and delivering events to be able to validate the use of such resources.

- Efficiency and effectiveness in our processes and systems are vital but planning for each event needs to start with clear objectives. As an event manager you may have to help your client through this process.

- We recommend that you develop an evaluation plan that runs throughout the event planning and delivery timeframe – be creative in what you measure.

- Consider how you can improve your event planning and delivery processes, how you engage with suppliers as well as their performance – and yours.

- If you build in improvements and reviews as part of the way your events team works, you will find that their creativity focuses on getting better at what you do – and that will make for happy clients.

Reference list

Bowdin, G, Allen, J, O'Toole, W, Harris, R and McDonnell, I (2011) *Events Management*, 3rd edn, Butterworth Heinemann, London

Elkington, J (1997) *Cannibals with Forks: The triple bottom line of twenty-first century business*, Capstone, Oxford

Jones, M (2014) *Sustainable Event Management: A practical guide*, 2nd edn, Routledge, Abingdon

Phillips, JJ, Breining, MT and Pulliam Phillips, P (2008) *Return on Investment in Meetings and Events: Tools and techniques to measure the success of all types of meetings and events*, Butterworth-Heinemann, Oxford

www.businesseventssydney.com.au/# [Accessed: 16.09.2014]

www.businesstourismpartnership.com/ [Accessed: 16.09.2014]

www.eco.co.uk/content/uploads/files/BS8901percent20Caseper cent20Study.pdf [Accessed: 16.09.2014]

www.eventroi.org/roi-week/faculty/ [Accessed: 16.09.2014]

www.iso20121.org/ [Accessed: 16.09.2014]

www.kirkpatrickpartners.com/OurPhilosophy/TheKirkpatrickModel/tabid/302/Default.aspx [Accessed: 16.09.2014]

www.livegroup.co.uk/ [Accessed: 19.09.2014]

www.telegraph.co.uk/news/picturegalleries/worldnews/10133833/Brazil-World-Cup-protests-teenager-dies-as-a-million-people-take-to-the-streets.html [Accessed: 16.09.2014]

Future-proofing your events

10

In the opening chapter, we proposed that a really great event will be remembered as something very special or perhaps as something quite different to the everyday routine by the attendees. Hopefully the people attending will then go away from the event and want to tell others (whether it be their friends, family or colleagues) about their great event experience – whether it be having heard from a great guest speaker, having visited an unusual location or venue, or having enjoyed an exciting evening's entertainment. Indeed it can have been any number of things that were memorable about their event experience. In this final chapter, we pose the question 'how do we keep it that way?' How exactly do we maintain that buzz and excitement around the events we are putting on, how do we keep people talking about our events and perhaps, most importantly, how do we keep people coming to our events? After all, as we have already mentioned earlier in the book, an event without any attendees isn't really much of an event at all.

'Future-proofing' is a buzz phrase in the vocabulary of management used to describe approaches and methods adopted by companies to ensure a viable future for their business. It is essentially about companies making sure that the goods and services they provide (in our case events) continue to be of value to their customers (in our case attendees) not only today and tomorrow, but also the following day and into the distant future. Those companies who invest time and effort in future-proofing recognize that past success does not mean future success is inevitable. We don't have to look far for examples of popular products that ceased to be of value to customers (ie these products became obsolete). It would have been hard to imagine several years ago that today we would no longer be watching video cassettes, sending off and developing film for photographs or checking the road map before setting off on a journey.

The largest and most successful companies are always thinking about the future. In fact, they are not only thinking about the future but they are preparing for what lies ahead. Take, for example, the large energy companies who, it seems, are continually seeking to diversify their energy sources by investing in renewable energy to keep the lights on in the future. So too, as event planners, we must strive to ensure a bright future for our events by creating events that remain relevant and appealing for attendees. While nobody can say with certainty what the future will bring (like you we don't possess a crystal ball), we are able to offer some suggestions to help ensure your events prosper in the future.

In the final chapter, we will be looking at:

● creating custom- and customer-made events
● trend-spotting to help prepare for the future
● creating future success through innovation.

Creating bespoke events

As already mentioned, at a very simple level, we can think about future-proofing our events in terms of the ability to continue to attract attendees (draw in the crowds!). Basic economic laws of supply and demand tell us that so long as an event continues to draw in the crowds then it will most likely continue to be put on. Conversely, if such a time arises that audiences no longer want to attend, then the future of the event is put in doubt. Don't fool yourself that an event is any different to a video cassette, photo film or road map!

In much the same way as made-to-measure suits and tailored clothes are designed to fit the customer perfectly, bespoke events are tailored to meet the specific needs of the attendees. Anybody fortunate enough to pamper themselves with a made-to-measure clothing service will have enjoyed the satisfying moment of putting on an item of clothing that fits perfectly. So too an event planner, who can deliver an event which fits perfectly with the needs of their audience, will be able to deliver that feeling of extreme happiness and satisfaction amongst the attendees. And of course, when you're able to generate such a feeling of happiness and satisfaction amongst the event attendees, then it is very likely that they will be back!

Below we look at two different types of bespoke event – 'custom-' and 'customer–made' – that can help to deliver higher levels of audience satisfaction which in turn will continue to draw in the crowds – future-proofing!

Custom

Large retail stores have long been interested in the buying habits and behaviours of their customers. By understanding what their customers like, as well as what they don't like, the stores are able to create the ultimate shopping experience. A couple of years ago when stories began to emerge of some retailers using new technology, such as Bluetooth in smartphones, to track a customer's movements and activity in store, there was a public outcry about privacy issues (although it could be argued that this is no different to what online retailers have been doing for years).

While many customers are still concerned about privacy issues, it does appear that the use of technology to track customers' movements and activity is being adopted elsewhere, perhaps most notably in the Disney Theme Parks. On entering the Disney Parks, customers receive their Disney World Magic Band which is used to gain entry to the park, to buy food and merchandise, and also to unlock their hotel room. And, of course, with customers wearing their Magic Band for the duration of their visit to a Disney World theme park, this makes tracking their movements and activity extremely straightforward (eg how many times did they go on a particular ride, where and at what time did they eat lunch and so on).

Tracking technology is not confined to retail stores and theme parks, with Radio Frequency Identification (RFI) wristbands featuring at some of the biggest UK music festivals, including Glastonbury, Radio 1's Big Weekend, the Isle of Wight Festival and T in the Park (Pike, 2014). RFI wristbands allow festival organizers to create a type of digital trail of festival goers that they can then use to improve the attendee experience at future events.

CASE STUDY 10.1   Standon Calling, the cashless festival

Libby Willetts, Managing Director at EMA Events, UK Centre for Events Management Graduate, 2010

Standon Calling is an award-winning well-established boutique festival held annually in Hertfordshire, with a reputation for booking artists before they hit the big time such as Bastille, London Grammar, The Noizettes and Mumford & Sons, alongside classics such as Public Enemy, Buena Vista Social Club and Super Furry Animals. The author of this case study, Libby Willetts from EMA Events has been involved as part of the delivery team for Standon Calling for the last four years in a variety of roles including traffic management, production-office management, event control and trader management.

In 2013 Standon Calling became the first UK festival to adopt an entirely cashless system, provided by cashless system operator Glownet.

Standon Calling Founder and Festival Director Alex Trenchard comments: 'Working with Glownet to implement the first cashless festival site in the UK has undoubtedly benefited the festival from both an attendee experience perspective, as well as allowing us to be better equipped with data to plan the festival year to year.'

The system operates RFID (radio frequency identification) technology, which works using a chip in the festival attendee's entry wristband. Money can be loaded onto the chip to pay for various items at the festival including food and drink. All traders are issued with a generic tablet device, customized with their point of sale details. This device then becomes their till point for the festival, with attendees scanning their wristband against the device to deduct their cash direct from the wristband.

The cashless system presents numerous benefits for all festival stakeholders including creating a safer site with less opportunity for crime associated with cash, both from an attendee and a trader perspective. Since introducing the system, Standon Calling has seen a marked reduction in reported crime at the festival. The RFID technology has also been seen to increase spend per head (11 per cent increase between 2013 and 2014) as well as helping to reduce ticket fraud. Moreover, such a system has great benefits for vendors at the event as they do not have change-management issues or have to store large amounts of cash over a weekend. And clearly there is a benefit for the festival as a whole as transaction times are shortened, which has obvious benefits for traders and attendees. At Standon Calling 2014 the Glownet system managed 53 vendors operating 150 devices to achieve an entirely cashless site.

From an event management perspective the system has a great level of reporting detail which is invaluable for a festival organizer. With clear reporting on spending habits at each vendor throughout the duration of the festival, as well as social demographic customer profiling, this enables a picture of the attendee experience to be built with patterns emerging of peak areas and spending habits. This has key benefits for event managers in equipping them with data to aid in the management of booking traders, site layout and crowd management. Moreover, from a safety aspect, the data available via the wristband chips have been used to combat crime, as well as to reunite parents with missing children.

The cashless system is still in its infancy and as with all technology the process will be refined over time to overcome some barriers which currently face the operating procedure, such as the ability to secure a reliable Wi-Fi/3G connection at festivals which typically take place in very rural locations. However, the growth Glownet has achieved since being founded in 2012 (£1 million investment and delivery of 20 cashless worldwide events) is evidence that this technology is going to become mainstream within the next few years.

Scott Witters, Director at Glownet comments: 'Glownet provides Festival Promoters with a solution that is robust, reliable and affordable, so that it not only improves the experience for all stakeholders but has a significant impact on the festival bottom line.'

Read more:

Glownet – **www.glownet.com/**.

Standon Calling Festival – **www.standon-calling.com/**.

EMA Events – **www.emaevents.co.uk**

Customer-made

It seems remarkably simple (almost too simple) but giving customers (in our case event attendees) a direct say in how products and services are created (ie customer-made) is a great way of ensuring a continued demand for them. It does indeed seem remarkably simple, but how many times have you heard that the best solutions are often the simplest? When you think about it, if you don't know what Christmas gift to buy for a friend, and you are worried that they might be disappointed with your choice of gift, what you should most likely do is ask them what gift they would really like. Say, for instance, that your friend tells you that they would like a new pair of gloves. Now, if you were a really good friend, then you might ask what colour and what size they would like. The more you ask them for their input, then the more likely you will be to get it right.

Asking customers to contribute towards the development of ideas and concepts is commonly referred to as the process of 'co-creation'. Through a series of steps, customers are invited to contribute, evaluate and refine ideas and concepts for new products and services, as well as experiences (eg events). An event planner, for example, is able to invite the target audience to contribute ideas for an event location or venue, guest speakers or entertainers, food and beverage choices and much more. The great thing is that not only do customers contribute ideas and concepts that you may never have thought of but, because they are ideas that they like, then you can be confident that the ideas are relevant and of interest to them, thus reducing the risk that a new idea won't work.

Top Tip

Above all else the co-creation process should be one thing: FUN! The more enjoyable it is for people to get involved, to share their ideas and to show off their creative talents, then the more likely it is that you will create a really great event. Social media networks, such as Facebook, Twitter and LinkedIn, make it really easy for people to contribute their ideas as well as respond to other people's suggestions during the co-creation process.

Trend-spotting

A key part of future-proofing is the spotting of trends which might have an impact (good or bad) on the events that you are putting on. While nobody can say with certainty what the future holds, it is unlikely that the future is going to be very like the past and, therefore, we need to spend some time understanding the trends and likely influences on the future of our events. Trend-spotting (also referred to as environmental scanning, horizon scanning or simply scanning) can be thought of as a form of early-warning system that lets event planners see potential threats and so avoid any nasty surprises. It is very easy to think about trend-spotting in terms of preparing for the worst but the likelihood is that many of the emerging trends and developments will impact favourably on an event and you must be prepared to capitalize on the opportunities presented.

If done properly, trend-spotting (scanning) can help an event planner answer such questions as:

- What are we doing at our events today that will probably no longer work in the future?
- What types of event are heading for obsolescence?
- Do we have a plan in place to capitalize on innovative and exciting opportunities?

If you feel like you have a good handle on such questions, then you may already be a skilled scanner. If, however, the thought of scanning for emerging trends and developments seems a little daunting (like it does to most of us), then, below, we provide two suggestions of what to look for to give you a good idea of the most important trends.

Mega trends

First, start with those trends that are impacting on everyone (one way or another), so inevitably they are going to have some sort of an impact on you – we call these the mega (or macro) trends. These are the global phenomena that make headline news each and every day – trends such as global population growth, resource scarcity, global sustainability, climate change or advancements in technology. Mega trends are easy to spot because they are happening already and, because these trends have built up such a momentum, we can be fairly sure that they are likely to continue well into the future. This sounds simple and straightforward but it is remarkable how many event planners continue to ignore even the most obvious trends.

The following case study focuses on one of the mega trends that we believe will continue to have a significant impact on the events industry in the future. While mega trends are probably already very familiar to you, the challenge is to put these into some sort of context by considering how these could impact (both well and badly) on the events that you are working on in the future.

CASE STUDY 10.2   China's emerging festival industry

Yanning Li, PhD Student at UK Centre for Events Management

Mainland China has become a big, targeted market for many industries and companies for more than a decade now. However, why is it an emerging market for events, what are the opportunities for events that we can see in that market and what is currently going on there for events? These questions are not easily answered.

Although statistics about China may not always be reliable, some figures can indicate the potential growth of the mainland China market. China's GDP in 2013 was around 56,884.5 billion RMB, with a 7.67 per cent increase (National Bureau of Statistics of China, 2014a), which shows a strong economic growth in mainland China. And according to the Tabulation on the 2010 Population Census of the People's Republic of China (the latest statistics up to 2014), the population of mainland China was around 1.33 billion (National Bureau of Statistics of China, 2014b). However, due to the difficulties in calculating China's population, it can be assumed that the actual figure is more than that. Furthermore, in 2013, the China government amended the one-child policy, and the country is now trying to implement a two-child policy. The new population control policy indicates a growing population on mainland China. And as we all know, numbers of people are very important to the success of events.

Finding statistics about China's event industry is very difficult, as there are very limited official statistics, and the collection of statistics in a newly developing industry, in a very big, chaotic country can be extremely complicated. Some information and knowledge about how the industry has been developing indicates good opportunities for event professionals. China's event industry has been developing rapidly since 2000. MICE (meetings, incentives, conferences and exhibitions), as narrower sectors of events have been paid more attention, especially the meeting, conference and exhibition sectors. Concerts and similar entertainment events are growing rapidly as well. For example, income from venues for artistic performance was about 2.8 billion RMB in 2012, while it was about 1.9 billion RMB in 2011 (National Bureau of Statistics of China, 2014c). A popular music concert ticket is generally priced from 200 RMB to 3,000 RMB or more. Music concerts are definitely a lucrative market. Live Nation is one of the companies from the West that is very interested in China's music event market. They have a joint venture company with the Beijing Gehua Culture Group in China and have organized many big concerts and music festivals. Since 2007, the number of festival events has started to increase very quickly, especially the music festival sector. The big, famous music festivals in mainland China, such as the Midi Festival and the Strawberry Festival, have grown from once a year to multiple times at multiple cities in just a year. As reported, the Strawberry Festival made over 4 million RMB in profits in 2013, in Beijing alone, attracting 240,000 visitors per year (Xiao, 2013).

Although the Chinese market is huge and growing, there are quite a few challenges. One of the biggest is the under-development of the supply chain. There have been problems with supplying items and services such as Bunkabin (a sustainable and temporary power source), temporary toilets and shower facilities, sustainable plates and cutlery, trackways, fencing, etc. There Is also currently a lack of expertise and knowledge in planning, operation, health and safety, sustainability, volunteer management, sponsorship management and many other aspects of the events industry. Events are in high demand in China and these challenges provide huge opportunities for China's event industry. China's event academia recognize that their event education is still developing (under-graduate courses have only been available since 2004). The changing political, social and cultural Chinese outlook has strongly influenced the Chinese people's preference for events, such as a growing demand for 'escape' (Wood & Li 2014). So expertise and knowledge from the West would definitely be a huge advantage when planning an event in China. Therefore more knowledge about China's policies and its socio-cultural context would definitely act as a competitive advantage in this big emerging events market.

Read more:

National Bureau of Statistics of China (2014a) [Internet] **http://data.stats.gov.cn/search/keywordlist2;jsessionid=43582E16D6B6C55EFDD5CCAFAC672F84?keyword=gdp** (Assessed at 2014-08-28)

National Bureau of Statistics of China (2014b) Tabulation on the 2010 Population Census of the People's Republic of China. [Internet] **www.stats.gov.cn/tjsj/pcsj/rkpc/6rp/indexch.htm** (Assessed at 2014-08-28)

National Bureau of Statistics of China (2014c) [Internet] **http://data.stats.gov.cn/workspace/index;jsessionid=43582E16D6B6C55EFDD5CCAFAC672F84?m=hgnd** (Assessed at 2014-08-28)

Xiao, X (2013) Observation: a total of 360,000 visitors by entry in Midi and Strawberry festival, music festivals making good money? [Internet] **http://music.yule.sohu.com/20130506/n374904301.shtml** (Assessed at 2014-08-28)

Wood, EH and Li, Y (2014) Music festival motivation in China: Free the mind, Leisure Studies

Micro trends

As well as looking at the mega trends, it is important for event planners to keep a close eye on new trends and developments specifically within the events industry. These industry specific movements and shifts are typically referred to as the micro trends. For event planners, a sound understanding of the industry situation as a whole is imperative to avoid their competitors stealing a march on them or, more worryingly, stealing their event attendees!

A PESTLE analysis, sometimes referred to as a PEST Analysis, is the most commonly used tool for understanding more easily the industry situation as a whole. PESTLE stands for Political, Economic, Sociological, Technological, Legal and Environmental factors. The questions to ask yourself are:

- What are the key **political** factors likely to affect the industry?
- What are the important **economic** factors?
- What **social** trends are most important?
- What **technological** innovations are likely to occur?
- What current and impending **legislation** may affect the industry?
- What are the **environmental** considerations?

Carrying out a PESTLE helps an event planner to determine how various types (or categories) of factors are likely to influence the future well-being of an event. The importance of each category of factors will vary and the same external factors will influence different events in different ways. For instance, an organization supplying products and services to an outdoor event might be more concerned about environmental issues whereas an organization providing online event software will pay more attention to technological developments. To understand further what PESTLE is and for tips on how to carry out a PESTLE analysis visit **http://pestleanalysis.com/**

Every event professional needs to develop his or her own list of 'go to' information sources to stay informed and to get updates on what is happening within the industry as a whole. Below we have provided a suggested list of what we consider to be the most appropriate sources. It is, however, up to you to choose the best sources to use depending on the type of work that you do and the types of events that you are involved in. As we've already said, if you don't keep a close eye on new trends and developments specifically in your industry, then you leave the door ajar for competitors to steal a march on you.

Sources of information to keep up with news and developments in the events industry

Industry magazines

Most industry magazines are published monthly and each will take a special focus on an area or topic that is particularly timely and relevant to readers. Mash Media, for example, are one of the UK's leading publishers for the events industry with monthly publications including *Access All Areas*, *Conference News* and *Exhibition News*. For more information **www.mashmedia.net/magazines.html**

Industry shows and conferences

Attending trade shows and conferences is a great way to learn about emerging industry trends and provides great opportunities to network and discuss these developments with industry peers. International Confex, for example, is the UK's leading exhibition for the meetings and events industry and has been running for over 30 years. For more information **www.international-confex.com/**

Face-to-face networking

Proactively networking with industry suppliers, customers and even competitors will help you to stay informed about current development and trends.

Online networking

Social media networks, such as LinkedIn and Twitter, are a great way to connect and get the latest updates from individuals and organizations in the industry.

Membership organizations

Joining a membership organization can help to keep you informed through regular updates such as newsletters and also provides networking opportunities. Meetings Professionals International (MPI), for example, is one of the leading membership organizations for Meetings Professionals around the world.

Market intelligence reports

Publishers of market intelligence reports cover a range of sub-sectors of the events industry including Conferences and Meetings, Weddings and Private Parties, Live Music Events and so on. Mintel, for example, is one of the UK's best known producers of market intelligence information.

Top Tip

If you are unsure about which are the best sources of information to keep up with news and developments for your industry sector, then ask a colleague whose opinion you value and respect. You could also ask them for recommendations of who to follow on twitter or which LinkedIn groups to join as well as the industry conferences they think are the best to attend.

Innovation as the key to future success

Probably the best way to know what the future holds is to create it yourself! So, for an event planner, this means going out and creating the events of the future. Be the first to try out new ideas. Be the first to test new ways of doing things. Put simply – become an innovator!

Whereas co-creation involves asking event attendees to contribute ideas towards developing an event, innovation is about giving the attendees something unexpected, something different, something that up until now they didn't even know they would like! Becoming an innovator involves continually striving to breathe new life into your events (whether the changes are large or small) to avoid stagnation and to maintain the buzz and excitement around an event.

Top Tip

To be an innovator you have to be brave because trying something new is never guaranteed to work out the way you hoped. The chances are that your 'big new idea' could be a flop! Being an innovator means being brave enough to say 'So what? I'll just have to try something different next time.' And maybe next time your idea will create the WOW factor you were hoping for. And, if not, well – there's always the next time...

Now, it is at this point, that the idea of creating the events of the future through innovation becomes a little daunting (it certainly does for us). Fortunately, though, it is possible to find ways to be an innovator without being innovative. Admittedly, this does sound a little strange but please read on...

Below we suggest two ways of enhancing creativity and innovation at your next event without being particularly innovative (at least in the purest sense of the word).

Imitate to innovate

To imitate someone is another (slightly nicer) way of saying to copy someone. But if that someone happens to have a creative and innovative idea that can add something new and exciting to your next event then we say go right on ahead and copy them. If all you do, however, is to copy ideas from other event planners (particularly those organizing similar events to you), then that is hardly going to be new and exciting for the attendees (more like tried and tested). But, if you look beyond the confines of the events industry, then you never know what exciting and inspirational ideas you might find.

The concept of imitating to innovate is based on the idea that the most important future trends and developments for the events industry are already here, and we just need to know where to look for them. That is to say, that the future trends and developments that will soon be shaping and influencing the events of the future are already happening in other industry sectors. So it could be, for example, that what is happening today in the world of fashion, film or music holds the key to future success in the events industry. Perhaps the latest trend at this year's London Fashion Week will provide an event planner with their 'next big idea' for finding a theme and decorating an event. Or perhaps the set for the latest blockbuster movie or popular music video will provide the inspiration for a new event location or venue. It's not always simply a case of copying exactly what others are doing but of using their innovative ideas as a springboard to come up with your own 'innovative' idea.

As we say, it is important to look beyond the confines of the event industry for new ideas and inspiration because only tracking developments in your own industry (micro trends) is likely to mean that you are missing out on bigger opportunities. We have already given the examples of looking to the worlds of fashion, film and music to provide ideas and inspiration for an event planner. These industries are often labelled 'creative' industries and considered to be 'ahead of the curve' or the 'trend setters'. As such, these would seem to be obvious places to look for ideas and inspiration. But, of course, looking in the most obvious places probably means that this is exactly where everybody else (including your competitors) is looking as well. It is important to realize that inspiration can come from anywhere, so it pays to keep your eyes peeled and search in the more unlikely areas. Could it be, for example, that your 'next big idea', will be inspired by robotic technology being developed in manufacturing or advancements in aerospace travel? Who knows? But what we do know is that by looking where others aren't then you might just spot a great new idea that others haven't seen.

Collaborate to innovate

Collaborative working is essentially about two (or more) parties cooperating to create something new. This textbook, for example, is the result of the collaborative efforts of two authors. There are two major benefits typically associated with collaborative working. The first is that it helps you to get the work done faster. The second is that you are able to capitalize on the strengths/talents of the other party. It is this second benefit that can enable an event planner to capitalize on the innovative capabilities of a partner organization to enhance the creativity and innovation for their next event. By drawing on the creative and innovative talents of their partner organization (someone able to imagine or think up an idea far better than their own) they can jointly create something new and exciting, something unique and unusual, something that will help create the buzz and excitement around the event that keeps attendees coming back time and time again (the essence of future-proofing).

Earlier in the book, we explained that putting on a successful event is only possible through the collaborative efforts of many different individuals and organizations. Here we suggest that by choosing to collaborate with partner organizations that are particularly creative and innovative in their approach will enable you to enhance the level of creativity and innovation at your events. For example, a conference organizer may plan a fairly routine (some might say uninspiring) event programme but, if they are wise enough to choose a venue with an award-winning chef who creates a dining experience to 'wow' the delegates, then those delegates will go away from the conference and tell others about their wonderful dining experience. While the chef clearly deserves the majority of the credit for his creative and innovative talents, the event planner too deserves credit for such a wise choice of collaborating with the particular venue and chef.

Chapter summary

- Future-proofing an event is about making sure that it remains relevant and appealing to the target audience not only today and tomorrow, but the following day and into the distant future.

- Simple economics dictates that so long as there is a demand for an event then it will most likely continue to be 'put on'. Conversely, if such a time arises that audiences no longer want to attend, then the future of the event is put in doubt.

- In much the same way as a made-to-measure suit will deliver superior customer satisfaction, creating bespoke events, tailored to the specific needs of the attendees, will deliver higher levels of satisfaction and are likely to generate repeat business.

- New technology, such as Bluetooth in smartphones and RFID wristbands, allows event organizers to track the movements of event attendees while on-site. Creating a digital trail of the event attendees allows organizers to use this data to improve the attendee experience at future events.

- Co-creation involves asking the target audience to contribute towards the development of ideas and concepts for an upcoming event. Social media networks, such as Facebook, Twitter and LinkedIn, make it easy for people to contribute, evaluate and refine ideas and concepts.

- Event planners need to spend some time understanding the emerging trends and developments which are likely to have an impact (good or bad) on the events that they are putting on.

- Event professionals should develop a list of industry publications, shows and conferences, networking events and other sources of information to help keep them informed and updated on what is happening within the industry.

- The future trends and developments that will soon be influencing the events of the future are most likely to be already happening in other industry sectors. Stay ahead of the curve by looking beyond the confines of the event industry for new ideas and inspiration that can enhance creativity and innovation at your next event.

- Collaborating with individuals and organizations that are particularly creative and innovative in their approach will enable you to enhance the level of creativity and innovation of your event.

Reference list

Pike, P (2014) Wear Your Tech, *Access All Areas*, **183**, September 2014

INDEX